About This Book

Why is this topic important?

Although many books have been written on the subjects of executive coaching and leadership development, none has focused on the challenge of how to reduce the time needed to prepare leaders for next-level positions. At the same time, organizations are beginning to realize how much the lack of good leadership talent within their pipelines poses a critical bottleneck to continued growth. Until now, this topic hasn't been effectively addressed. While organizational leaders often participate in formal development and training programs, they frequently lack the tools they need for taking charge of their own development. In the same way, managers are held accountable for the development and retention of their people, yet are often placed in a "sink or swim" position by not being given adequate training for making this happen. For their part, many HR and OD leaders are struggling to figure out ways to develop their organizational leaders despite the lack of time and resources. This book attempts to meet these needs by providing leaders and their managers with a self-directed development toolkit that they can use for accelerating leadership development on the job and become better prepared to tackle broader leadership responsibilities within their organizations. There is no magic here—only an organized and systematic plan of attack that encompasses all developmental steps, from initial goal setting to personal brand management.

What can the reader achieve with this book?

This book has been written for several audiences. If you are a leader who wants to advance your own career while strengthening your performance, then you will find that this book can help you in a number of ways. It will show you how to construct well-focused development goals, how to enlist your manager as a partner in your development, how to convert job assignments into developmental opportunities, and how to strengthen your own personal "brand label" as a professional. If you are a manager, you will learn how to coach and assist your team members at each stage of their development process, how to convert job assignments into developmental opportunities, and how to stage feedback and coaching conversations in a way that supports good work relationships.

If you are a learning and development, OD, or HR leader, then you'll find that this book can serve as an excellent learning resource for conducting workshops on leadership development, or for supplementing your leadership coaching programs. [For additional assistance, feel free to reach me through the contact information provided in the back of this book and I'll be happy to talk to you about the workshops that I run on the subject of accelerated leadership development.] Finally, if you are a university instructor or private consultant who conducts coaching certification programs, I believe that you will find this book to be a good supplemental resource to your own program materials. I am currently using this book myself in the coaching certification program that I teach for students at Southern Methodist University.

How is the book organized?

This book is comprised of two parts; a Participant's Guide and a Manager's Guide. If you are focused on accelerating your own development as a leader, then you will want to spend all of your time working through the Participant's Guide. Each section of this guide provides detailed guidelines and exercises for establishing development goals, translating those goals into a viable action plan, and overcoming frequently encountered barriers to personal development. If you are a manager who is attempting to accelerate the development of your team members, then you will want to follow up your completion of the Participant's Guide with a careful review of the Manager's Guide. The Manager's Guide provides suggestions for supporting leader development at each stage of the process, from helping team members to prepare for developmental job assignments to guidelines for providing feedback and career guidance. Each chapter also identifies some of the most common pitfalls that managers are likely to encounter at each stage of the development process and steps you can take to avoid or minimize them.

About Pfeiffer

Pfeiffer serves the professional development and hands-on resource needs of training and human resource practitioners and gives them products to do their jobs better. We deliver proven ideas and solutions from experts in HR development and HR management, and we offer effective and customizable tools to improve workplace performance. From novice to seasoned professional, Pfeiffer is the source you can trust to make yourself and your organization more successful.

Essential Knowledge Pfeiffer produces insightful, practical, and comprehensive materials on topics that matter the most to training and HR professionals. Our Essential Knowledge resources translate the expertise of seasoned professionals into practical, how-to guidance on critical workplace issues and problems. These resources are supported by case studies, worksheets, and job aids and are frequently supplemented with CD-ROMs, websites, and other means of making the content easier to read, understand, and use.

Essential Tools Pfeiffer's Essential Tools resources save time and expense by offering proven, ready-to-use materials—including exercises, activities, games, instruments, and assessments—for use during a training or team-learning event. These resources are frequently offered in looseleaf or CD-ROM format to facilitate copying and customization of the material.

Pfeiffer also recognizes the remarkable power of new technologies in expanding the reach and effectiveness of training. While e-hype has often created whizbang solutions in search of a problem, we are dedicated to bringing convenience and enhancements to proven training solutions. All our e-tools comply with rigorous functionality standards. The most appropriate technology wrapped around essential content yields the perfect solution for today's on-the-go trainers and human resource professionals.

Pfeiffer *Essential resources for training and HR professionals*
www.pfeiffer.com

ACCELERATING YOUR DEVELOPMENT AS A LEADER

A Guide for Leaders and Their Managers

Robert Barner

Pfeiffer

A Wiley Imprint
www.pfeiffer.com

Library of Congress Cataloging-in-Publication Data

Barner, Robert (Robert W.)
    Accelerating your development as a leader : a guide for leaders and their managers / Robert Barner.
        p. cm.
    Includes index.
    ISBN 978-0-470-59364-6 (cloth); ISBN 978-0-470-93701-3 (ebk); ISBN 978-0-470-93703-7 (ebk)
    1. Leadership.   2. Personal coaching.   3. Executive coaching.   4. Management.   I. Title.
    HD57.7.B36647 2011
    658.4′092–dc22

                                                        2010043314

Acquiring Editor: Matthew Davis
Marketing Manager: Brian Grimm
Editorial Assistant: Lindsay Morton
Production Editor: Michael Kay
Editor: Rebecca Taff
Manufacturing Supervisor: Becky Morgan

Printed in the United States of America

Printing   10 9 8 7 6 5 4 3 2 1

CONTENTS

PART I: PARTICIPANT'S GUIDE   1

Participant's Preface   3

1   Managing a Company of One   7

2   Closing the Gap   17

3   Building Your Plan   38

4   Leveraging Developmental Assignments   58

5   Accelerating Your Learning   85

6   Managing Your Personal Brand   122

PART II: LEADER'S GUIDE   161

Leader's Preface   163

1   The What and the Why of Managerial Coaching   165

2   How to Implement Coaching   175

3   Helping Others to Identify Developmental Gaps   188

4   Helping Others Build Their Plans   196

5   Helping Others Leverage Developmental Assignments   205

6   Helping Others Accelerate On-the-Job Learning   217

7   Coaching Others on Brand Management   231

About the Author   240

Index   243

PART I

PARTICIPANT'S GUIDE

PARTICIPANT'S PREFACE

Why This Book?

I was motivated to write this book for the same reason that I have written five previous business books, namely that I tend to get frustrated when I'm looking through hundreds of titles on a given topic and I cannot find what I'm looking for. In this case the topic area was high-potential development, particularly those actions and tactics that can be used to reduce development time for exceptional performers, while better preparing them for next-level assignments.

Unfortunately, what I found was that, while many books have been written on the subjects of executive coaching and leadership development, none has focused on the subject of how to reduce the time needed to prepare high-potential leaders for next-level positions. That's a shame, since leaders who are thrown into HIPO pools are often given few tools to support their development, with the exception of a few formal leadership development workshops. In the same way, managers who are expected to coach and sponsor these high-potential leaders are seldom adequately prepared to meet this challenge. They are held accountable for the development and retention of their people, yet placed in a "sink or swim" position for making this happen. As for executives and HR leaders, they

3

want to understand the leading trends, tools, and techniques that guide their industry. That's especially true for the many HR generalists and leadership development professionals who are attempting to quickly graft on the skills of OD and talent management as a way of taking on broader roles in their organization.

So having waited around (less than patiently, I'm afraid) for someone to put together book that focuses on the subject of high-potential development and coming up short, I decided to write one myself.

A Little Bit About Me

So what are my qualifications for writing this book? Well, for a start, I like to think that I represent a good balance between applied practice and academic scholarship. As a practitioner I have worked in the fields of organization and leadership development for more than thirty years and have spent fifteen of those years holding the top OD/LD position for six different companies. That means I have managed talent reviews and succession plans, have formed, managed, and coached high-potential leaders, and have also hired (and occasionally fired) executive coaches. I currently work as a management consultant, specializing in the areas of talent management and high-potential coaching, a consultancy practice in which I spent several years at an earlier part of my career.

On the scholarly/academic side, I hold a doctorate in human and organizational development from Fielding Graduate University and am currently a university instructor at Southern Methodist University in Dallas, Texas. As part of my academic responsibilities, I created and currently direct a coaching certification program for our university, which has focus areas in the subjects of coaching assessment as well as transitional, developmental, and performance coaching. More than two hundred individuals have completed the program since its inception over three years ago.

The five previous books that I have written on leadership development, team building, and talent management have been translated into three foreign languages for distribution throughout the UK, Europe, Scandinavia, and India. I have also written chapters for seven texts, and I have written more than thirty articles for leading trade and academic journals. Apart from my writing, I have presented on the subjects of leadership development and executive coaching at a number of international conferences, including those sponsored by The American

Society for Training and Development, The Society for Human Resource Management, the National OD Network, and the International Forum for Visual Facilitators.

I mention these facts because I want you to understand that I have stepped up and tested out a lot of what you'll read about in this book with those professional business and academic learning communities with which I am involved. In short, I have thought carefully about both the theory and conceptual framework that forms the contents of this book and have successfully applied those concepts within a number of business settings, ranging from engineering to media, insurance, and hotel franchising. After thirty years in this field, I continue to enjoy my work, since I'm a firm believer in the concept of life-long learning.

How to Use This Book

If you are a leader who wants to advance your own career and strengthen your performance, then I would encourage you to take the time to complete the action steps that I have placed in each chapter before advancing to the next chapter. My reason for suggesting this is that a book on leadership development is a bit like a book on exercise or dieting, in that it is really difficult to change any area of your life simply by reading about innovative change techniques. The hard part is that you actually have to put these ideas into practice. If you are using this book as a self-study guide, then I would recommend that you purchase a second copy for your manager, since the second part of this book provides a number of guidelines and suggestions for the steps managers can take to support the development of their team members. Another option is to find a peer or associate who would be willing to serve as troubleshooter and sounding board as you formulate and implement your development plan.

If you are a manager, you can use this book to help you coach and develop your people. I would recommend that you start off by working your way through the first part of this book and apply the ideas that you will find there to support your own professional development. Once you have accomplished this, proceed to the second half of the book, the Leader's Guide, and read about the steps you can take to support your team members' development process.

There are three reasons why I suggest this approach. First, by going through the exercises yourself, you might be able to gain something of personal value. Second, you will also gain a better feel for the concepts and guidelines that I will be introducing to your team members. Finally, if your team members know that you are actively engaged in your own development, they will be more likely to model your approach and apply these new ideas to their own development.

If you are a leader in learning and development (L&D), OD, or HR, then you will find that this book can serve as an excellent learning resource for conducting a workshop on leadership development. If you want something more extensive, feel free to reach me through the contact information provided in the back of this book and I will be happy to talk to you about the workshops that I run on this topic.

Finally, if you are a university instructor or private consultant who conducts coaching certification classes, you might also want to consider using this text as a supplemental resource to your own program materials. I am currently using this book myself within the coaching certification program that I teach at Southern Methodist University.

That's about it. If, after reading it, you have any questions or want to find out a little bit more about my approach to executive coaching, my contact information is provided in the back flap. Enjoy!

CHAPTER ONE

MANAGING A COMPANY OF ONE

Put Yourself in the Driver's Seat

If there's one thing that our increasingly volatile business environment has taught us, it is that the future is unpredictable. Simply speaking, I know of no organization these days that operates under the stable-state conditions that allow for the creation of reliable career paths. Faced with uncertain business conditions and a competitive field that seems to change on a daily basis, companies are trying to keep pace with these changes by continually adapting their organizational structures, leadership roles, and key business processes. The by-product of these changes is that we've reached a point at which it is a bit unrealistic, if not naïve, for anyone to expect that his or her employer will able to provide a reliable roadmap to advancement and career fulfillment. Instead, it is up to each of us to take the initiative to self-manage our own development as professionals and organizational leaders. This book lays out a simple, coherent approach you can use to jump-start your career and accelerate your development as a leader, while avoiding common (and often painful) missteps.

Now, in asking you to slide into the driver's seat I am not suggesting that your manager, HR department, and senior executives don't care about your growth as a professional—far from it. What I am saying is that there are several reasons why you benefit when you take the lead in directing your own development:

1. *You are the expert on you.* As helpful as other people want to be, the simple fact is that you know yourself better than anyone else does. As we'll discuss in the following chapters, your organizational stakeholders do play important roles as guides and advisors. They can keep you informed of important business developments that could affect the shape and structure of your organization, provide you with a fuller picture of your organization's changing expectations of its leaders, or alert you to development opportunities that might lie outside of your immediate job function. At the same time, it is a little unrealistic to think that your managers or HR leaders possess your level of insight when it comes to understanding such things as what provides you with satisfaction and meaning in a career or the types of work/life tradeoffs that you are willing to make to pursue a challenging developmental or promotional opportunity. In other words, as you continue along your career journey your managers and HR leaders can provide useful travel directions and help you anticipate those bumps that may lie hidden along the road. What they cannot do is tell you the direction in which you should head; that is your responsibility. So an important part of taking charge of your development is learning how to clearly identify, define, and communicate to your key organizational stakeholders what is most important to you in meeting your development needs.

2. *Self-development fosters self-discovery.* All too often when professionals set out to self-assess their development needs or to explore available development options, they fall into a trap that I call "surface skimming." By this I mean that they try to employ a simple, paint-by-the-numbers approach to self-development. While they may perform a cursory scan of their company's training catalogue or read a few recommended books on leadership, they seldom go further in the discovery process.

That is a big mistake, because at the core of development is the willingness to ask yourself a few key questions that force you off of autopilot and get you to take a fresh look both about what it is that you really want at this point in your career and the value you could potentially add to your organization. Critical questions include: (1) What it is that uniquely defines you as an individual and an exceptional performer? (2) Which of your strengths provide the building blocks for your long-term career success? and (3) How are you viewed by others in your organization? As you go through the remaining chapters I will invite you to explore these and several other questions that I routinely pose to my own coaching clients. If you make the effort to actively engage in these questions, you will find that you will discover a lot more about what it is that can make you an exceptional professional in your field.

3. *It is the only way to keep pace with change.* If you think that development is all about promotion, then think again. Taking control of your development is absolutely necessary when you are attempting to keep pace with rapid changes in your professional function, organization, and industry. Failing to take this step is a bit like failing to examine your 401(k) plan every few months to make certain that you are obtaining the best yield from your fund portfolio. Most of us would agree that in today's volatile investment market that isn't a smart move for financial planning. Similarly, it does not make a lot of sense for leadership development. It may be that you are an HR leader who has just started dealing with international employee relations, or a marketing leader whose company is quickly migrating toward online marketing. Whatever your leadership role, my guess is that your employer is expecting you to quickly graft on new technical and leadership skills that can help you to adapt to changing work conditions. If this is the case, the exercises that you will encounter in this book will help you build the kinds of technical and leadership skills you need to stay ahead of these changes.

4. *It saves time and effort.* When leaders lack a carefully targeted development plan, they tend to employ a "scattershot" approach to leadership development. The end result is that they experiment with a wide range of development activities, from taking a smattering of online courses to acquiring a senior-level mentor, in the hope that something will eventually "stick." A faster, more efficient method involves pinpointing and behaviorally defining your most important development needs, then using techniques such as leveraging "naturally occurring events" (more on this in Chapter 5) to fold leadership development actions into planned job activities.

Also, keep in mind that, like you, your manager is also continually under a time crunch. Therefore, the best way to gain your manager's support on your development and career goals is to make certain that before the two of you engage in a development conversation you have first done your homework. By this I mean carefully thinking about where you want to focus your development efforts and the types of assistance (shadowing opportunities, short-term assignments, etc.) that you actually need from your manager and senior stakeholders.

5. *Passivity is a loser's game.* Each year many organizations engage in something called a leadership talent review (LTR), which is intended to evaluate the performance and leadership potential of their managers and professionals. Not too long ago, leadership potential was defined in terms of the competencies, skills, and experience that an individual had acquired. While these factors are still deemed important, these days, when evaluating leadership potential, executives are placing greater emphasis on each individual's level of demonstrated learning agility. By learning agility I am referring to a person's ability to aggressively learn on the job and readily adapt to new and challenging circumstances. (I will talk more about learning agility in Chapter 5.) Quite often, in order to gauge an individual's degree of learning agility, executives raise the following questions during LTRs:

- "How invested is this person in her own development?"
- "How self-aware is she about her impact as a leader?"
- "How much insight does she have about her own development requirements?"
- "How did she perform when she was thrown into xyz assignment?"
- "How well has she adapted to (a new boss, a difficult work assignment, directing an organizational change, etc.)?

In attempting to answer these questions, senior executives tend to give a high level of attention to the level of thought and effort that leaders appear to put into their own professional development. From my own experience as a talent management leader and executive coach, I can tell you that nothing is more unimpressive than a person who, during the initial coaching session, comes across as being completely clueless about his or her own development needs. The opposite is also true. If you are willing to invest time and effort in formulating and executing your development goals, then you will find that this extra effort helps to distinguish you from the rest of the pack.

Accelerated Development: Is It Possible and Desirable?

In summary, the person who needs to direct your leadership development process is you. "All well and good," you say, "but is it really possible to compress the time that would typically be required to develop myself as a leader?" The answer to this question is an unqualified "Yes!" Some people doubt that it is possible to accelerate the time needed for leadership development. These individuals still adhere to what I call the outdated "cooking school" philosophy of leadership development. You can hear this assumption reflected in such comments as, "She's a strong performer but she still needs a little more seasoning" or "Experience has shown us that it takes five years for an engineer to be ready to take on a project manager role here."

Statements such as these imply that a standard and invariable "cooking time" is required for a professional or leader to reach a certain level of development. I would argue that, while these types of comments may be appropriate to the preparation of soup, they are not applicable to the area of leadership development. The reason is that organizations typically rely on certain accepted rules-of-thumb for gauging a professional's readiness for advancement, based on the typical time that it has taken for managers in similar roles to take on broader organizational rules. Those rules-of-thumb, however, are based on anecdotal data from professionals who have typically been given little or no targeted developmental support. This assumption falls apart when we take the time to show individuals how to build effective self-development plans and then give them the tools they need to successfully execute against those plans.

In my thirty years as an internal talent management executive and executive coach, I have discovered that it is, indeed, possible for you to accelerate your development as a leader. While I would be the first to admit that leadership development is partially contingent upon a few variables that are beyond your control, such as the availability of unique job assignments, at the same time certain influential factors lie directly within your control. By learning how to manage these factors, you can discover how to leverage your strengths as a leader, more quickly prepare yourself to take on broader leadership responsibilities, and make a bigger impact on your company's performance. What is more, it is possible to do all of this without shortchanging the effectiveness of the development process.

The secret lies in taking a targeted and disciplined approach to your own development. As an analogy, consider the area of physical fitness. I feel good about the fact that, now in my mid-fifties, my running distance and workout levels in resistance training are close to what they were thirty years ago. At the same time, I have seen certain people regularly attend the same gym that I do year after year without making any improvements to their heath. Why is this? Well, let me share a few observations:

- You cannot get optimal results unless you have first established a clear set of goals. People who only vaguely define their fitness goal as "getting fit" seldom do. A more precise fitness target would focus around making improvements to one of three pillars of heath: flexibility, aerobic endurance, or muscular strength. Taking muscular strength as an example, you get even better results when you target specific muscle groups for improvement.
- Moreover, you need to continue to focus your efforts during the execution phase of your plan. For example, it takes a lot longer to build muscle tone if you use sloppy form. Good form involves restricting your movements to those isolated muscle groups on which you are focusing your improvement efforts.
- You can't push yourself toward good results if your attention is spread, for example, if you are simultaneously talking on a cell phone while doing aerobics.
- Finally, you will find it difficult to achieve good results with a hit or miss, skip the gym for three weeks and then kill yourself with a four-hour session approach to training.

In short, while you cannot control your genetic makeup or certain pre-conditions that could influence your overall health, I do believe that by implementing these types of simple workout guidelines the average person can dramatically reduce the time required to meet his physical conditioning goals. The same holds true for leadership development. By leveraging the following factors that are directly within your control you can get better results, in less time:

First, you need to clearly identify the most important changes that occur to leadership requirements and job demands as you go from your current role to other job roles or the next leadership level in your organization. Simultaneously, you also need to understand the types of leadership adaptations that are required if you are attempting to migrate from your current work setting to other organizational settings in your company. We'll discuss how to master these challenges in Chapter 2.

Next, you need to create a development plan that goes beyond fuzzy language to include a detailed behavioral description of your development goals and targeted priorities for action. You also need to know how to approach organizational stakeholders to ensure that you receive detailed, timely, and value-laden feedback on your development needs. We'll cover these development challenges in Chapter 3.

A key part of any development planning process is learning how to make the most out of developmental assignments, such as leading a cross-functional project team or being loaned out to another department. In Chapter 4 you will learn how to partner with your manager to prepare for development assignments and to conduct debriefing and feedback sessions to gain the most effective learning from these assignments. You will also learn when and how to use developmental assignments as test points for gauging your readiness to tackle new work challenges. You will also learn how test points can help you lower the risk level associated with making major career moves by providing you with opportunities to conduct previews of new work settings or leadership roles. Finally, we will discus how test points serve as avenues for showing your organizational stakeholders that you are ready to take on bigger assignments.

Chapter 5 will introduce you to the concept of learning agility and explain how you can become more learning agile by taking advantage of a variety of learning opportunities, such as social networking and self-directed learning. You will also be introduced to several techniques that you can use to shorten your learning curve on the job. These techniques include using naturally occurring events as a scaffold for development activities, obtaining fast-cycle development feedback, and making more effective use of practice sessions.

Your career success is partially contingent on how you are viewed by others in your organization. In Chapter 6 you will explore your personal brand; those leadership behaviors and interpersonal styles that characterize how you come across to others in your organization. In this chapter you will also learn how to leverage your brand identity to support your career goals and how to aggressively address any aspects of your leadership style that could potentially hamper your progress.

Used together, these six chapters provide a solid framework for accelerating leadership development—one that puts you in the driver's seat of more effectively managing your own career. To make it easier for you to apply this book, the same four-step learning process will be incorporated in each of the remaining chapters. First, an Introduction provides an overview of the development stage covered in the chapter. You are then provided with General Guidelines for applying this stage of the development process. I will then share with you an illustrative example that will serve as a Case in Point for better understanding how that stage folds into the overall development process. I will then challenge you to take a few Next Steps for moving forward and applying these development stages. In addition, if you are using this book as a coaching and development vehicle for certain members of your work team, you will find the Leader's Guide in the back of this book to be very helpful.

Case in Point: Letting Go of the Past

Sally was a VP of operations, having been promoted into this role after transferring from the position of an operations director in one of her company's divisions. By the time that I had began working with her as a coach, her performance had begun to backslide. Her manager felt that she had the potential to continue to advance in the organization, but for some reason she was finding herself stuck in a performance rut. My initial conversation with this client was very telling. She spent a lot of time talking to me about how frustrated she was that her current manager didn't seem to have the same degree of respect for her as did her previous boss. She also complained that in her new role she was somewhat removed from the senior team, while in her previous role she had been able to communicate freely directly with the company president and senior executives. When she was notified that she been selected for her company's high-potential program, instead of being excited, Sally indicated frustration. She explained that, having already completed a high-potential program in another company division, she felt that she was simply repeating a phase in her development.

Furthermore, Sally was having difficulty adapting to her new role. Instead, she kept insisting that she could turn around her performance if she was only given the support she needed to implement the kinds of changes that she had made in her previous position. Sally's problem was that she was having a difficult time accepting that she was now in a new leadership role that came complete with a very different set of organizational expectations and success measures. In her previous role she had managed a fairly narrowly defined work function and had worked within an established function that had in place strong process controls and adequate staff support. In this previous role Sally had made her reputation by being a team builder and organizational cheerleader and by finding innovative ways to muster the full support of her work team. In contrast, within her new role Sally was expected to set up new procedures and process controls for a totally new distribution and call center. Most of what would be needed wasn't built yet, and she would need to aggressively recruit and develop her staff to fill a number of position vacancies.

Eventually, Sally made a successful transition, but before she could do this she had to agree to leave her old job behind and move on. As I explained to her, taking accountability for your professional growth is a bit like swinging out on a trapeze bar. You cannot take hold of the empty bar without first letting go of the one you are holding. Before you continue on to the next chapter, take a few minutes to ask yourself, "What bar are you still holding onto? What aspects of your current job do you need to let go of if you want to take on a broader, more expansive role in your organization?"

The Next Steps

I mentioned earlier that senior executives are beginning to place increased emphasis on an individual's learning agility. The chart on the next page summarizes six characteristics of learning-agile professionals. As a starting point for your own development, why not ask your manager or a few selected peers or other managers whom you trust and respect to use the learning behaviors listed in this chart to share with you how they view your learning agility.

Here are a few tips to make the process easier:

1. Rather than ask other people to rate you on each of these factors (people tend to be a bit noncommittal when a friend or colleague asks them for written feedback), a more effective option is ask your colleagues to identify one behavior in which you excel and another one which, if strengthened, would yield the greatest impact for you.

2. If you want your feedback providers to give you an example that illustrates a strength or development need, don't ask them to pull these examples from your past behavior. Once again, that question will make many people feel that they are providing you with an evaluation of your performance. Instead, ask: "Looking ahead, could you give me an example of the type of situations in which this behavior would be especially important were I to take on broader, more complex job roles within our company?"

Learning Factors and Behaviors Related to Learning Agility

Learning Factor	Related Behaviors
Self-Insight	I look for feedback that can provide me with a better understanding of my development needs.
	I know the organizational context in which certain personal characteristics (how hard I sell ideas, my listening ability, ability to build rapport, etc.) work for or against me.
	I solicit input from a variety of organizational stakeholders.
Adaptability	I am flexible with regard to looking at a number of career paths and options.
	I readily adapt to new circumstances, managers, etc.
	I don't require a "paint-by-numbers" work situation; I can easily deal with high-change, uncertain work settings.
Scope	I can view business issues from the perspective of the next level (understand how those issues would appear to leaders at my manager's level).
	I progressively work toward taking on a broader range of increasingly complex work responsibilities.
	I don't get lost in complexity.
Perspective	I understand the business context for decisions.
	I remain current on issues and trends within my industry.
	I factor into account the long-term implications of my decisions.
Impact	I can influence the decisions of others.
	I know when and how to navigate the organization and enlist the support of stakeholders.
	I can make a compelling business case for new initiatives.
Risk Taking	I am able to step out of my comfort zone to tackle new challenges.
	I am willing to make tough tradeoffs (relocation, job security) to advance my career and grow on the job.
	I "play without a net"; in other words, I am fully accountable for my actions.

CHAPTER TWO

CLOSING THE GAP

Take Aim at Your Career Target

When leaders come to me for coaching, it is usually because of one of two reasons. Some individuals have what I refer to as a remedial focus to executive coaching. That is, they are trying to resolve certain leadership style or behavioral issues that, if addressed, can help them turn around performance problems. In contrast, professionals who are already doing well in their current jobs approach executive coaching from a developmental perspective. These individuals are looking for ways to prepare themselves for broader leadership roles, either by expanding the value that they add within their current roles through promotional moves or through transitions into very different work settings within their companies.

The first step in both remedial and developmental coaching is to determine the gap that exists between current and desired performance. These two perspectives differ, however, in terms of the nature of the performance gaps that they address, with the result that they have different starting points for coaching. If you were approaching this book from a remedial perspective, I would suggest that you begin your planning process by meeting with your manager to discus those areas in which you are, or are not, currently meeting the performance expectations for your job. As it is, I am working off the assumption that you are a good performer.

If I am correct, then the starting point for building your acceleration plan involves developing a more complete composite profile of your ideal career target. By "career target" I am referring to the next position that you want to hold, be that a promotional move or a lateral transfer into another work area.

As you read this you may be thinking, "My career plans are a bit fuzzy at the moment and I haven't really done a lot of thinking about my career target. Is this step really necessary? Can I skip this first step and proceed directly to development planning?" In response I would suggest that you cannot take aim unless you first set your sights on a clear target. If we assume that an important part of your development plan will require you to take on special assignments or projects that could last several weeks or months, then neither you nor your company can afford the wasted effort that would result from taking a scatter-shot approach to professional development.

Not long ago this point was illustrated during a talent review and succession planning session that I facilitated for the executive team of a biotechnology company. At one point during the meeting, the discussion turned to Laura, a finance director who was extremely well respected by several members of the executive team. The company's CFO had identified Laura as being a successor to the VP of finance position and had also suggested that Laura had the long-term potential to eventually be a potential successor to his own role. Another of Laura's advocates, the company divisional president to whom Laura reported, had listed her as a successor for a significant leadership role within his operations department. Laura also appeared as a successor candidate for two other senior positions. It was at this point in the meeting that we discussed how unrealistic it was to think that Laura would be able to simultaneously prepare for four very divergent leadership paths.

Part of the problem was attributable to Laura herself who, in an effort to keep her options open, had intentionally been quite vague in expressing career priorities. During my follow-up coaching session with her, I helped Laura see the advantage of establishing a well-defined career target. While I respected her desire to keep her options open, I explained that, without additional clarity, her lack of direction could create a stumbling block to her development. As it stood now, if she had to chose between shadowing the SVP of sales on an extended negotiation and contracting process with a large pharmaceutical company or supporting the EVP of operations in developing a cost model for a new product distribution system, would either she or her employer know which option afforded the her best long-term developmental payoff? Given the time and effort required to secure and plan for these kinds of assignments, did she really want to risk disappointing her executive sponsors?

Does Your Career Target Reflect Your Priorities?

Quite often, in development planning we stay so focused on the task side of the equation that we never stop to ask ourselves two fundamental questions:

1. "At this point in my career and my life, what is most important to me in terms of both my career and my personal life?"
2. "Are these priorities reflected in my long-term career goals?"

These questions are important because, while we continually change over time, we seldom pause to give ourselves permission to determine whether those changes are reflected in our long-term personal and career goals. One way of getting in touch with your career priorities is to consider the types of career tradeoffs that you are willing to make over the next two years. The following questions can help prime your thinking a bit in this area:

Representative Career Tradeoffs

- If you are the parent of pre-school children would you be ready to relocate if a great promotional opportunity were part of the package? Do you think you would be as ready to move once your children were old enough to begin school?
- Are you willing to become a road warrior at this point in your life if that is what is required to get ahead?
- How about taking on a job that would require you to sleep next to your BlackBerry or iPhone so that you could immediately respond to a barrage of late-night emails from around the globe?
- Have your stress tolerance and energy level gone up or down over the past few years? Based on your answer to this, how willing would you be to move into a high-pressure job over the next few years?
- When you get beyond title and compensation, what really provides you with enjoyment at work? What makes you miserable? Does your career target reflect these factors?

- When you look back over the past several years, which of your jobs provided you with the greatest degree of personal satisfaction? What was it about the job that provided that high level of satisfaction? Is this factor baked into the selection of your career target?

While these aren't questions that your HR department or manager are likely to ask, they are questions that you need to honestly explore by yourself. Without a little time for personal reflection, it is easy to put yourself on "automatic pilot," only to find yourself stumbling when a major career opportunity suddenly comes your way.

Over the past twenty years, I have seen several leaders derail themselves from fast-track progressions because these questions remained unexamined until promotional opportunities fell into their laps. Within a few days one manager had to make decisions regarding taking on an expatriate assignment for two years, while another faced a promotional opportunity that required him to transfer his family across the coast, and a third was asked to fill a newly created position that required 24/7 attention. Quite often, blinded by the lure of title and trappings, I have seen professionals who are faced with these types of decisions make the wrong moves, only to immediately experience a high degree of buyer's remorse.

Please understand me here; I am not saying that you should turn down these types of career moves when they're offered. My message is only that, if you do have some constraints regarding the types of advancement opportunities that you are willing to consider, then take the initiative to discuss these matters with your manager before your company places you on the short list for consideration for a new career opportunity.

Case in Point: Tom

After graduating at the head of his class from a top-rated MBA school, Tom entered his company's fast-track development program. During his first year with the company Tom was ranked in the highest potential category of all thirty program participants. The CFO of Tom's company took Tom under his wing and assigned him some fairly significant projects having huge revenue and cost impact. Tom waltzed through the projects and in the process earned high marks from everyone regarding his many technical skills, from valuation analysis to managing financial negotiations with a few key business partners. The CFO was very pleased, and although Tom was relatively new to the company, plans were already in place to move Tom into a director role once he had completed the end of his remaining year of the fast-track program.

Yet something was missing. When I asked people about Tom they told me that, even though he was very polite and agreeable, they knew almost nothing about him. He had a tendency to avoid all small talk and spent most of the day buried behind his computer. Although Tom performed exceptionally well when he was working with data, he never took the lead when he participated in team brainstorming sessions, nor did he attempt to take the lead role when assigned to projects with his peers. At one point, Tom was invited to attend the CEO's annual planning session (a high-status event typically restricted to senior executives). I observed him spending his break time playing with his BlackBerry rather than taking the opportunity to reach out and introduce himself to key executive stakeholders.

During one of my first coaching sessions with Tom, I shared my concerns and asked him to discuss his career goals. I explained that unless he said something to the contrary, he stood a good chance of moving up the standard career path within his department, which would mean taking over a large chunk of the daily operation of his company's finance or accounting departments.

Tom admitted that he didn't find this career target very exciting. He told me that what he really enjoyed was the chance to engage in strategic analysis, not the day-to-day management of a large group of people in the operational side of the business. This area of work was simply too pedestrian for his tastes. His idea of a perfect job was to work in a McKinsey-like think tank, where he would provide recommendations for addressing large business problems, not slog through the tedious implementation of those solutions. In Tom's company that meant taking on a director role in the company's very small strategic planning group. Even though I explained that this would mean a dead-end move into a niche area, Tom was adamant that this move would be well-aligned with his true passion. I passed the word on to the CFO and we set Tom's plans accordingly.

Tom was honest regarding his career goals and values, and his honesty served him well. If he had allowed himself to be recommended as an eventual successor to the CFO position and then turned down the next logical advancement opportunity leading to this position, he would have embarrassed his senior sponsor and seriously curtailed his chances for advancement. The moral is: When identifying your career target, be true to yourself.

Keep the Big Picture in Mind

In coaching high-performing leaders on selecting career targets, one of the most common mistakes that I encounter is the tendency for clients to become obsessively concerned with short-term and relatively trivial concerns, such as position title or how much of a compensation increase would accompany a given move. If you are serious about your career and feel that you have the ability to go far in your organization, then you need to be thinking in terms of where you'd ideally like to be five to ten years down the path. Only after you have this long-term target in mind should you consider moving backward to identify short-term moves that support this long-term goal.

To an outsider these moves may, at first, seem counterintuitive since they may not produce a short-term payoff. Don't be concerned; stick to your long-term game plan. If a novice chess player were to observe two masters at play, the new player might not understand why one of the experienced players opts to sacrifice a pawn early in the game. The difference is that experienced chess players are able to think several moves ahead and to continue to revise their strategy as the game unfolds. They are able to keep the big picture in mind as they play.

One of my coaching clients, David, was a very intelligent, high-performing director of product development. Shortly before I had begun working with him, his company had been acquired by a much larger corporate entity. A few months earlier, David had been identified by his employer as a fast-track candidate for a senior executive position within the corporate office's product development function. Unfortunately, even though David had experience in managing a few small product lines, he lacked the experience of managing multiple products through the pipeline, particularly those involving rather complex execution strategies. As a result, David's manager recommended that for his next assignment he consider transferring to a product line director position within the corporate office. His response was less than enthusiastic.

"But I am already a director of product development," he told me.

"Yes," I countered, "but you have to understand that even though the title's the same, the two positions aren't equivalent. The scope of what you are currently managing is rather small, while this next position will provide you with an opportunity to take on much larger projects associated with a significantly higher revenue stream. It will also put you in the lineup for the VP of product development position, should that position open up."

"But I am ready for that now," he argued. "Besides, given the relocation allowance involved, I don't see how I am going to come out that far ahead on the move to corporate, even with a 15 percent bump in salary."

And so it went. You see, David was so preoccupied with title and status that he couldn't keep the larger picture in mind. Instead, he tried to hold out for the hope of a promotional opportunity at his acquired company, even though I warned him that the organizational trend was that most of the VP-level jobs would be migrating to the corporate office over the next two years. For all I know, he's still at the company at the same position.

Don't make the same mistake of viewing "career growth" as a progressive, time-bound movement by title and grade. When opportunity comes knocking, keep the big picture in mind.

Job Demand Features: The Heart of the Crucible

The secret to making intelligent choices regarding your professional development is to take the time to construct a composite profile that clearly identifies, from all of the many defining characteristics of your career target, those few elements that represent the most important demand features associated with this position. Demand features are job characteristics that:

- Present you with the biggest adaptive challenges, in other words, work situations that are difficult to master and that typically require you to build totally new skills;
- Have been important in determining the success or failure of people who have held this position;
- Are aspects of the job that are likely to receive the greatest amount of attention from your executive team; and
- Are the features to which your managers are most likely to attend when evaluating your performance.

To better understand what I mean by demand features, think of your career target in terms of the metaphor of a crucible. A crucible is the heat-resistant part of a container where different materials are fused together to form something new. In life, the crucibles we encounter are those situations or critical life events that force us to adapt and grow—in effect, to become something different. In our personal lives, such life events might include becoming a parent for the first time or overcoming a serious medical problem. In the world of work, a leadership development crucible can be viewed as any new leadership assignment or position that requires us to succeed by using different kinds of leadership behaviors, applied within different work contexts, to meet different kinds of performance expectations. These three elements of behavior, context, and expectations fuse together to form those job demand features that are catalytic to true professional growth.

Over the remainder of this chapter, I will introduce you to a simple process that you can use to identify the crucible that is associated with your next career target, as well as the development gaps that you will need to close to better prepare for this assignment. We'll also talk about how to go about reaching alignment with your manager and other stakeholders regarding how they view these new leadership challenges. For now, I want you to briefly describe your intended career target on a piece of paper. If that target does not currently exist in your organizational structure, then select a position that comes as close as possible to the job target that you envision or take a minute to construct your own job description. Completing this simple action will help you keep this career target in mind as you progress through the rest of the chapter.

The First Element: Leadership Behavior

In order to identify those leadership behaviors that represent important demand features of your career target, you need to consider where your target sits within your company's leadership hierarchy. While it is true that every promotional change involves some degree of adaptation, the biggest adjustments occur when you jump to a level that represents a major expansion in the type of leadership work that you will be required to perform in your new job. The authors of *The Leadership Pipeline* have suggested that there are six major promotional steps that characterize major movements through any organizational leadership pipeline. These six shifts involve the following progressions:

- From managing one's self (individual contributor) to managing others
- From managing others to managing managers

- From managing managers to becoming a functional manager
- From becoming a functional manager to becoming a business manager
- From business manager to becoming group manager, and finally
- From being a group manager to becoming an enterprise manager (CEO)

Each of these promotional transitions carries with it a very different set of leadership adjustment demands. As an example, consider what happens when someone is promoted from managing managers to leading an entire function. As a new functional manager, the leader now has complete responsibility for the costs that roll through her function. In addition, this may well be the first time that this leader is responsible for managing sub-functions that lie outside of her area of expertise. Thus, someone who is promoted into the job of a vice president of finance may have come up through the ranks having obtained a strong background in financial analysis. At the same time, this person may have had relatively little exposure to performing valuations on perspective acquisition targets, although this financial sub-function may now directly report up to the VP. In the same way, one seldom encounters a head of HR who has had in-depth exposure to all HR sub-functions, including compensation, employee relations, leadership development, employee communications, and talent acquisition.

To manage such a broad range of work activities, new functional managers find that they must rely more on the expertise of others and base decisions on information that is indirectly accessed, as it is filtered (and frequently distorted) through multiple work levels. Functional managers must also understand the subtle interdependencies that exist between their own functions and other company work groups, and how to manage lines of influence across their organization. Finally, they are now at the level where they must begin to shift their focus of attention from inside the company to the external business environment, as they consider how to bring about performance that can beat the competition. While it is beyond the scope of this book to summarize the distinct leadership challenges that are associated with each turn in the pipeline, I heartily encourage you to purchase *The Leadership Pipeline* and pursue your own studies in this area. The point that I am trying make here is that each step forward in these management levels requires a qualitative shift in leadership thinking and the willingness to engage in very different roles and leadership behaviors.

Along with the changes to leadership behavior that occur as you progress through each stage of the leadership pipeline, each job has certain requirements that are unique to that particular position. Mapping out these requirements helps you to clearly pinpoint your development requirements and puts you in a more competitive position to go after these jobs.

How do you go about finding out about the types of leadership behaviors that are unique to a given leadership position? A safe starting point is to ask your HR manager for a copy of the job description for your current career target, then compare it with the job that you are currently performing. While this approach will provide you with some general information on skill gaps, formal job descriptions usually provide only a broad overview on a position. To obtain a more granular picture of your career target I recommend that you ask the following questions of your manager, peers, and other managers who are in positions to understand both the work you do and the work that is expected to be performed within your target position.

Questions for Identifying the Unique Demand Features of Your Career Target

- What has made the difference between people who have succeeded or failed in this position? For example, would I find that successful and unsuccessful leaders differed greatly in terms of how these two groups of leaders managed work relationships, stakeholders, or work priorities?
- Is there someone who currently holds, or who has previously held, this position whom you view as being an exemplar—someone who is a strong role model for "how to do it right"? What is this person's secret to success? Can you give me an example?
- What do you see as some of the biggest differences between the skills, competencies, and experience required for my current job and those required to succeed within my career target? Can you give me an example?
- If I were to move into this job tomorrow, what aspects of the job do you think would come easy to me? What do you think would be a big learning area for me?
- If I were to step into this job, are there any nasty surprises waiting for me (things such as difficult political issues, resource constraints, or ambiguous priorities)?
- Who else within our organization really understands the requirements for this position? Would you be willing to help me reach out to this person to obtain more information?

The Second Element: Organizational Context

In identifying career targets we may find that we've set our sights on positions that will force us to operate in very different organizational settings. The same job requirements, set within different organizational contexts, can transform those requirements into completely different types of job challenges. Let's consider the adaptive challenges posed by three changes in organizational context—namely those represented by different organizational cultures, different strategic priorities, and different organizational structures.

Different Organizational Cultures. Every organization likes to believe that it is dominated by a singular corporate culture that defines the norms for how its employees are expected to work together. These organizational values are often written on large posters, loaded on corporate websites, or make their appearance on coffee mugs and other company giveaways. There is nothing wrong with these actions, since they simply attempt to convey the types of corporate values and culture that senior executives hope to build in their organizations. All well and good, but as your personal coach I am going to ask you to treat these statements with a certain amount of caution. First of all, while they convey the espoused organizational culture, they do not provide a lot of information about the types of behaviors that are actually rewarded in an organization. Consider the organizational value of teamwork. I have yet to see an organization that does not have teamwork (or some version of this word) listed as one of its corporate values. Yet the word has little meaning unless we first "unpack" it and consider what it means in terms of expected employee behavior.

I know of one organization in which being a team player means "playing nice in the sandbox." Leaders are expected not to aggressively disagree with or challenge others in public forums such as interdepartmental staff meetings, even if they feel that other managers are not meeting agreed-on commitments. Instead they are expected to deal with such issues either by conducting private off-line meetings with the offending managers or by escalating their concerns through the formal chain of command.

I have also worked with another company in which being a team player is largely defined in terms of meeting group commitments. As a result, professionals and leaders are encouraged to openly confront other leaders in departmental or project meetings if they feel that those individuals are not meeting their team commitments. Given this norm, group meetings are frequently confrontational, and leaders are expected to hold their own in public debate. Both of these companies have teamwork etched in as one of their core values, yet they express this value in very different ways, resulting in very different sets of expectations of their leaders.

We also have to consider that most large companies are not dominated by a uniform corporate culture, but instead show wide fluctuations in culture by work levels and sites. This tends to be particularly true for those companies that have been formed through rapid acquisition and those that span diverse international locations. As a result, you are quite likely to find yourself faced with some important differences in organizational culture when your career target involves both a promotional jump and a transition into another company work location.

One of my colleagues, the head of HR for a large, privately held company, tells me that her HR leaders must deal with the continual tension of managing functions that straddle North America. Those functional elements that reside in the company's U.S. division are dominated by a sub-culture that is very process-driven. On the other hand, employees in the company's Canadian location place less emphasis on adhering to uniform, formal HR policies and more on maintaining informal networks. Given this culture, the Canadian HR managers are used to customizing policies to meet one-off requests by their internal stakeholders. How do these differences show up in developmental challenges? Namely, anyone who hopes to move into a senior HR leadership role must be able to balance these different organizational cultures, which are expressed in the conflicting needs for administrative standardization versus personalized customer responsiveness. The moral is that any internal career move that requires you to perform within a different organizational culture requires a significant adaptation of one's interpersonal behavior and work style—adaptations that you can begin to prepare for with a little creative planning.

Different Strategic Priorities. A move to another part of your company may also mean adapting to different strategic priorities. For example, many corporate portfolios contain both fast-growth and mature companies. Within fast-growth companies there tends to be more forgiveness when it comes to following set processes and procedures because the company's erratic growth jerks tend to keep people focused on doing whatever is needed to capture and manage the next big contract. In these organizations, professionals and leaders tend to be pushed through the leadership pipeline at an aggressive rate and will frequently be thrust into promotional assignments or asked to direct large projects with little advanced preparation. Work hours tend to be long, and 24/7 operations are not uncommon as leaders try to keep up with customer demands, operational limitations, and the swelling mass of new employees.

For mature organizations, the situation is very different. Faced with receding margins and difficult competition, these organizations typically attempt to achieve a high level of standardization and process control to reduce costs while maximizing operational efficiency. Needless to say, each of these organizational settings requires a very different set of leadership skills and is likely to operate within a very different set of organizational norms. The same can be said about start-up businesses and organizational turnarounds.

The question that you need to answer is whether pursuing your career target will require you to make a move into a company unit that has a very different culture and/or different strategic priorities. To get a better understanding of the types of changes that you are likely to encounter you might consider presenting the following questions, both to selected leaders and peers within your own work unit as well as the work unit that you have targeted:

Questions for Identifying an Organization's Culture and Strategic Priorities

- What are some of the interpersonal behaviors that typically pose challenges for leaders in ... [name of the target organization]? (Examples would include how people deal with conflict, how they are expected to balance risk taking with fast decision making, and whether they feel free to skip chain-of-command and talk directly to senior-level leaders.)
- What are some of the biggest adjustment difficulties that have been encountered by leaders who have transferred over from our organization to ... [name of the target organization]?
- Every company has certain unspoken norms, or rules of the game, that define what is viewed as exceptional performance and how employees are expected to work together to accomplish things. What are some of the biggest differences that you see between the norms that characterize my organization and those that are unique to ... [name of the target organization]?
- Most organizations can be classified as being in a start-up mode, a growth mode, a mature market, or a turnaround. How would you classify ... [name of the career target]? Given this, what are the organization's strategic priorities; what seems to be getting a lot of attention on the executive agenda?

Different Organizational Structures. The last contextual change that you need to consider when pondering an internal move is whether or not making this move will place you into a very different organizational structure. A classic example involves transfers between field and corporate locations. Professionals who make the move from field offices to corporate centers can easily lose patience with the slower speed of decision making. They soon learn that to accomplish things in their new setting they must develop the tenacity required to wade through more intricate corporate politics and approval processes. For recent transfers it can feel as if every small decision needs to be taken to committee for review and that it takes forever to reach a simple decision. In addition, the lines of influence are not so clearly demarcated as they are in field roles, meaning that it is easy to overlook getting buy-in for an important decision from a key stakeholder. People who make field-to-corporate moves can also discover that because of their increased visibility they are under increased scrutiny from senior executives. They can end up feeling as if they've just moved into a fishbowl in which their every move is watched by others. Finally, such transitions typically require a higher degree of finesse when it comes to one's social behavior. For example, a leader who is loud and brash may find that this behavior is frowned upon at corporate dinners or off-sites.

Leaders who are transitioning from corporate sites to field environments face very different adjustments. These leaders may not be fully prepared for the relentless pace of implementation in the field, where time frames from inception to execution are contracted. They also need to be able to find innovative solutions to work problems, despite lacking the resources and staff support that were more available in their former corporate roles. Corporate transfers can also feel that they are cut off from contact with senior corporate executives (out of sight, out of mind). Finally, corporate transfers may find that they have to work to gain acceptance from people in the field who, while perhaps lacking in academic credentials or fancy titles, have proven themselves time and again in tough jobs.

Transitions between corporate and field positions are only one type of adjustment that can accompany a career move. Additional changes include the shifts between staff and line roles, between home office positions and expatriate assignments in other countries, between organizational units where you are reporting to a single manager and matrix organizations involving multiple reporting lines, and between established jobs and new positions. Before going further you may want to go back to the career target position that you had identified earlier and note whether the transition into this position would require you to make a move into a very different organizational structure.

The Third Element: Performance Expectations

In preparing for your career target, the third contextual change you may encounter is a change in performance expectations. The question of how success is defined in your target position reveals what is considered important in that organizational setting, and it has direct implications for how you need to approach your development planning.

Assume that you are working in a sales role in which your sales bonus is directly tied to your ability to generate overall top-line revenue. Eventually, you'd like to take on a different sales role in a different company division and, after little probing on your part, you discover that the president of this division is very concerned about the company's profit margins. Part of this concern is based on the assumption that the division's sales force does not always cut profitable deals. Accordingly, sales reps and leaders in this division receive bonuses, not on top-line revenue, but on net profit. What is the implication for development planning? Well, I would argue that to succeed in this position you'd have to be able to have a solid understanding of pricing and full product costs, with more emphasis placed on your ability to negotiate contract terms and conditions. You'd also have to know when to walk away from an unprofitable sale.

It is helpful to obtain the perspectives of your manager and other knowledgeable leaders in your company regarding the types of performance expectations that you would be likely to encounter were you to transition into another organizational area. At the same time, when you raise this subject your listeners might think that you are talking about performance standards, for example, whether your current organization has looser or tougher standards than does the organizational unit in which your career target is located. To get around this problem consider providing a few comparative examples, such as the ones shown below.

PARTICIPANT'S GUIDE

Comparative Performance Expectations

1. Risk taking versus caution:
   a. Some organizations reward aggressive risk taking.
   b. Other organizations reward caution over risk taking; in these organizations you are more likely to be remembered for the mistakes you have made than for the large "wins" you have generated.

Continued

2. Effort versus outcome:

   a. In some organizations leaders make a mental note of who puts in the most hours; 24/7 performance is highly valued and performance is equated with one's number of work hours.

   b. In other organizations leaders don't pay attention to your work hours; rewards are based solely on whether or not you excel on your goals.

3. Task versus process

   a. In some organizations how you interact with others, and your ability to build friends and allies, is extremely important.

   b. In other organizations you are forgiven if you alienate others in the organization if, by doing so, you are able to achieve your goals.

4. What versus how

   a. In some organizations performance reviews focus entirely on what you have accomplished.

   b. In other organizations annual reviews are balanced, with weight given both to what you have accomplished and to how you have achieved it (for example, in an effort to boost performance did you create higher attrition within your work group?).

5. Customer-focus versus profit

   a. In some organizations people are expected to go the last mile to please the customer. In such organizations "customer heroes" are applauded, even if their actions cut into the profit line.

   b. In other organizations there is more emphasis on pleasing the customer only if those actions don't cut into the profit line.

Case in Point: Jamie

I know of a media company that created a new director-level position to manage the dissemination of news information across the traditional media silos of newspaper, broadcast, and Internet. Jamie, one of the company's assistant news directors, conveyed to me his interest in applying for this position. Jamie already knew that the new job required the technical skill of being able to repurpose news, such as reducing extended story content intended for one of the company's newspapers into the leaner, more crisp format that works well for the Internet. During our first developmental coaching session, I encouraged Jamie to probe further to identify other leadership behaviors that would be critical to success on this job. In doing so, he discovered that the job also required a leader who had good influence skills. These skills were important because the new director would have to balance the often conflicting needs of different power groups, while having no authority over those groups. The news content director would, for example, have to know how to explain to a broadcast news director why it didn't make sense to hold off an important storyline for five hours until the station's next scheduled televised news program, when there were important advantages to be gained by breaking the news story immediately on the station's Internet site.

Jamie was already aware that these same skills of influencing and political savvy were required of many other director-level positions in his company. At the same time, through additional questioning, he found out that there were several reasons why these general leadership skills took on unique demand features within the new director position:

1. The new director would be managing a totally new work function that lacked historical credibility (some managers doubted the need for such a position, while others were threatened by the fear that it was going to intrude on their sovereign turf).
2. The new position stood at the cross-hairs of a broader ongoing organizational battle regarding the role that online news should play in supplementing traditional broadcast and print news.
3. Being a totally new work function, the company lacked a consistent set of procedures and policies regarding how news resources were to be shared across the silos of broadcast, print, and Internet.
4. The director role would not be a stand-alone position. The new director would also need to be able to quickly hire and manage a team of three people who would have the same prerequisite technical and interpersonal skills.

Because of these factors, success in the new director role would be strongly contingent upon Jamie's ability to demonstrate his skills as an organizational influencer. By constructing a more complete description of the job requirements for this new position Jamie was better able to determine whether he still wanted to apply for the new job when it became available. He also gained a better understanding of the types of skill gaps that he needed to close to prepare for this new role and the type of self-branding that would help him to sell his value as a candidate to executive stakeholders.

Your Next Steps

To help you implement this first step of your development acceleration process I am going to ask you to take on the following two assignments. You will get a lot more out of this book if you complete these assignments before moving on to the next chapter.

Assignment One: Describe Your Ideal Career Target

To begin your first assignment, select someone you trust such as your life partner, a family member, or a close friend. This could also be a co-worker who has agreed to work with you as a peer coach. In a peer coaching arrangement you and your selected co-worker agree to read through this book and to meet on a regular basis to discuss the completion of your respective Next Step assignments. It is not important that the person you select have an intimate understanding of your current job or your career target, His or her role for this assignment will be merely to meet with you for an hour and take the role of a troubleshooter and sounding board as you discuss the career target.

In presenting your summary to your listening partner, attempt to complete the following sentences:

1. "The one thing that sets my career target apart from any other position, in terms of the types of work activities and environment that I find rewarding and satisfying, is ..."

2. "In order to be ready to take on this role, the biggest skill gaps that I would need to close are ..."

3. "To succeed in this role the most difficult adjustment that I would make (culture, strategic priorities, organizational structure) would be ..."

4. "The major challenge that I would face in succeeding in this role would be ..."

5. "The one thing that I still don't know about my career target is ..."

6. "The three people in our organization who are in a position to tell me more about my career target are ..."

7. "The leaders in our company who would be most influential in evaluating my readiness to take on this new role are ..."

Encourage your listening partner to stop you and ask for clarification whenever your answers appear to be vague or ambiguous. Your partner can also help you by asking additional questions.

Assignment Two: Conduct Three Informational Interviews

Your second assignment involves interviewing three key leaders within your organization regarding their views on the major demand features (leadership behaviors, work context, performance expectations) that characterize your career target. I would recommend that one of these leaders be your manager. Others can be

- Knowledgeable co-workers
- A fast-track leader, someone who has successfully made a similar transition
- A key leader within your target organization
- An HR leader who directly supports managers within your career target

Please keep in mind that these don't have to be formal interviews. A lot of times you can scan your electronic calendar and identify upcoming events (project team meetings, staff meetings, town halls, sales conferences, etc.) during which you are likely to come into contact with those key leaders and professionals who can provide you with good information on your chosen career target. Consider reaching out to these individuals through a quick phone call or email. Ask them if they wouldn't mind setting aside a few minutes immediately before or following these events to talk with you about a position or organizational niche in which you have a strong career interest. As you conduct these informational interviews, you may want to use the following form for collecting and consolidating information on your chosen career targets.

Informational Interview Form

My career target is ...

The three individuals in the best position to provide me with information on this career target are ...

Based on my interview data, the two leadership and technical gaps that I need to close in order to be fully prepared for this position are ...

Based on my interview data, the biggest adjustment that I would have to make (new organizational culture, different strategic priorities, different organizational structure) to succeed within my career target would be ...

After you have completed the interviews, look for consistent themes that run through them. Then try to identify the two greatest development gaps that you will need to close in order to prepare for this role. Also identify any additional questions that still need to be addressed before you can develop a clear picture of your target.

CHAPTER THREE

BUILDING YOUR PLAN

Essentials of Good Development Planning

In the last chapter we discussed the importance of establishing a clearly defined career target. If you completed all of the suggested "next step" actions that were recommended at the end of the chapter, you should now have a better idea of the skill gaps you need to close in order to prepare for your next career move. In addition, if your selected career target lies within a very different organizational setting, you have probably discovered the gaps you will need to close to successfully adapt to this new work environment.

The second step in accelerating your development is to construct a written development plan that can help you close those gaps. A written plan is more than a check-the-box exercise. Few people would play golf without keeping score or would undertake an intense fitness program without maintaining some record of their progress. The same is true with professional development. A written development plan provides a method for you to periodically check your progress against your development goals. In this regard, having a written plan is one way to nudge yourself out of complacency if you find yourself procrastinating on carrying out development actions. The simple step of constructing a written plan is one way to secure your commitment to your goals and maintain the momentum in your development process.

In addition, as with any planning document, taking the time to write out your plan will help you clarify your thinking regarding your development goals and options. Most of my coaching clients find that, by stepping away from their plan for a few days and then going back to it, they approach it with a fresh and more objective perspective. A written plan provides a baseline that you can continue to refine and adjust over the next few years. In doing so you may find that, over time, you end up revising the priorities that you had originally assigned to your development goals or find ways to overcome stumbling blocks that had originally seemed insurmountable.

Finally, consider the fact that constructing a good development plan is one way for you to clearly communicate your developmental priorities and planning process to your manager, senior executives, and any co-worker you might use as a coaching partner. This feature is particularly important when we are trying to gain the support for our plans from senior leaders who are time-limited and who expect us to be able to come to the table with a well-developed plan of action for anything that we are undertaking.

It may be that you have already taken the time to put together a preliminary development plan. If so, you might want to refer to that plan as you read through the remainder of this chapter so that you can see how it measures up against the following five characteristics of good development plans. Over the remainder of this chapter, we will see how these five characteristics come together to support the development process.

The Five Characteristics of Good Development Plans

1. Starts with Outcomes—Your planning process proceeds from a detailed description of the work challenges that you will be able to master and the work outcomes you want be able to achieve as the result of completing your development actions.
2. Focused and Precise—Your plan is limited to two behaviorally defined areas for improvement.
3. Actionable—You have identified the most important actions that you and others will take to support your development goals and the most appropriate sequence and timing for completing these actions.

Continued

4. Aligned—Your stakeholders are in agreement regarding your plan outcomes, proposed development actions, and the support roles that they will be asked to play to make your plan a success.
5. Based on Feedback—You have identified others within your organization who are in the best position to provide you with developmental feedback and the types of feedback that you need to obtain from them. You continually revise your plans based on available feedback.

Performance Outcomes

I frequently hear people complain that their managers and senior sponsors don't support their professional development. I would argue that your manager and executive stakeholders will support your development plan, if they see a strong connection between your professional growth and their need to meet critical performance objectives. Unfortunately, quite often we fail to make a good business case for our development plans. Instead, proposed development plans are presented as a wish list that appears to be totally detached from key work requirements. The most ineffective planning process relies on an *activity-based development model*, such as the one shown in Figure 3.1.

As you can see from the figure, people who engage in activity-based development planning attempt to start their planning process by generating a list of development activities. Ask such a person to describe his or her development plan and you might hear something like:

- "I want to take a course on listening."
- "I feel like I need more exposure to our company's sales function."
- "I understand that our company is putting together a leadership workshop, and I would like to attend."

Because these development actions are totally disconnected from the performance requirements for a given career target, if you ask these individuals to explain how their proposed development actions support their

FIGURE 3.1. Activity-Based Development Model

core development needs, the answers you hear are usually vague and lack in-depth thinking:

- " My manager has told me that I need to become a better listener."
- "Getting a better understanding of our sales process will help me understand our customers."
- "I want to become a stronger leader."

If you go one step further and ask these individuals to describe how these development needs link to their career targets or how their organizations benefit from their suggested development actions, you will usually find that they are completely stumped. They don't understand the relationship between personal development and business requirements.

You can gain a marginal increase in the effectiveness of your development process by making use of a *needs-based development model*, such as the one below. On the plus side, this approach offers the advantage of starting with a review of one's development needs before generating a list of development activities. Once again, however, performance outcomes are treated as an afterthought and don't guide the development process, as in Figure 3.2.

To accelerate your development, I recommend that you make use of an *outcomes-based development planning model*, as shown in Figure 3.3. This approach begins with envisioning how you would like to be able to perform differently a year from now, after undertaking a dedicated development process. The second step involves determining the skills, knowledge, and contextual understanding you will need to develop to achieve these outcomes. Only then should you focus on identifying those actions that can help you achieve your development goals.

Development Activities

Anyone who has ever fired a gun at a moving target knows that you have to lead your target; that is, you have to anticipate its trajectory and aim

FIGURE 3.2. Needs-Based Model

FIGURE 3.3. Outcomes-Based Model

slightly ahead of it. In the same way, professionals who make use of an outcome-based development model recognize that career targets are not static. Rather, when these individuals identify a career target that lies two to three years down the path, they continually adapt their development plans and career goals to take into consideration changes in market conditions, business requirements, and organizational structure. In this way they ensure that they can succeed in the evolving job role that they've selected.

Case in Point: Randy

Randy was one of two marketing directors employed by a direct marketing consulting firm. For two years he and a second marketing director had worked together under the guidance of their general manager to launch the company's first successful online marketing function. The new function provided a number of specialized services to mid- to small-size companies, including data-mining and analytics, creating or redesigning clients' websites, building microsites to support special client marketing campaigns, designing online newsletters, and conducting targeted email campaigns.

Randy had identified his manager's current job, the GM position, as his desired career target. He intended to make certain that if this position were to become available he would be viewed as the logical replacement. He also knew that due to the successful launch of online marketing function his company was seriously discussing the option of transforming the function into a separate business unit. This change would mean that, instead of being subsumed as an expense burden under the company's corporate marketing department, the function would stand alone as a revenue-making unit. Given these changes, Randy realized that not only would he have to convince his executive team that he had the skills needed to perform the GM role as it stood today, but he would have to demonstrate that he was able to take the next step and transform this start-up into a fast-growth revenue-generating unit.

During our first few coaching sessions, Randy and I worked together to identify the most important outcomes that he needed to derive from his development process. These included:

- Being able to develop a strategic plan that would establish a viable path to profitability (P2P) for the newly created enterprise. The plan would have to include a solid revenue model, with agreed-on progress dates for gauging success.
- Building and managing a greatly expanded team. This would be particularly true for the group's production function, which was responsible for the design, installation, and testing of new online tools and services.
- Identifying expanded client market and sales priorities for the growing firm.
- Negotiating service support from the company's other business functions.

Of all of these challenges, the one that represented the biggest development gap for Randy was the first one, that of establishing a viable path to profitability. He explained that this task would be particularly challenging, given that many of his function's products and services were currently bundled together with other company services, such as direct mail campaigns, under a consolidated fee structure. In addition, up to this point Randy's work team had lacked a high degree of discipline in how they approached their pricing. Because good project and cost controls weren't in place, the production team often found itself going well over the allocated hours that had been established for projects, with the result that the group lacked good historical data on which to gauge their pricing when bidding on new projects.

Using this information as his focal point, Randy identified two development outcomes that he wanted to achieve over the course of the next twelve months:

1. Developing a more accurate financial model that would be scalable to address the increasingly larger projects that his function would be assuming
2. Implementing more effective project controls so that his group could anticipate the financial impact of such things as schedule slips, cost overruns, and unplanned change requests

To obtain these outcomes, Randy felt that he needed to become stronger in understanding financial modeling and project controls. I cautioned Randy that whatever financial planning model was eventually adopted for his function would need to have buy-in from several other business groups within his company. Given this, a second development area would involve being able to form influential partnerships with selected stakeholders.

Randy's last step involved brainstorming with me and his manager a list of actions that could support his development goals, including:

1. Attending an outside training seminar that dealt with how to establish and monitor a path to profitability
2. Requesting that one of his company's finance managers help him perform a baseline assessment on his function's current financial planning model and recommending improvements to that model
3. Beginning to develop stronger relationships with a few identified key stakeholders over the next few weeks

By starting with his desired performance outcomes, before identifying his development needs and related development actions, Randy established a strong business case for his development plan. He was able to use this case to gain his general manager's support for his plan, while at the same time positioning himself as being a strong business leader who was giving close attention to the evolving role of his work function. Randy's thinking process is summarized in the table below.

TABLE 3.1. Randy's Thinking Process

Desired Outcomes	Development Needs	Development Actions
1. Develop better financial model	1. Understand financial modeling and project controls	1. Attend training seminar on path to profitability.
2. Implement effective project controls	2. Form influential partnerships with stakeholders	2. Review current financial planning model and recommend improvements to that model.
		3. Begin to network with identified key stakeholders

Is Your Plan Focused and Precise?

One of the reasons why professional development plans become side-tracked and lose momentum is that people tend to use vague and ambiguous terms to describe their development needs. If not addressed, this pitfall can easily lead to communication breakdowns between you and your manager. For example, let's assume that your manager has previously suggested that you need to develop a stronger "executive presence." You thank your manager for her feedback and admit that this was actually a developmental area that you had already identified for improvement. The problem is that, while on the surface it may sound as if the two of you are in agreement, you may each hold very different views regarding how this goal of "developing a stronger executive presence" is supposed to show up as changes in your leadership behavior.

Not too long ago the manager of one of my clients used this term to describe my client's development needs. When I pushed the manager for detail he explained that he wanted to see my client perform better during executive presentations. As it stood, when presenting to senior leader she tended to be nervous and fidgety and use a lot of non-words ("So the main point, is uh, its like."). Another one of my coaching clients in the same organization also had a manager who had identified the lack of executive presence as a development goal. In this case, however, the underlying behavioral issue was very different, in that this individual tended to dress sloppily (loud ties, wrinkled dress shirts) when appearing in front of his executive team or corporate customers.

The fact is that the term "executive presence" is just one of several non-descriptive adjectives that I have seen loosely thrown around during executive talent reviews or coaching sessions. The fuzziness of developmental labels is one of the reasons that I don't rely heavily on leadership competency models in executive coaching. There is nothing wrong with using competency models; it is just that they tend to be fairly redundant and won't provide you with the level of detail you need to formulate effective development goals. Almost every competency model that I have seen contains sections on problem solving, communication, team building, vision, strategic thinking, and customer focus. (Have I left out anything?) Unfortunately, once executives and HR leaders use these labels, they feel that they have a good handle on a development dimension and stop there. The fact is that having someone sum up your development needs in terms of a generic list of competencies does not tell you a lot about the kinds of

PARTICIPANT'S GUIDE

performance results that you are expected to obtain through the application of these global skill sets.

The problem of ill-defined development needs becomes even more problematic when other people, such as additional managers, senior-level executives, or HR leaders, weigh in with their own views regarding your development needs. If you don't take the time to ensure that all of your stakeholders share the same understanding of what you mean by a given leadership development area, you create a number of problems for yourself:

- Some of your stakeholders will feel that you aren't making a serious effort to develop on the job, since they aren't seeing the behavioral changes that they had expected.
- Also, you will end up spending a lot of time and effort on development actions that are not taken seriously by your stakeholders, because you fail to address what they perceive as fundamental development issues.
- Finally, this kind of hit-or-miss approach to development takes a lot longer. It will eventually burn you out, given the shear amount of effort that you will end up wasting on development actions that don't truly address the underlying concerns of your stakeholders.

Case in Point: Mindi

Mindi was an operations VP who reported up in a matrix organization to both a division president and her company's SVP of operations. She was considered to be one of the most intelligent people in her department and also demonstrated great business savvy in her day-to-day dealings with other managers. During our initial session Mindi told me that she felt ready to take on a broader leadership role in her company, but that she was concerned that one of the things that might hold her back was that she had trouble delegating.

"I guess that I am just a micromanager," she confessed to me. "Can you give me some one-on-one training on how to delegate more effectively?"

"Sounds reasonable," I responded, "but before we go down that path, let's unpack the word 'micromanager.' If you are finding it hard to delegate, it could be due to one of four reasons. First, if you are a perfectionist it may be that you are fearful that if you don't do it all yourself your team will send out work that is sloppy or incomplete. A second reason could be that you believe that the people you have working for you aren't strong enough to tackle tough projects without a lot of direction. I have also seen situations in which leaders try to delegate but fail to set clear goals, standards, and guidelines. When this happens, associates can feel that they have to keep checking in with their managers in order to gain clarity on what it is that they are supposed to be doing. Finally, it could be a problem of focus. If you are facing a huge plate of work with ever-changing demands, then you may be finding it difficult to discern which of your many work tasks and projects are truly critical and require your personal intervention. So Mindi, given these possibilities which do you think it is?"

After thinking about it for a moment, she said, "A little of each, I think."

That answer wasn't good enough for us to move forward, so instead of running off in all directions we spent more time discussing representative performance examples until we had a more detailed picture of her development needs. Only then was Mindi able to define the development issue of poor delegation in a way that was really meaningful for her.

Is Your Plan Actionable?

It is important to identify development goals and supporting activities on which you can truly take action. To ensure that you do this, avoid development goals that imply changes to your intentions or internal psychological processes, rather than observable behaviors. The goal statement, "I want to become more self-aware" says little. Trying to act on this goal is a bit like nailing gelatin to the wall—it simply won't hold. If you are unsure about whether or not one of your development goals is actionable, ask yourself the following questions:

- If I improve or strengthen myself in this area, how will it be apparent to others?
- How will these improvements show up in my performance?
- How would I go about describing improved behavior to others?

In addition, avoid the pitfall of framing your development goals in terms of what you should stop doing, such as:

- I want to stop interrupting people when they are talking.
- I want to stop criticizing my team members in public.
- I want to stop procrastinating on difficult decisions.

The problem with these types of goal statements is that nature abhors a vacuum. If you simply attempt to stop doing something, you will inevitably fall back into that behavioral pattern again, unless you substitute an alternative behavior for it. The reason is that stopping something does not necessarily tell us what we need to be doing differently. Telling someone that he should stop being so "aggressive" or "arrogant" does not provide him with a lot of insight as to exactly the kinds of behavior that he needs to demonstrate. Does being arrogant mean presenting issues as if one has all of the answers, denigrating the past efforts of others, making condescending comments to other people at work, or a little of each?

You can go further in development planning by converting "stops" to "starts." For example, the goal of "stop interrupting people when they are talking" could be better cast as "start giving people an opportunity to complete their thoughts before offering my own ideas and opinions." Likewise, the goal of "stop criticizing my team members in public" could be converted to "start identifying appropriate times and places for providing one-on-one feedback to my team members."

Is Your Plan Aligned?

Always keep in mind that the success of your development plan is contingent upon whether you have the support and buy-in from key organizational stakeholders. Particularly important among these are your manager, your HR leader, the senior executive who directs your function or department, and those senior leaders whom you directly support. It is in your best interest to make certain that these individuals understand and agree on your proposed plan outcomes, goals, development actions, and the roles that you may be asking them to play in supporting your plan. Never assume that they are interpreting your desired outcomes and development goals in the same way. Starting with your manager, take the time to review your written plans with each of your stakeholders to ensure that they understand the chain of logic that links the elements of your performance outcomes, development needs, development goals, and support actions.

Case in Point: Carlos

Carlos was the news director for a television station who was considered to be a strong, innovative leader. During a coaching planning meeting,

Carlos' manager made the comment that one of the areas on which he wanted Carlos to work was his indecisiveness. Interestingly enough, the company's HR leader, who was also present during the discussion, strongly disagreed with this statement. She claimed that, judging from the comments that had trickled back to her from Carlos' team, he was "more of a shoot-ready-aim kind of person."

As a starting point for making sense of these different perspectives, think about what typically comes to mind when you hear the word "indecisive." For many people, this word calls up the image of someone who is unable to make decisions or who procrastinates in taking action. That was also my initial assumption, until I had a chance to meet with Carlos and several members of his work team. In doing so I found that it wasn't so much that Carlos didn't make decisions, but rather that he quickly made them and continued to reverse them with every new tidbit of information that came his way. He would develop a plan for the morning news lineup and then completely change it after someone on his team would alert him to a creative idea that a competitive station had just adopted. Then someone else would confront him about the logic of that change and he'd reverse himself again.

As a news director at his station, Carlos wanted to appear supportive and responsive to every member of his team, with the result that he found himself continually shifting direction with each new piece of advice. All of this was occurring in a work environment in which he had only a few hours to move from the initial inception of a newscast to final production. Changes that rolled in toward the end of the production process caused huge rework for everyone. Carlos and I were able to put together a development plan to address the issue, but only after we got past the surface-level description of the problem to its underlying nature.

Is Your Plan Based on Feedback?

One step you can take to ensure that key organizational stakeholders are aligned on your development plan is to solicit their collective feedback on your strengths and development needs. While you can wait for these individuals to provide this feedback, there are several reasons why it is to your advantage to initiate these feedback discussions.

Some managers are uncomfortable with the idea of giving feedback because they are concerned that their comments may not be well received. As a result, they either postpone giving feedback until the yearly performance review or they couch their feedback in such general, subtle terms as to render it useless. Soliciting feedback enables you to select a venue, such as an informal luncheon meeting, that can create a more relaxed and open setting for these discussions.

Other managers may have difficulty clearly communicating their developmental concerns and suggestions. When this occurs, development needs are poorly conveyed through fuzzy language, in statements such as "you need to develop more executive presence" or "you need to learn to communicate better." This kind of feedback is too vague and ambiguous to provide anything of developmental value. Soliciting feedback allows you to think about how you can frame the wording of your questions in such a way as to increase the likelihood that you can obtain detailed and useful information about your development needs.

Taking the initiative to solicit feedback also helps you to position yourself as a self-learner who is receptive to input from others. As we will discuss later in Chapter 6, this can be a very important part of your personal brand.

A final consideration is that soliciting feedback also allows you to direct the feedback discussion to future needs. If your manager is attempting to deal with a number of day-to-day performance challenges, her feedback is likely to focus on what you can do to become stronger in your *current* job. The problem with this is that your career target may require a very different set of skills and experience than those employed in your current position. Soliciting feedback allows you to direct the feedback discussion on those competency and experience gaps that you need to close in order to be better prepared to take on future roles and assignments.

Guidelines for Soliciting Feedback

Here are six guidelines that I would urge you to follow when soliciting feedback from others:

1. *Solicit feedback from a wide range of providers.* Don't be so preoccupied with getting feedback from your senior executives that you ignore useful guidance from others in your organization. Your co-workers can provide a lot of useful feedback on your interpersonal and leadership style, while leaders who have intimate knowledge of your career target can provide valuable information on the evolving job demands and work challenges that are associated with this role. Give particular attention to identifying feedback providers who have knowledge of both the

unique skill and experience requirements of your career target and your own skill set.

2. *Set the stage.* Take a minute or so at the start of your feedback meeting to explain the purpose and intent of the discussion. Let your feedback provider know that you are not asking for an evaluative appraisal of your performance over the last year, but for help in identifying the kinds of skills and abilities that can help you move closer toward your career goals.

"Tamara, at some point in the future I would like to be qualified to move into a product line director role. Given your familiarity with this role and your knowledge of the job challenges that I face in my current position, I was hoping to get your feedback on one or two development gaps that you think that I need to close if I want to succeed in the product line director role. Would you have some time over the next few days to discuss this?"

3. *Unpack fuzzy language.* When soliciting feedback from others, look for ways to break down vague or confusing feedback statements into behaviorally specific language.

"You mentioned that one step that I could take to prepare for this role would be to get a better read on our largest manufactures. Could you tell me a bit more about what you meant by this?"

"Can you point out someone at the next level whom you regard as being an exemplar in the use of this skill area? Is there a project or decision that this person has recently managed that you feel could provide me with an excellent demonstration of how this skill is successfully applied?"

"You had suggested that I need to be thinking about developing stronger project management skills. There are a lot of skill components and responsibilities that are associated with project management, from stakeholder management to resource forecasting. What, specifically, are the one or two areas in which you think I could benefit the most from development?"

"You have mentioned that to move into the area of business development I need to become stronger in the area of financial analysis. I believe that I am already applying this skill to some degree in my current job. Can you give me an example of how financial analysis is applied differently within a business development role?"

"You said that one big job challenge that I would face if I were going to make the move from our division to Alpha division, would be that this change would take me away from selling discrete products such as valves or pumps, to selling more sophisticated automation solutions. I understand this, but I am unsure what you meant when you suggested that this would require me to make use of a completely different sales model. Could you say a little more about that?"

PARTICIPANT'S GUIDE

4. *Ask context-defining questions.* Ask questions that tell you more about the conditions under which a given skill or ability would be expected to be applied within your career target.

"You had mentioned that, even though I am currently responsible for managing some of our smaller regional accounts, the position of national accounts director involves account management challenges that are much more complex. Can you give me an example?"

"You had said that if I eventually want to work on our client engagement team then I would have to be prepared to work in a high-stress environment. How do those stressors translate into the kinds of work challenges that I would likely face on a day-to-day basis?"

5. *Ask for three types of feedback.* Feedback comes in three basic flavors. The most common type, *performance feedback*, gives us information about how we have performed on a given task or project. While this feedback is essential to the success of any organization, it suffers from the disadvantage of being delivered only after our work has been completed. As a result, it requires us to learn from our mistakes, rather than adopt a preemptive approach to learning. It is also difficult for most of us to accept this type of feedback when it is given to us, since we tend to equate it with a personal assessment or evaluation of our overall capability. An alternative is to ask for *in-process feedback*, which allows us to examine our performance while a task or project is underway. An example would be asking someone to review the first draft of a report or presentation before you go further on these projects. The most useful developmental feedback, *anticipatory guidance*, is designed to help you think about how you can prepare yourself to deal with future challenges. An example is presented below:

"I have been asked to run the cross-functional process improvement team that will be working on streamlining our distribution system. As someone who has seen me conduct several team meetings, what suggestions do you have for steps that I could take to strengthen my performance in this role?"

6. *Avoid debate.* When people provide you with feedback, you will occasionally hear something that challenges your view of yourself. In these situations, it is easy to get caught up in a debate and try to prove to the speaker why her views are not accurate. If you do this, you will lose trust with your feedback providers, who will feel that you are not sincerely looking for ways to strengthen yourself as a professional, but rather merely looking for affirmation and encouragement. When you receive feedback, summarize what you have heard, thank the individual who gave it to you, and move on without extended debate.

Case in Point: Paul

Paul was a vice president of sales and marketing for one of three divisions within a large healthcare company. His goal was to eventually become the president of his division. In addition, should the situation evolve where the top sales leadership position for each division were to become consolidated under the direction of one corporate-wide senior vice president of sales, this newly created position would be Paul's secondary career target.

During our initial coaching session, I discussed with Paul a problem that he needed to overcome, which was that his executive team was beginning to question his ability to contribute as a strategic thinker. Paul disagreed entirely with this assessment and challenged me to provide an example. In response, I mentioned feedback that I had been given about two staff meetings that had recently taken place. During these meetings, Paul had participated with several corporate executives and the VPs of sales and marketing for the company's other two divisions in detailed discussions regarding how to advance a new physician sales program. Paul was surprised to hear that his performance in these sessions hadn't been viewed as impressive, since he felt that he had contributed several creative ideas.

To understand Paul's confusion, you have to understand that Paul frequently met with other department heads or direct reports in his small division to tackle tough work problems. During these sessions, he tended to engage in informal brainstorming sessions, in which roughly formulated ideas would be quickly tossed on the table and later screened for feasibility. When Paul tried to apply this approach to his work within the more complex cross-divisional meetings he was now attending, the result wasn't very effective. When the hard questions began to fly, like a deer in the headlights, Paul tended to freeze up and fumble his responses. Eventually, days or weeks later, he'd arrive at a thoughtful response, but quite often by this time the team would have already moved ahead in its thinking.

Paul's problem was that his view of strategic thinking was limited to the kinds of spontaneous brainstorming that, while effective within his small divisional unit, weren't sophisticated enough to be useful to the larger corporation. In the minds of his executive team, being strategic didn't just mean generating creative ideas on an impromptu basis. It also meant doing your homework to anticipate, in advance of these executive discussions, the kinds of questions that you would be expected to answer if you wanted to demonstrate that you could take a creative idea and successfully execute against it. For Paul, these questions might include how he planned to manage costs and resources, the potential operational impact of proposed change initiatives on other large-scale projects that were already underway, and his ability to produce hard data showing that the company's customers would be receptive to his new idea.

As I explained to Paul, while no one expected him to have all of the answers to these types of questions, he was expected to have at least given them serious consideration and be prepared to discuss how he would plan to go about getting the answers. Once Paul understood how this view of strategic thinking shifted as he made the transition from informal divisional brainstorming to more complex company-wide problem solving sessions, he was able to begin to develop a solid plan to accelerate his development and increase his chances of successfully attaining his career target.

How to Leverage Your Strengths

Over the last few years there has been a lot of discussion regarding the value of using a "strength-based approach" to development planning. This approach is based on the premise that over the course of many years each of us has developed certain core strengths. Given this, does it not make more sense to select career targets that maximize your strengths, rather than waste time attempting to work on converting your weakest areas up into strengths? The answer is that it depends on the situation. The best of all worlds is when you have selected a career target that will employ only your strengths. Unfortunately, the more common situation we are likely to encounter is one in which at least some of our weaknesses must also be addressed to meet the minimal performance standards for those desired positions.

The best way to answer this question for yourself is to first use your informational interviews to break down the skill areas required for success within your career target into three categories: those that are viewed by knowledgeable people as being essential for success, those that are considered to be of moderate importance, and those that are relatively unimportant. You can then use your feedback interviews to see whether you are viewed as strong, moderate, or weak in each of these skill categories. By loading your information into a nine-cell table, such as the one in Table 3.2, you can obtain a rich assortment of data from which to make career and development decisions.

TABLE 3.2. Value of Skills to Your Career Target

Your Strength in Each Skill Area	Value of Skills to Your Career Target		
	Unimportant	Moderately Important	Essential
Strong	1 Deemphasize	2 Ignore	3 Leverage These Skills
Moderate	4 Ignore	5 Fourth Developmental Priority	6 Second Development Priority
Weak	7 Ignore	8 Third Developmental Priority	9 First Developmental Priority

Work to Move Cell 6 and Import a Complementary Skill Set or Select a Different Career Target

Consider these nine cells as a game board, with each cell calling forth an optimal developmental move or action. To start off, you want to leverage those skills (Cell 3) that are both essential to your career target and in which you excel. This will involve maximizing your use of these skills and showcasing them whenever possible. Your two danger points are found in Cells 9 and 1.

I would recommend that any skill deficiency that falls into Cell 9 should be your top developmental priority. This cell represents those essential skill areas on which you are currently weak. You have two options here. First, given that this is one of your weakest competencies, it would require tremendous effort to convert this area into a core strength. A more reasonable option would be to work hard enough to bring the skill up to minimally acceptable standards (move to Cell 6), while at the same time hiring an employee or consultant who has exceptional skills in this area and who could bring the overall performance level of your team up to the level of Cell 3.

Applying this same rationale, I would suggest that your next two developmental priorities are found in Cells 8 and 5, respectively. Ignore skill areas in Cells 4 and 7, given their lack of importance, and ignore skills found in Cell 2, since you are already strong in this area.

That only leaves Cell 1, which I have identified as your second danger area. The reason that I say this is that all of us have the tendency to fall in love with those skills that we enjoy doing and in which we excel. The problem is that if this skill area is irrelevant to your career target, you may be focusing on it at the expense of other job responsibilities that need your full attention. All of us have seen managers who, once promoted, run into trouble because they cannot leave their old jobs behind. To avoid this issue, once you make a career move you need to be conscientious about slough-ing off those job responsibilities and skill areas that are no longer relevant to your changing job role.

Not long ago I coached a senior leader who was brought in to head up a new business development function. One of this individual's first projects was to develop and execute the integration planning process for one of his company's new acquisitions. During the integration process, the acquired company continued to have a number of operations problems. When these issues arose, instead of delegating them to the company's operations department the leader did what he was best at and applied his twenty years of operations excellence to helping the acquired company in its daily fire-fighting activities. This created a huge time-management issue for the senior leader and led to a number of delays in the completion of certain critical stages of the integration project. Once the leader saw the problem for what it was, he developed a written plan for systematically divesting himself of the operations responsibilities and focusing his efforts on the integration process.

Your Next Steps

Over the next two weeks, I am asking you to take the following action steps to support your professional development:

1. Conduct at least three feedback interviews. One of these should be with your manager, while the other two should be with organizational leaders who are familiar with both your career target and your own work performance. Use the questions provided in this chapter to guide your interview process.
2. From these questions, see whether you can identify recurring themes regarding your key strengths and development needs, with particular attention on those areas you need to development to support your long-term career goals.
3. Load this information into a nine-cell grid, such as the one found earlier in this chapter.

4. Determine the initial development actions that you should take to support skills that fall within each cell, with particular attention on those skills that fall within Cell 9.

5. Incorporate this information into a preliminary development plan, such as the model found in Table 3.1. If done correctly, this should show the connections between your desired performance outcomes, your development needs, and supporting development actions. We will extend our discussion of development actions in the next chapter.

PARTICIPANT'S GUIDE

CHAPTER FOUR

LEVERAGING DEVELOPMENTAL ASSIGNMENTS

Why Developmental Assignments Often Disappoint

So far we've discussed how you can accelerate your development as a leader by identifying your career target, prioritizing your development needs, and crafting a detailed development plan. The next step involves identifying the types of job assignments that can support your professional development. The right job assignment can help you assess your readiness to take on broader leadership responsibilities while at the same time broadening your skill base. Well-constructed developmental assignments can also serve as a proving ground for demonstrating untested skills and leadership capabilities to your manager and your senior sponsors. In addition, the right assignment can help lower the risk level for making a major career move, by providing a realistic preview of what is involved in tackling a new job setting or taking on a new leadership role. In this chapter we'll look at how to identify assignments that are truly developmental. You will be introduced to guidelines for extracting the greatest developmental value from job assignments and for fully leveraging assignments to meet your career objectives.

The unfortunate fact is that all too often job assignments fail to live up to their potential as developmental vehicles. I am sure that at some point in your career you have experienced the following scenario. Your boss mumbles something to you about how lucky you are to be afforded the opportunity to take on a unique "developmental opportunity." Soon afterward, you find yourself being parachuted into a totally unfamiliar job situation. It is not long before you begin to feel like one of the characters in a Dilbert cartoon. First, your manager immediately disappears from view, leaving you foundering in the new work setting without feedback or direction. To make things worse, the people you are supposed to support don't appear to be very grateful for your help. Furthermore, the new job opportunity consumes far greater time than you had anticipated, to the extent that it starts to interfere with your ability to meet the requirements of your full-time job.

Being the intrepid professional that you are, however, you suck in your breath and plunge into it. After diligently working on the assignment for several weeks or months, you finally complete it, only to find that little has been said about all of the hard effort that you have invested. Worse still, although you know that the assignment has presented you with a variety of new job challenges, looking back on this work experience, you find it hard to articulate what you have actually taken away from it. In fact, when all is said and done, you find that you don't really feel more "developed," just more stressed-out and fatigued. Upon careful reflection you realize that the assignment wasn't really related to, or supportive of, your career goals. After having weathered this type of situation is it any wonder that many professionals come to view the term "developmental assignment" as some kind of Machiavellian code for "getting shafted"?

So what went wrong? Why do developmental assignments so often disappoint us? To answer that question let's deconstruct the way that developmental assignments are typically selected, staged, managed, and reviewed. Before we do that, please take a second to recall a tough job assignment that you completed during the past two years that fell short of living up to its promise of providing a good developmental experience. With that picture in mind, use the following questions to determine why this assignment may have failed to provide sufficient professional growth. Each question speaks to a different problem that can reduce the developmental impact of job assignments. These problem areas, and suggestions for addressing them, are discussed in detail over the remainder of this chapter.

Questions to Ask Regarding Developmental Assignments

Selecting the Assignment

❒ Does the assignment provide opportunities to close development gaps and build critical leadership competencies?

❒ Does the assignment stretch you to build critical skills?

❒ As part of your selection process have you carefully considered the scope* of the assignment?

Staging the Assignment

❒ Has your manager discussed with you how to use the assignment as a leadership learning opportunity?

❒ Consider those organizational leaders with whom you will be working during the assignment. Do they understand how the assignment supports your development needs and the roles you would like them to play in providing you with feedback and coaching?

❒ Can these organizational leaders serve as good models of the leadership competencies that you want to develop?

Managing the Assignment

❒ Have you and your manager clearly defined the competencies that you need to build during the course of the assignment?

❒ Have other responsibilities been temporarily lifted off of you so that you can focus on the assignment?

❒ Have you and your manager jointly identified key test points or aspects of the assignment that will constitute the greatest test of the skills that you are attempting to develop?

Following Up on the Assignment

❒ At the close of the assignment did you establish a method for receiving detailed developmental feedback on your performance?

*The term "scope" refers to whether the assignment will take place within your work group, will require you to work extensively with other departments or functions, will involve projects that span your organization, or will involve development activities that occur outside of your organization.

❐ Did you take the time to reflect on what you learned from the assignment?

❐ Did you conduct a follow-up meeting with your manager to discuss how you could apply the "lessons learned" from this assignment to future work challenges?

Selecting Developmental Assignments

Seven Criteria for Evaluating Developmental Assignments

During the next twelve months I am sure that you will find yourself involved in dozens of job tasks and projects. Not all of these assignments have the same developmental value. One key step you can take to accelerate your development as a professional is to determine which assignments are likely to have the greatest developmental yield. Leadership research over the past twenty years suggests that work assignments that help people to grow in their jobs fulfill at least some of the following seven criteria. You may want to refer back to this list to screen and prioritize potential job assignments:

Does the assignment...

❐ *Foster new skill development?* The assignment should provide you with an opportunity to tackle unfamiliar work challenges and to assess your performance on new, previously untested skills.

❐ *Involve a high, but realistic, degree of stretch?* The key point here is the word "realistic." The assignment should push you out of your comfort zone while not representing a challenge level that is so steep as to represent a sink-or-swim assignment. One of the ways of assessing this is try to gauge the speed and amount of learning that you will need to master to stay on top of the assignment.

❐ *Extend your organizational knowledge?* The right assignment can give you experience and exposure to other parts of the organization and provide you with a better understanding of the challenges and business perspectives of these organizational units. Such assignments could include being temporarily loaned out to another function, making a shift from a line to

Continued

staff position or visa versa, exposure to international business units, or making the shift between corporate and field offices.

❏ *Require you to perform without a safety net?* In other words, the outcomes of the project are considered important to the organization and will be directly visible to key organizational sponsors. Keep in mind that this is a two-edged sword. With visibility and exposure comes a higher degree of risk. If project success matters to your senior managers, then you will also need to be willing to accept the consequences of failure.

❏ *Provide a realistic job preview?* The assignment should provide you with a realistic preview of at least some of the work challenges and job conditions that you are likely to face in your career target. This might include being placed in a position that requires continually juggling between tasks, dealing with high-stress work situations, or having to navigate through a political minefield.

❏ *Expand your sources of feedback?* The right job assignment should enable you to obtain unambiguous feedback on your performance in new and challenging job situations from leaders other than your manager. Such opportunities are particularly important when you find yourself working with leaders who will eventually have the opportunity to weigh in on their assessment of your leadership potential.

❏ *Include effective mentoring?* Many job assignments give you the opportunity to learn from, and be coached by, a leader other than your manager. In the ideal scenario this is a manager who has gained organizational respect as an exceptional performer and who is willing to take the time to serve as a good mentor.

What Do You Want to Take Away from the Assignment?

Using these seven selection criteria as a starting point, you can go further in your selection process by pinpointing what you hope to learn from your job assignment. One approach for doing this is to use your organization's leadership competency model to identify key competencies that relate to demand features of your career target. As an alternative approach, consider selecting one or two of the nine leadership development themes that are described in the following list. During my own thirty years as a senior HR leader and executive coach, I have found that these eight leadership themes often take on critical importance when senior executives are attempting to determine whether leaders have what it takes to make it to the next level in their organizations.

Working Through Messy Problems	Effective leaders are able to successfully tackle complex, ill-defined problems that have no readily available prescriptive, cookie-cutter solutions. These are often problems that an organization has encountered for the first time. These types of problems have developmental value because they push a leader's thinking. They require the problem solver to identify the critical parameters of a complex situation, to carefully define the problem, to explore innovative solutions, to assess the varying risk levels associated with the implementation of those solutions, and to gain alignment from different stakeholders on the proposed solution.
Influencing Without Authority	A critical leadership skill involves being able to sell ideas, negotiate tradeoffs, and balance the competing interests of leaders across the organization. This skill is particularly challenging when one lacks direct authority to drive results through positional power and authority. The best leaders are able to maintain a high level of credibility and trust with stakeholders from other organizational groups and to gain the commitment of those groups to reach business objectives.
Managing Change	The growth of international efforts, the challenges brought about by acquisitions and mergers, the introduction of new product lines or markets, and continual revisions in both organizational structure and leadership benches are but some of the difficult and stressful organizational changes that need to be managed in today's organization. Companies are looking for leaders who can step out in front of such changes and successfully obtain results, while retaining employee commitment for change.

Thinking
Strategically

Good leaders wear bifocals, in that they are able to simultaneously keep one eye on the long-term trajectory of their organization while keeping the other eye focused on day-to-day expediencies. Thinking strategically means being able to not only develop long-term overarching objectives that constitute a winning game plan for a function or business unit, but also being able to understand the long-term ramifications of short-term decisions. It also involves being able to sift out, from a variety of confusing data, those informational components that are essential to making good business decisions.

Working with
Diverse Groups of
People

Organizations are becoming increasingly diverse with respect to ethnic, cultural, and generational diversity. However, an often-overlooked aspect of diversity involves the ability to work with cognitive diversity. This is the term that researcher Paul Paulus of the University of Texas has coined to describe situations in which we find ourselves working with people who think quite differently and who approach problems from very divergent perspectives. An example would involve an IT leader's ability to understand the perspectives of other departments in arriving at a plan for implementing an enterprise-wide technology change.

Working Across
Silos and
Functions

A critical leadership competency is the ability to accomplish projects that span organizational boundaries. Such projects could include getting commitment from other functions on key initiatives, achieving alignment on seemingly contradictory functionally driven objectives, or managing process improvement projects that extend across the white space between functions.

Developing Expertise Beyond Your Function	Effective leaders understand that their success in influencing actions across their organizations is strongly dependent on their ability to speak the language of other functions, understand business issues that span organizational boundaries, and align their requirements with the needs and priorities of other work groups. For an HR leader, this might involve the ability to build a business case for an HR initiative that is based on a solid knowledge of financial analytics. For a sales leader, the same skill might focus on understanding how a new product launch will create a downstream impact on engineering, manufacturing, and distribution.
Managing Through to Execution	When executives discuss whether an individual has the potential for taking on broader leadership roles, a key question that is frequently asked is, "Has this person demonstrated the ability to get things done?" Anyone can come up with good ideas, but a relatively rare skill is the ability to find ways to creatively work around cost, time, and resource constraints to see an idea through to implementation. The development of this skill area is particularly important if you work in a function such as process improvement or strategic planning, where the bulk of your time involves strategy development and problem analysis, rather than business execution.
Taking a Broader Perspective	Some of the most productive leadership developmental assignments are those that force us to examine our work from a broader organizational perspective. In part, this means being able to think at the next level; that is, to understand the issues, concerns, and leadership thinking that drive your manager's decisions and priorities. It also means being able to move beyond a narrow parochial view of your job to see how your work is viewed from the perspectives of your internal stakeholders and external customers. Finally, it involves developing an understanding the potential impact of broader organization-wide business objectives and change initiatives.

With these nine developmental categories in mind, it is time to identify a developmental job assignment that might be right for you. Tables 4.1, 4.2, 4.3, and 4.4, shown on the next few pages, list thirty-one potential job assignments. You can see that these assignments have been divided into four categories based on their scope of impact. Table 4.1 provides examples of assignments that are carried out within the scope of your current work group. Table 4.2 shows job assignments that require you to work through other work groups or business units, while Table 4.3 shows assignments that extend across your organization. Finally, Table 4.4 shows developmental assignments that take place outside the boundaries of your company.

While there is no cookbook formula for determining from which category you should select your job assignments, as a general rule of thumb as you move up the scale from assignments that occur within your job area to organization-wide projects, you begin to encounter job assignments that are more complex, require greater strategic ability and business savvy, have broader organizational impact and accompanying risk, and extend over a longer period of time.

Assignments that occur outside of your organization, such as the nine shown in Table 4.4, represent a wide range of complexity and sophistication. External assignments offer several unique advantages over their internal counterparts. First, some of these assignments may provide your first exposure to broad-based high-impact decision making. An example would be taking on a role as a board member for a non-profit organization and helping that organization formulate its strategic, three-year plan. Some external assignments, such as coordinating a national conference for a professional association, can expose you to a diverse set of leaders who have very different leadership experiences and skill sets. Assignments such as representing your company at a trade conference can help you stay current on industry best practices and bring you into contact with professionals who have very different leadership experiences and competencies. In addition, external assignments provide you with low-risk opportunities to experiment with, and acquire, new skills before you attempt to apply those skills within your organization. Examples would include strategic planning, financial modeling, and selling a business case for change to an executive team. As a final consideration, external assignments usually require little in the way of company resources and frequently do not require the approval of your manager or senior executives.

TABLE 4.1. Suggested Development Actions Within Your Current Job

How You Learn	Work with complex, messy problems	Influence without authority	Manage change	Think strategically	Work with diverse work groups	Work across silos and functions	Develop expertise beyond your function	Manage through execution	Take a broader perspective
					What You Learn				
Step in when your manager is on vacation	X	X				X			X
Direct a process improvement project	X		X		X	X	X	X	X
Build a business case for a new capital expense	X	X						X	X
Help your manager in annual revenue or budget planning	X			X					X
Facilitate a strategic planning session for your team	X			X					X
Manage key consultants or vendors	X	X						X	
Mentor a junior-level team member or intern					X				

TABLE 4.2. Suggested Development Actions That Engage Other Parts of Your Organization

How You Learn	What You Learn								
	Work with complex, messy problems	Influence without authority	Manage change	Think strategically	Work with diverse work groups	Work across silos and functions	Develop expertise beyond your function	Manage through execution	Take a broader perspective
Lead a cross-functional project team		X	X	X	X	X	X		
Be on loan to another function		X			X	X	X		X
Contribute to a business process outsourcing project	X	X	X	X	X	X	X	X	X
Direct a distributed work team		X			X				
Direct a system change	X	X	X	X		X	X	X	
Perform a best practices study on another organization					X	X	X		X
Direct an infrastructure project			X					X	
Join an international project	X	X			X		X		X
Assume P&L responsibility for a project				X				X	X

TABLE 4.3. Suggested Development Organization-Wide Development Actions

How You Learn	What You Learn								
	Work with complex, messy problems	Influence without authority	Manage change	Think strategically	Work with diverse work groups	Work across silos and functions	Develop expertise beyond your function	Manage through execution	Take a broader perspective
Work with HR on revising your performance management system	X	X	X			X	X		X
Troubleshoot issues with customers or franchisors	X	X			X	X	X		X
Work with HR on your company's employee engagement project	X		X		X	X			X
Work on an enterprise-wide system change	X	X	X	X			X	X	X
Support an acquisition	X		X			X	X	X	X
Direct your company's United Way campaign		X			X	X	X	X	

TABLE 4.4. Suggested Development Actions Outside of Your Organization

How You Learn	Work with complex, messy problems	Influence without authority	Manage change	Think strategically	*What You Learn* Work with diverse work groups	Work across silos and functions	Develop expertise beyond your function	Manage through to execution	Take a broader perspective
Serve as a board member	X	X	X	X	X		X		X
Be the liaison to another organization		X			X	X			
Teach at a local college					X				
Take on a leadership role in a civic group		X			X	X		X	
Coordinate a professional conference		X			X			X	
Become an advisor to a non-profit	X			X	X		X		X
Join an advisory council for a local college		X			X				
Represent the company at a trade conference					X				
Present to a professional association					X				

Matching Developmental Assignments to Project Lifecycles

If may be that your job assignment will require you to participate with several other professionals in the completion of a long-term work project. Given this situation, one way to accelerate your learning is to identify the stage in the project lifecycle that will be most likely to require the skills that you are attempting to develop. Consider the case of a business process outsourcing (BPO) project, which could easily require twelve to twenty-four months from inception to full implementation. If you wanted to assist in a company BPO project, it might be unrealistic to assume that you could commit your time in all project activities over the full course of the project. A more effective approach would be to offer your assistance during BPO project steps that will make particular use of the types of leadership competencies that you are trying to develop.

Let's take a minute to see how this would work. Listed below are nine sequential steps in the BPO process and the types of leadership competencies that become especially important within each of these steps. Take a moment to review this list and consider which of these steps would provide you with the strongest development experience. For the job assignment that you are considering, you could generate a similar competency breakdown based on input from other leaders who are close to the project. You would then need to determine where these steps are likely to occur over the course of the year so that you can plan to set aside time on your work calendar to accommodate your involvement in the project.

Leadership Competencies That Could Be Developed Through a BPO Process

Steps in the BPO Process	Related Development Opportunities
1. Performing a high-level opportunities audit to determine what value creation could be potentially achieved through improvements to service efficiency, process optimization across businesses, labor cost reductions, and the integration of technology platforms	Working with messy problems, financial analysis, strategic thinking, developing expertise beyond your function, taking a broader perspective
2. Developing a business case to justify the need for business process outsourcing and selling this case to senior management	Executive presence (selling the concept to senior-level stakeholders and internal customers and support groups), strategic thinking, developing expertise beyond your function, communications skills

Continued

Steps in the BPO Process	Related Development Opportunities
3. Selecting an outsource provider who can serve as a business partner throughout the project	Problem analysis, innovation, decision making, negotiation (both external negotiation with alternative vendors and internal negotiations with internal customers regarding tradeoffs among alternative vendors).
4. Mapping key processes to compare current versus desired state, identifying key improvement opportunities, and determining which processes should be outsourced	Problem and financial analysis, process analysis, working across silos and functions, influence without authority.
5. Developing a financial model (or several alternative financial models) to evaluate overall costs and potential payoffs associated with the outsourcing, including staff reductions, technology integration, facilities consolidations, and the creation of dedicated service centers	Developing expertise beyond your function, financial analysis, taking a broader perspective, thinking strategically.
6. Negotiating with the selected outsource vendor and internal departments regarding the contract terms and conditions, the creation of service level agreements (SLAs), associated process measures, service level reporting requirements	Negotiation, financial analysis, project management
7. Managing the vendor throughout the BPO lifecycle from initial pilot launch within a given process or functional unit to full implementation	Working across silos and functions, influencing without authority, performance management
8. Developing and implementing a comprehensive communication and change plan to manage BPO implementation across the organization and to secure the commitment of leaders and employees to the change process	Change management, managing through to execution, influencing without authority. Project management; communication skills (both formal presentations and written communications) working across silos and functions, working with diverse groups of people
9. Periodically following up on and reviewing the status of the BPO project in terms of both the resolution of change management issues and the ability to the project to reach stated results, such as SLA measures and cost reduction	Analytics, financial reporting, data synthesis, mediation skills (resolving the resolution of sticky problem issues)

Staging the Assignment

Challenging job assignments frequently arise in response to the sudden emergence of a difficult business problem or the need to stay abreast of an emerging business challenge. In these circumstances managers tend to be so focused on getting the job done that they don't stop to consider whether a given assignment represents a good match to a leader's development needs. Because of this, it is to your advantage to jointly identify with your manager the types of job assignments that can support your development needs. Likewise, before you take on a new job assignment it is helpful to discuss with your manager how you can use the assignment as a leadership learning opportunity.

You may be thinking that you are not in a position to negotiate job assignments with your manager—you simply have to take what is assigned. If this is a concern, let me suggest another way of viewing the situation:

- If you take the time to reach out to your manager and discuss your development needs, you make it more likely that your manager will give you job assignments that represent the best possible learning opportunities. In addition, your manager will be in a better position to represent your interests when senior executives are discussing whom to assign to high visibility work projects.
- You may be able to negotiate the timing of an assignment. Sometimes delaying a project by a few weeks can help free up the time needed to allow you to focus your full attention on it.
- If the assignment involves a large project, you may be able to negotiate the role that you play in the project or the project steps that you would like to support. The aim here is to focus your efforts on those project steps that can provide you with the clearest test of critical leadership competencies. Viewed from this perspective, if you were attempting to develop stronger planning skills, then you would want to take part in the initial planning phase of the project. On the other hand, if you were working on communicating more effectively with senior executives, then you might want to volunteer your time to help the project team develop a strong business case for presentation to senior management.
- You may be able to negotiate the degree to which you will be released from other job duties to focus on the assignment. One way of setting the stage for this portion of the discussion is to see whether you can

identify the more routine aspects of your work that could serve as developmental assignments for more junior members of your work team.

- Cross-functional projects often involve opportunities to travel to other divisional locations or vendor or customer sites. See whether you can negotiate the time and travel budget you will need to expand your understanding of other parts of your business.

In short, it is certainly true that you aren't always to pick and choose the job assignments that you are given. On the other hand, by discussing your development needs with your manager you increase your chances of being able to identify the kind of job assignment that best supports your professional development, and you ensure that your engagement in the assignment yields the most productive results.

Having said that, how you approach your manager is equally important. First, do your homework. Use the development matrixes shown in this chapter (Tables 4.1 through 4.4) to begin to identify development opportunities that correspond to your most important development needs. If you have already identified a potential job assignment, find out everything you can about that development opportunity before approaching your manager. To illustrate, if the job assignment involves joining a cross-functional process improvement team, you might want to uncover the following:

- The project's intended outcomes and success measures
- The name, title, and respective leadership roles of the project leader and other team members
- The project's expected duration and completion data
- The time commitments expected of project team members, including off-site travel to other organizational units, best practice reviews with other companies, vendor site visits, etc.
- Who will be paying for this off-site travel (sometimes each function is expected to support travel costs for its respective project representatives, while in other projects such costs are covered by dedicated project funds)
- What you think you can contribute to the project in terms of company knowledge, industry knowledge, technical skills, and leadership competencies
- What you hope to gain as a result of your participation in the project
- Who the project stakeholders are and how they expect to be kept informed of the team's progress

- The final review and approval process to senior managers (Will the final deliverable be a written set of recommendations, a formal presentation, or both?)
- Whether the project will be limited to the development of a set of recommendations or whether it will also include the creation of an implementation plan and managing the execution of this plan
- Any recommendations you have for balancing your workload throughout the period that you will be involved in the project
- The potential impact that being involved in the project is likely to have on your work/life balance (for an international project this might involve making yourself available to other team members sixteen hours a day, or being willing to commit to an extended travel schedule)

While it may be difficult to gather all of these facts before sitting down to discuss your proposed assignment, the more information you have available the easier it will be for you and your manager to reach a decision regarding the appropriateness of the job assignment.

During this discussion your manager may suggest job assignments that you hadn't previously considered. In anticipation of this, take some time in advance of the discussion to determine how you would prioritize your various development needs. As a final consideration, think about how you will start the conversation. I suggest that you lead by talking about how your involvement in the assignment can help your work team and organization, before explaining how you hope to personally gain from your involvement in the assignment. Starting the meeting in this manner establishes a solid business framework for the developmental assignment and shows your manager that you have given some thought as to how your company can benefit from your assignment.

Keep in mind that your proposed developmental assignment may involve a project that is under the direction of someone other than your manager or that will require you to work extensively in another business unit or work function. In such cases, it will be important for you to encourage those other leaders to support your development. Ideally, your manager should discuss with these leaders the roles that you would like them to play as mentors or feedback providers over the course of the assignment. If your manager does not take this initiative, you may need to be prepared to step in and explain to these potential mentors and feedback providers what you hope to take away from the assignment and the types of feedback and coaching that you are seeking from them.

Managing the Assignment

Establishing Test Points

One way to accelerate your development over the course of an assignment is to work with your manager to identify valid test points, those steps in the assignment where new competencies and knowledge will be really put to the test. Test points provide a means to gauge the progress that you are making in your development efforts. In addition, test points indicate to your key stakeholders where within an assignment they should focus their feedback and developmental coaching.

To give you a better understanding of how test points are applied, let's consider a quick example. Assume that you are trying to strengthen your ability to communicate in a compelling way when you are making formal presentations to senior executives. Your manager suggests that, while you do well in presentation design and delivery, you encounter difficulties in the question-and-answer phase of a presentation. More specifically, you tend to become flustered when senior executives pose questions that you hadn't anticipated. If these questions are presented in a confrontational or challenging way, you may even find yourself becoming defensive and argumentative.

To increase your skills in this area, you decide to participate in a cross-functional team that is attempting to address a recurring customer service problem. In researching this project, you quickly learn that your team is expected to make three presentations to your executive team. Their first presentation will involve identifying the underlying causes of the problem. The second presentation will involve proposing a plan for resolving the problem. During the team's final presentation, which will occur about three months after a solution has been successfully implemented, the team will be asked to describe the results of their problem-solving strategy. In reviewing the project, you conclude that the first and last sessions, which will be primarily focused on sharing information, will be relatively easy for you to manage. It is during the second presentation, when you ask for time, resources, and process changes to address the customer service problem, that you anticipate that you will encounter some push-back from your senior managers. Given these facts, you conclude that it is the second presentation that will constitute the best test point for gauging your progress in managing the Q&A portion of your presentations.

Defining Success Measures and Obtaining Feedback

It is important that you reach agreement with your manager, and any other leaders who will be providing you with feedback on assignments, on what constitutes successful performance on the assignment. The box below contains a simple template that you can adapt for arriving at this agreement. The second box shows how success criteria could be established for measuring performance within the previous example on delivering a presentation to senior executives.

Template for Establishing Success Measures

Within this particular phase of the assignment:

_____

It is important that I am able to produce the following results:

_____

Through the application of the following competencies: _____

_____

With success determined by: _____

Example: Delivering a Presentation to Senior Executives

Within this particular phase of the assignment: *managing the Q&A session of the second presentation to our senior team*
   It is important that I am able to produce the following results: *remain calm and focused and provide persuasive answers when addressing executives' questions*
   Through the application of the following competencies: *responding effectively to questions and challenges*
   With success determined by: *follow-up feedback that I receive from selected participants*

PARTICIPANT'S GUIDE

One way to increase your knowledge on how you are performing in a developmental assignment is to identify more than one type of feedback source. Your manager, senior executives, peers, internal customers, and direct reports can all provide different unique perspectives on your performance:

• Your manager has observed your performance over a wide range of activities and has a solid understanding of your baseline performance as you launch into new learning areas. As a result, your manager can help you gauge the progress that you are making over time in strengthening certain knowledge areas or competencies.
• Your senior executives have the broadest, most extensive perspective regarding business strategy and the interdependences that exist among different business units and functions. Because of this, they can provide excellent feedback on your ability to exercise strategic thinking, demonstrate business acumen, build a business case for new initiatives, and present yourself well to executive leaders.
• Your internal customers have observed how you perform as a service provider and as a representative for your work group and function. They can speak to how well you understand the concerns and perspectives of other work functions and units. They can also provide feedback on the degree to which you respond in a timely way to requests, collaborate across work functions, meet commitments, and negotiate and manage service levels.
• Your peers collaborate with you on a daily basis to achieve team results. They are probably the best group of people to provide feedback on the degree to which you maintain composure in high-stress situations, resolve work conflicts, and influence without authority.
• Your direct reports have a first-hand view of your leadership style and management performance. They can provide useful feedback when it comes to understanding how well you provide clear direction, set priorities, respond to employee concerns, and coach and develop the members of your work team.

In summary, when looking for feedback on your performance in developmental assignments, consider choosing individuals who are in the best position to provide relevant feedback on the types of competencies that you are trying to develop.

It is also worth repeating that effective feedback does not always occur at the end of a job assignment. It can also involve having someone pull you to the side during an assignment to provide suggestions and guidance regarding ways that you can improve your performance over the remainder of the assignment.

Several years ago, I participated in a six-month, part-time assignment as a member of cross-functional process improvement team. After a couple of weeks on the project, I was beginning to feel very proud of all of the hard work that I was contributing to the project. It was at that point that one of the other team members pulled me aside one day to give me some useful advice. She told me that no one on our project doubted that I was fully committed to our team's success. On the other hand, several team members felt that I was so preoccupied with making sure that our team was meeting its objectives that I tended to come across as being overly critical of other team members. This feedback certainly wasn't what I wanted to hear, but after giving myself some time to reflect on it, I decided that she was right. From that point on, I altered my communication style and started to ask other people on our team for more help in making sure that we met our commitments. Receiving this feedback early on during the project was a lot more valuable to me than it would have been had it been presented to me after the project had concluded.

Reviewing the Assignment

Sometimes the hectic pace at which many of us work causes us to jump so quickly from one job to another that we don't take the time at the end of a developmental assignment to pause and consider what we've taken away from what we have just experienced. This reduces the developmental impact of assignments because it is often in the review process that the deepest learning takes place. There are three steps you can take at the close of any project to accelerate your development:

Step 1: Reflect

Set aside time to privately reflect on what you learned from the assignment. I am talking here not only about any technical skills or knowledge areas that you might have developed, but also what you learned about yourself as a professional and leader. When we think about the concept of "professional development," we usually restrict our thinking to building up knowledge areas or grafting on new professional or leadership skills. The fact is, however, that the most demanding developmental assignments often do much more than this. They place us in situations that are highly stressful, test our resiliency, and force us to work outside of our personal comfort zones. Here are some of the questions that you might want to consider asking yourself:

1. If you could replay any step in the assignment, what would you have done differently, and why?
2. Looking back on this learning situation, were there any surprises? Did you learn something about yourself that you hadn't really noticed before? For example:
   a. How well did you manage the stress of the assignment?
   b. How flexible were you in coping with change?
   c. How well do you handle being in a work situation in which you don't know all of the rules, are missing important background information, lack sufficient resources, or are forced to work with difficult people?
3. Did the experience uncover any serious development gaps that you now need to close?
   a. Are these technical skills gaps, the need for increasing your knowledge of certain business processes, or the need for developing specialized expertise?
   b. Do you now know what you need to do to close these gaps?
   c. If not, do you at least know whom you can reach out to in your organization for help in formulating a development plan for improving in these areas?
4. You took on this assignment, in part, to obtain a realistic job preview of your career target. What did you learn from this preview?
   a. Has your experience in this assignment altered your initial career goals and development plan?
   b. Did you learn something about your career target that you hadn't known before?
5. Did the feedback that you received from others align with your own views on how you felt that you performed in the assignment or did you uncover any "blind spots"? These are feedback areas that may have been completely different from the way that you view your own behavior.

Step 2: Solicit Feedback

Take the time to circle back around to your feedback providers to find out how they feel you performed during the assignment. When soliciting feedback, ask precise questions that help you to understand how you per-formed within the test points of your assignment. Consider the following two questions:

- The question, "Overall, how do you think that I did in managing the contract process with Alpha Group?" is vague and requires your feedback provider to evaluate your performance over the entire length of the assignment. As a result, the response you get may not directly touch on the development area that you are trying to assess.
- A more effective question is: "One of the things that I wanted to learn from my work in managing the contract process with Alpha Group was how to negotiate complex service level agreements with outside vendors. Having seen me in those negotiations, could you tell me how I did and anything that I could do to improve my effectiveness in this area?"

Step 3: Consolidate Lessons Learned

The final step of the review process involves sitting down with your manager and sharing both your own self-reflections on the assignment as well as the feedback that you have obtained from others. This information can help the two of you to plan further development actions and to identify the "lessons learned" that you can apply from this assignment to future work challenges. During this discussion, don't be surprised if your manager asks you some of the five self-reflection questions that I have listed in Step 1. The assumption here is that, if you are treating the job assignment as a learning opportunity, then you will take the time to seriously reflect on what you have learned from this assignment and do some serious thinking regarding how this learning can be applied to your development process.

Case in Point: Ken

Ken wanted to become stronger in the areas of project management and influencing without authority. As one of three leaders in his company's corporate training department, Ken decided that a developmental assignment that could help him meet these goals would to take the lead in launching a new learning management system (LMS) that would serve all divisions within his organization. An LMS is the software system that houses online training for an organization and supports such features as the online registration of participants, data collection on training usages and associated costs, and the validation of participant learning through online testing. The project extended over eighteen months and had a number of components that made it particularly challenging:

- The project would require a massive corporate expenditure for the purchase of a new learning management system at a time when the organization was facing a severe budget crunch.
- The project would involve a review of alternative LMS vendors, contract negotiations and pricing discussions with these vendors, and the securing of a contract agreement with a selected LMS vendor.
- The project would involve the implementation of a single LMS platform across multiple national site locations and installation into all corporate divisions.
- One of these divisions already had its own LMS, although this system was rather antiquated and wasn't robust enough to support the needs of the entire corporation. A second division was already reviewing LMS vendors, with the intent of setting up its own LMS. Neither division wanted to relinquish its plans in order to participate in a corporate-wide LMS project.
- Implementing the project would require the integration of the first division's online training database into the database that would be established for the new corporate system.
- The implementation process would require careful consideration regarding cost allocations back to the divisions and a rollout plan for bringing each division onto the system.

In reviewing the project with his manager, Ken decided that his project management skills would be tested both in the creation of a project implementation plan and in the continual adaptation of this plan to meet changing circumstances. He decided that the one project step that would most severely test his ability to influence without authority would be the stage at which he had to secure divisional commitment to the project team's recommendations for the proposed LMS provider and to agree to the associated costs that would be allocated back to each division. Ken then spent a lot of time with his manager identifying those divisional stakeholders who would need to be approached individually in advance of this critical project meeting. He also used these discussions to determine how best to identify and address each stakeholder's concerns regarding cost allocations, divisional input into the design of the LMS, and the proposed rollout schedule.

Attention to these details helped Ken to substantiate the proposed benefits of the new LMS, including cost reductions that would be achieved by preventing the creation of redundant systems at the divisional level, economies of scale achieved through contracting with a single online training content provider, extending technical training to employees across the entire organization, and obtaining better data for the tracking and managing of online training costs and usage.

Apart from his manager and internal divisional customers, Ken sought out feedback from the program manager who was assigned to support him on the project. In reflecting on the project at its mid-point (it is still under-way), he concluded that two of the big learning areas that he took away from the project were (1) the importance of finding ways to help divisional stakeholders gain greater ownership and control of the implementation process and (2) the need for spending more time with those same stakeholders in troubleshooting potential obstacles and risks to the project and in finding ways to mitigate those project risks.

Your Next Steps

Over the next two weeks, use the examples provided in this chapter to identify a list of potential developmental job assignments. Then, working with your manager, use the selection criteria presented in this chapter to select an appropriate developmental assignment. You can use the form provided on the next page to create a plan to help you manage the assignment. Your last step is to schedule one opportunity over the next few weeks to obtain developmental feedback from at least one of your feedback providers.

Project Management Plan

Specific Development Areas to Be Addressed:

Summary Description of the Job Assignment:

Start Date and Estimated Duration of the Assignment:

Required Adjustments (balancing workload, travel, costs, etc.):

Test Points:

Success Measures:

Feedback Providers (may include your manager, senior executives, peers, internal customers, and/or direct reports):

CHAPTER FIVE

ACCELERATING YOUR LEARNING

Acceleration = Agility + Efficiency

You have already learned how to accelerate your development by constructing a solid development plan and using job assignments to jump-start your development efforts. In this chapter you will learn how to strengthen your development by accelerating your on-the-job learning. To do that I will discuss how you can take steps to increase your learning agility by exploiting available avenues for learning and improving the efficiency of your learning process. When brought together, these two components act as a powerful learning accelerator for not only increasing the speed at which you learn, but also how thoroughly you acquire and apply new work skills and information.

Are You Learning Agile?

Over the past ten years a number of research studies have demonstrated that there is a direct link between an individual's leadership potential and that person's ability to learn and profit from experience. Individuals who have a high degree of learning agility are characterized by the ability to aggressively seek out learning, to develop robust strategies for learning, and to adapt what they have learned to future situations. Strengthening your learning agility is one of the most powerful steps you can take to accelerate your workplace learning and advance your career. To do this you first need to understand how it is that you currently learn from experience.

Robert Eichinger and Michael Lombardo, the founders of Lominger International, have performed extensive research on learning agility. (Their research and that conducted by their parent corporation, Korn/Ferry International, is referenced at the end of this chapter.) Eichinger and Lombardo have suggested that learning agility is comprised of four major components:

- *Mental Agility*—The degree to which individuals examine problems from innovative perspectives, work well with problem complexity and ambiguity, and are able to discern meaningful patterns in information.
- *People Agility*—The degree to which individuals work well with diverse people, remain calm and composed when confronted with volatile situations, exhibit a high degree of self-knowledge, and are flexible in their willingness to assume a variety of work-related roles.
- *Results Agility*—The degree to which individuals exhibit a high level of drive, deliver on results when placed under challenging conditions, and inspire confidence in others.
- *Change Agility*—The degree to which individuals exhibit a high degree of curiosity, enjoy experimenting with innovative ideas, and are able to introduce new perspectives to work challenges.

To aid in the assessment of learning agility Eichinger and Lombardo have developed CHOICES®, a multi-rater instrument that evaluates these four components in terms of twenty-one dimensions that are evaluated through raters' scores on eighty-one statements. Research using this instrument has shown that individuals who score high in learning agility, as identified through CHOICES, received higher ratings on their leadership potential, when compared to their low-agility counterparts. Eichinger and Lombardo also found that when high and low learning agile performers were promoted into broader leadership roles, those who were highest in learning agility also received higher ratings on their first performance reviews within their new positions.

Related research has shown that learning agility is a distinctly different construct than that of intelligence and that the degree to which a person displays learning agility is independent of that individual's IQ. A recent research report by Korn/Ferry International, the parent company for Lominger International, notes studies showing that ratings of learning agility, as evaluated by CHOICES, are also independent of a learner's age, gender, and cultural origin.

Together, these findings mean that our ability to learn and profit from experience is not hard-wired into us at an early age, nor is it totally constrained by factors that are outside of our control. In other words, if you are willing to diligently work at it, you can increase your learning agility and discover how to take away more from your encounters with new and challenging work experiences.

How to Assess Your Learning Agility

So how can you increase your learning agility? Before answering this question, it is important to understand that research suggests that learning agility is not an all-or-nothing personality construct, but an approach to learning that is comprised of a number of highly differentiated behaviors. Eichinger and Lombardo's initial research in this area has shown that individuals vary widely in the scoring patterns that they have on the four dimensions of Mental Agility, Results Agility, People Agility, and Change Agility. Moreover, people differ widely in the degree to which they engage in each of these learning behaviors. The implication here is that you can be learning agile with respect to some aspects of work-related learning (being able to quickly adapt to change), yet still engage in other behaviors (being reluctant to seek out information and feedback from others) that act as a drag on your overall learning ability. Since each of us has a distinctly different set of learning strengths and weaknesses, it is easy to see that the more detailed information that you can obtain on your individual learning style, the easier it will be for you to develop an action plan for accelerating your development.

An important related research finding is that people sometimes have difficulty evaluating their level of learning agility. One of the most interesting findings from the Korn/Ferry study cited earlier involved comparisons of self and other ratings. Those individuals who were rated as highest in learning agility by their managers, peers, and direct reports tended to be more conservative when estimating their own level of learning agility. The opposite was also true, in that those individuals who received the lowest learning agility ratings from their managers, co-workers, and team members tended to rate themselves extremely high in learning agility.

I know that it sounds a bit strange and perhaps counter-intuitive to suggest that the people with whom you work may have a more accurate sense of your learning agility than do you, but pause for a moment and reflect on it. When I use the term "learning agility" I am not talking about the type of academic learning that occurs when you go off-line and privately analyze information or add to your knowledge base. Instead, your ability to learn at work depends heavily on your ability to capture, coordinate, and consolidate information and actions from a wide range of people. During those interactions, other people have many opportunities to observe the degree to which you appear to be receptive to new ideas, invite input on problems, and express a willingness to experiment with new work methods. These individuals have a first-hand view of how you present yourself in such situations and the degree to which your work behavior supports or impedes your learning.

Your manager, peers, direct reports, and internal customers are also in good positions to directly observe the output of your learning. By this I mean that the true test of workplace learning isn't your ability to acquire new knowledge and skills. Instead, it reveals itself in your ability to adapt and refine your leadership behavior to the ever-changing demands of your job, based on that learning. So while other people may not know what is going on inside your head, they can directly observe those learning behaviors that are both a necessary prerequisite to learning and a direct result of that learning. In addition, the degree to which you communicate to others that you are learning agile has a huge impact on strength of your personal brand (a subject that I will be covering more in the next chapter).

In summary, in order to assess your learning agility you need to know the kinds of behaviors that work for, or against, your ability to learn on the job. You cannot figure this out by privately mulling about it; instead you must ask others for feedback. The most effective way to solicit such feedback is through use of a multi-rater instrument such as CHOICES, which has been specifically designed to target behaviors related to learning agility. If this instrument is unavailable to you, an alternative option is to reach out to your manager and co-workers to obtain an informal assessment of your learning agility. A detailed process for conducting a learning agility self-assessment is provided at the end of the chapter, under the section entitled Your Next Steps.

How to Strengthen Your Learning Agility

Let me say it again—learning agility is not hard-wired into the brain. It is a set of learning behaviors that, when employed, can increase both your access to opportunities for learning and your ability to extract the most from learning experiences. With that in mind, here are a few steps you can take to become a more learning agile person:

First, aggressively seek out new learning experiences. Learning agile people are, by definition, individuals who aggressively explore new learning opportunities. The challenge we sometimes run into is that we may not recognize a learning opportunity when we see it. If this sounds paradoxical, consider the following quote, attributed to Thomas Edison: "Opportunity is missed by most people because it is dressed in overalls and looks like work." As an executive coach, I have seen many situations in which people overlook learning experiences because such opportunities (1) require a lot of work, (2) involve significant and complex business problems, (3) can expose them to the possibility of failure, and (4) often involve the tedious process of enlisting the help of other people in supporting these learning opportunities. Simply put, new work-related learning experiences frequently require a lot of heavy lifting, and that is something that we can easily talk ourselves out of.

One of the most effective ways to overcome self-induced procrastination on a workout program is to set and track your progress against written fitness goals. In the same way, the starting point for activating learning agility is to set down in writing a few structured learning goals, and then regularly track your progress against these goals. An excellent technique for starting this process, one that I refer to as "The Resume Test," is discussed at the end of this chapter in the section entitled "Your Next Steps."

Draw information from a variety of sources. Over the past twenty years Ronald Burt, a professor at the University of Chicago, has developed and tested a very sophisticated organizational model of communication that deals with something that he calls "structural holes"; these are those white spaces on the organization chart where good ideas seldom penetrate beyond organizational silos. Professor Burt has found that some people tend to spread ideas within their well-trod social networks. The problem is that, for most of us, almost all of the people who make up our social networks are located within our work functions or departments, and not necessarily where our ideas are needed most within our organizations. Learning agile performers are very adept at reaching out beyond these constricted networks to know where and how to spread good ideas. For such individuals, "networking" is not about how many connections they have on their Facebook pages. Instead, they put careful thought into determining who within their organizations could benefit from different kinds of information and expertise, paying particular attention to those higher-level influential managers who reside outside of their reporting structure.

When it comes to developing creative ideas, they also know the best places to search within their organizations to quickly identify the right expertise.

Burt's research has found that, because these professionals know when and how to span organizational boundaries, they are able develop a high level of "social capital." In other words, their organizations view them as extremely valuable and reward them accordingly. Burt's research has found that people who are effective boundary spanners have greater influence in their organizations, receive more in compensation, and have a faster promotional track. Later on in this chapter I will provide detailed suggestions for improving your effectiveness in social networking.

Learning from other sources also means that you continually seek out new informational sources. On a regular basis, purchase a magazine that you typically don't read, such as *The Economist, Smithsonian,* or *Fortune,* one that can help keep you abreast of trends and new developments in other areas. A couple times a month I like to hit the magazine section of a local bookstore, where I intentionally spend a few minutes trolling through magazines that span a wide range of reading interests. I often glean a lot of good ideas through this kind of idea scavenger hunt. As another option, occasionally conduct an Internet search on a new idea or concept that is floating around your organization and see where your search leads you. If you attend the same professional association each month, mix it up a bit and attend one that is outside your usual target zone. If you are somewhat shy about doing this, ask your friends and co-workers what professional associations they belong to and attend as a guest. As a final thought, universities are a great place to discover speakers in a variety of fields, ranging from international economics to anthropology.

Exploiting Available Avenues for Learning

When it comes to workplace learning, it is easy to fall into the habit of relying on a few trusted avenues for learning, at the expense of ignoring others that may be more effective. Each of the following learning options offers different advantages in terms of its time requirements, relative effectiveness, cost, availability, and the extent to which it supports a flexible learning process. Take a few minutes to scan through the following list to identify learning approaches that you could more effectively leverage.

Organizational Training

Most organizations offer a variety of formal training programs for both professionals and leaders. Unfortunately, not all organizations do a good job of giving employees advance notice of their offerings. Quite often professionals find themselves informed of training options at the last minute, leaving little time for juggling work schedules to accommodate training offerings. Companies typically identify their annual course offerings for the forthcoming year in the last quarter of the proceeding year. Because of this, the October through December months are a good time to contact your training or leadership development department to inquire about planned training offerings so that you can determine how to make the most effective use of your time and training budget.

In two situations getting advance notice on upcoming training programs is particularly important. The first is when your company will be providing training in areas such as project management or change management in advance of major change initiatives. Being one of the first people scheduled for such training ensures that you have advance notice regarding important changes that are rolling through your organization. Similarly, organizations frequently time the introduction of certain technical or sales training programs to coincide with the onset of new product launches or technology platforms. Once again, being one of the first people in the training queue means that you have a tactical advantage when it comes to understanding the long-range implications of such innovations.

Another useful hint is to ask your training manager to provide you with course outlines or samples of training content from upcoming training programs so that you can determine which training courses best meet your development needs. This information usually provides more detail on course offerings than is found on company online training sites. In addition, find out well in advance whether the courses that you want to take require offsite travel and associated travel costs or extensive pre-work such as the completion of cases or multi-rater reviews. Finally, talk to your co-workers to find out whether they felt that certain training programs were worth the time invested.

If your manager asks you to participate in a leadership development program, be careful about turning the offer down. Some leadership training programs are rather exclusive, with invitations extended only to those individuals who are viewed as being high-potential leaders. Turning down an invitation for such a program might convey to your manager that you

PARTICIPANT'S GUIDE

aren't fully invested in your own development—or that you have no interest in advancing within your company.

Aside from helping you build skills and organizational knowledge, formal training programs also provide excellent opportunities for networking with professionals outside of your work function. Before attending a course, take the time to scan the course roster to see whether you can identify individuals you may want to include in your professional network.

Professional Conferences

Professional conferences offer an excellent avenue for professional development. In addition, they provide a means for networking with professionals outside of your organization and represent a strong avenue for building technical and industry skills. The problem with professional conferences is that they offer a wide smorgasbord of offerings—far too many for any one person to absorb in a few days. You can take several steps to make the most out of professional conferences. First, go online to the professional organizations with which you are affiliated to check on the dates and locations for conferences that are planned over the next twelve months. This can help you review all available offerings before making any decisions regarding attending a conference. Checking ahead can also help you assess the potential impact of conference and travel time on your work schedule.

If you are considering attending a conference, expand your search to include trade conferences as a means of helping you build technical skills and keep you abreast of changes within your industry. If you are unsure as to which conference sessions you should attend, discuss this with your manager. You can also perform an online search of the conference speakers to see what they've written and their principal areas of expertise. As a final step, you can review the speaker rosters to see whether any of your organization's senior executives are scheduled to appear as presenters.

If your company is experiencing a budget crunch, you might find it difficult to gain approval to pay for the cost of the conference and associated travel. To address this constraint, first explain to your manager that the conference that you are requesting provides an important avenue for addressing important development needs and is the result of a thorough review of several conference alternatives. Then spell out the benefits that attending the conference will have for your organization.

To save on travel costs, look for conferences that will be conducted close to one of your company or customer site locations. Also keep in mind that regional conferences, which tend to be less expensive and require less travel, can be low-cost alternatives to national conferences. As another option, many vendors sponsor free user conferences that provide both product demos by vendors, as well as guest speakers on a host of topics tied to the vendor's area of expertise. Also, if your department currently has a budget for training but you are concerned that next year funding for training may not be readily available, you might find it wise to register and pre-pay for conferences that you want to attend next year under this year's training and travel budgets. Once those expenses have been accounted for, it is unlikely that anyone will cancel your travel plans. Finally, if you have never done so, give some serious thought to presenting at a conference. Often a speaker's registration and travel costs will be covered by the conference sponsors. This is also one of the most effective ways to build your professional reputation outside of your organization.

Conferences offer an excellent means of expanding your professional networks. Attendee rosters are usually passed out during conference registration. Use these to identify a few individuals whom you'd like to seek out during the conference as potential additions to your professional network. Also, keep in mind that attending a conference with someone else in your organization can be an excellent way to strengthen organizational relationships.

Always bring your business cards to professional conferences. When other people give you their cards, take a second to jot down on the back of each card how you and the other person met and any professional interest areas that you may have in common. Consider using downtime at a conference as a means of socializing with and getting to know other attendees from your organization. Conference proceedings are frequently consolidated in an online format or are provided in the form of CD disks. These proceedings can be very useful reference tools for covering conference sessions that you aren't able to attend.

Formal Education

If you haven't already done so, make sure that you take advantage of your company's tuition reimbursement benefit. Not doing so is like leaving money on the table. As a first step, check with your company's tuition reimbursement office or your HR manager to learn about the guidelines that you need to follow to receive tuition reimbursement. Often these guidelines involve obtaining approval by both your manager and HR department in advance of college registration. Organizations vary widely regarding the percentage of total educational costs that they will reimburse and the conditions that have to be met (such as maintaining a minimum grade point average) in order to obtain reimbursement for college courses. Consider taking advantage of your organization's tuition reimbursement program even if you are not interested in obtaining another degree. Find out whether your company will reimburse you for specialized courses within a degree program or for taking executive education courses.

If you are considering pursuing your education, it pays to shop around. Colleges vary widely with respect to tuition costs, the breadth of their course offerings, the selectivity of their selection processes, and the extent to which they make use of online, evening, or weekend intensive sessions to accommodate professionals' busy work schedules.

Since an important part of what any educational experience offers you is the ability to network, before committing to a course of study check on the profile of the typical student who attends a given academic program. Quite often, the students who gravitate toward evening and weekend courses are experienced first-line, middle, and senior managers who are attempting to further their career goals through part-time educational coursework.

Self-Directed Learning

The last few years have witnessed an explosion in self-directed training options. The best starting point for exploring self-directed learning is to contact your corporate training department and find out how to access any online courses that may be available through your organization's learning management system (LMS). You can supplement this by exploring some of the many self-directed training programs that are available through CD and online options. An example is the text-based and online self-study programs in project management available through the Project Management Institute (www.pmi.org/Pages/default.aspx). If you are a busy professional and don't have a lot of time for reading, consider subscribing to a service such as Soundview Executive Book Summaries (www.summary.com) which, for an annual subscription fee, can provide you brief summaries of the key learning points of on a variety of business books. Soundview's formats include print, online, CD, and the option of downloading materials through iTunes.

Some universities are now offering both paid and free video lectures through avenues such as iTunes U. In addition, you can gain access to a variety of top-notch speakers on a number of topics through both iTunes and YouTube. If you want to watch and listen to speakers who are regarded as thought leaders in their fields, then I heartily recommended that you check out the TED website (www.ted.com) and review the many free video lectures that are available to you there for downloading. TED is a nonprofit organization that is focused on the dissemination of innovative ideas. It began in 1984 as a conference devoted to Technology, Entertainment, and Design, but the scope of its speaking presentations now extends from oceanography to biotechnology. TED also conducts multi-day conferences each year. (If you are lucky enough to get into one of these conferences, don't pass up the opportunity.)

Another way to track leading-edge trends is to check out white papers and case studies that are available through the websites of some of the major consulting houses such as McKinsey, Accenture, Deloitte, Hewitt, and The Boston Consulting Group. Some of these materials are available without charge, while others require an annual subscription rate. Harvard Business School Publishing has a massive array of cases and thought pieces on every conceivable aspect of leadership.

Finally, don't forget to periodically go online and check out your own company website. During a recent consulting session, I asked the executive who had brought me into a consulting project what she thought about a new product line that was currently under review by her company. In response to her blank look, I directed her to the investor section of her corporate website, which contained a podcast on the subject by her CEO. If nothing else, I would advise you to check out any quarterly analyst calls that might be posted on your company website in streamed audio format.

Shadowing and Modeling

Two closely related methods for speeding up learning are through the use of shadowing and modeling. *Shadowing* involves following someone around and observing that person in real time as he or she engages in a work situation. A common example of shadowing is the use of a sales ride-along. In one form of the ride-along, a sales representative accompanies the manager on a customer call to observe that manager's sales approach. The opposite situation can also apply, in which a sales manager observes a sales rep complete a call and afterward provides the rep with feedback on his or her performance. *Modeling* is somewhat different in that it involves having an experienced performer schedule time to go offline and demonstrate the use of a certain skill within a mock situation.

In order for either method, to work three conditions have to be met. First, the manager or more experienced co-worker who is providing the shadowing or modeling has to be an exemplar who is highly skilled in the competency area that you want to develop. It is also important for you to clearly define your learning objectives in advance of the session. If you need to improve your skills in cold calling, it would make little sense spending time shadowing a sales manager during the close of a sales call. Finally, you need to ensure that, immediately following the shadowing or modeling experience, you and your manager set aside time for a debriefing and review session.

Shadowing and modeling are both useful, but each has it is own unique advantages. Shadowing allows you to observe a skill carried out within an actual work situation. On the other hand, one drawback with shadowing is that you have to wait until a shadowing opportunity is available. Sales calls occur frequently, but if you were attempting to shadow someone who was directing part of your organization's annual planning process, you could easily end up waiting a year for this type of opportunity to present itself. Also, when shadowing someone, you must pick a work situation in which you can remain somewhat unobtrusive and where your presence will not compromise the work performance. For example, if you were an HR professional, it would be difficult to create a situation in which you were able to shadow an HR leader as this person directed a sexual harassment investigation.

While modeling does not present you with full exposure to a real-life situation, it offers the advantage of allowing you to practice the skill area that you are modeling "offline" in a safe environment. If someone is modeling for you how to complete part of your department's annual budgeting process, you are less likely to feel uncomfortable asking a lot of questions about how the process works. During modeling you also have more control over how you "direct" the work situation; that is, you can ask your model to illustrate only that portion of the skill area that poses the greatest challenge to you. You can then stop the action as it takes place to discuss what you are observing. For modeling to be effective, it is important that you ask your model to "think aloud." Many people attempt to demonstrate work skills without explaining why it is they are doing what they are doing. From the observer's point of view, the model appears to start at point A and then magically complete the work task at point Z. Whenever you engage someone as a model, your challenge is to have the person verbally walk you through both the "what" and the "why" of the work so that you can follow the logic of how he or she progresses through a series of complex decision points or action steps. Finally, when making use of either shadowing or modeling, you can further accelerate your learning by staging a practice session immediately following your observation period. In summary, the steps involved in modeling are

- Clearly define the skill area that you want to observe.
- Watch and (if possible) ask questions as you observe.
- Listen to the person think aloud as he or she progresses through the steps of the skill area.
- Practice the skill yourself.
- Obtain immediate feedback on how close you came to approximating the behavior that you were observing.

Practice Runs

A large part of professional learning involves developing a strong platform of communication and relationship skills. One of the best techniques for simultaneously building these skills while lowering the risk level for applying them in difficult work settings is to schedule practice runs with your manager, a trusted friend, or even a small group of co-workers. Examples include situations in which you want to prepare yourself to make your first presentation to an executive team, negotiate pricing with a key customer, deliver a tough performance appraisal, or manage a conflict with someone in another department.

You can take several steps to get the most out of a practice run. First, plan in advance. If you want someone to spend an hour to help you practice negotiating with your customer, be considerate and give the person advance notice to put this on his Outlook calendar. Similarly, if you want to practice making a presentation you will probably want to reserve a conference room and an LCD display.

Next, try to make your practice session look and feel like the actual thing. If you are preparing for a large presentation that will take place in the company auditorium, then practice in the auditorium. If you are want to prepare to manage a conflict with someone, then describe that person's communication style to your practice partner so that your partner can display that style during your practice session. In other words, anything that you can do to make the session "real" helps you to master the skill that you are trying to develop, while reducing any anxiety that you might have about tackling something new and different.

Another suggestion is to make certain that the people who support you in a practice session are not passive observers but are, instead, actively engaged in helping you test and develop your skills. Going back to the presentation example, you could start your practice session by brainstorming with your practice partners the types of questions and objections that you might encounter in your upcoming presentation. Have them use these questions to test your ability to manage your question-and-answer session.

As a final suggestion, whenever possible, record or videotape your practice run so that you can subsequently review it and make additional improvements.

Increasing the Efficiency of Your Learning

Along with exploring additional avenues for advancing your work-related learning, there are also a variety of methods you can use to increase the efficiency of your learning process. Please don't be misled by the term "efficiency of learning." I am not talking here about ten ways to think smarter or clever techniques for increasing your memory. Instead, I am talking about six steps you can take to make certain that you learn what you need and obtain that learning in the most effective way possible.

Calibrate Your Learning Requirements

Years ago I read a study that contrasted the managerial approaches of two past presidents: Jimmy Carter and Ronald Reagan. The author suggested that of the two, President Carter probably had the higher IQ, as well as a stronger capacity to wrestle with complex issues. Reagan, however, had one strong advantage when it came to running the oval office. While Carter conscientiously attempted to wade through four-hundred-page reports on international and domestic issues, Reagan demanded that such reports contain two-page executive summaries, which he used to guide his decisions. This makes sense when you consider the overwhelming array of data that a U.S. president has to deal with on a daily basis. Some historians have suggested that Carter's desire to wade into the details of each decision was a big factor in the problems that he encountered during his presidency.

The moral of this story is that, when attempting to accelerate your learning, it is important to quickly gauge the extent to which you need to master a new learning area. Failure to do this can lead to two potential problems: If you underestimate the learning requirements for certain areas, you will end up developing only a superficial grasp of those areas. The flip side is attempting to be "master of all" and, in the process, finding yourself overwhelmed by a variety of new learning challenges. When coaching leaders, I find that it is useful to classify learning challenges within the four levels of learning mastery shown in Table 5.1. I then ask the person whom I am coaching to use this system to set more definitive learning goals.

The four levels of learning mastery are important to consider whenever your development goals involve acquiring skills and knowledge that are required at higher organizational levels. The reason is that quite often you may not know what level of skill mastery is actually required to succeed within a higher-level position by observing the job from the outside. You could, for example, easily assume that success in a certain leadership position requires an in-depth mastery of certain database systems. The reality might be that the most successful managers in this function have only a broad, general understanding of those systems; that is, while they know how to interpret reports generated by those systems, they have no actual knowledge of how to operate those systems (Level 4). Instead, they know enough about the database systems (Level 2) to understand the types of reports that their direct reports should be able to generate from those systems and to evaluate the quality of these system outputs. To ensure that you have a clear read on the actual level of knowledge required for success in a given leadership position, I strongly suggest that you conduct detailed interviews with people who currently hold those jobs and use the four levels

TABLE 5.1. The Four Levels of Learning Mastery

Level	Your Goal
Level 4	Your learning goal is to strive to become an expert in this skill or knowledge area, requiring no outside assistance or support.
Level 3	Your learning goal is to be able to master basic components of actually implementing the new skill or knowledge level, given some guidance and support by others.
Level 2	Your learning goal is to learn enough about the new skill or knowledge area to be able to interpret the quality of work in this area that is performed by other people.
Level 1	Your learning goal is to know a few general facts about how the new skill or knowledge area (a new product, work method, technical skill, or leadership responsibility) operates and how performance within this area can affect the overall success of your work team and organization.

of skill mastery to calibrate your learning requirements for these next-level positions.

Mine Your Social Networks

One of the fastest ways to accelerate your learning is by making the best possible use of your social network as a learning avenue. Think of your network as a kind of neural net that can help you quickly connect to the information and resources that you need to expand your professional expertise. Networking requirements increase the more you become involved in the kinds of multi-faceted work challenges that require integrated data from a number of sources. When used correctly, the people in your network will not only provide you with useful information, but they will help you to establish a more complete map of your information requirements.

Let me share an illustrative example from my own experience. Not too long ago someone in my HR network contacted me to ask for my opinion on a commercially available online learning management system (LMS). I had my own opinions about the system, but instead I referred my colleague to two best practice reviews that had been conducted on several of the most prominent systems and the metrics that these authors had used for reaching their rankings. I was also able to put the caller in touch with two of my corporate clients who had used the system in question. Together, these components allowed the caller to create a kind of mental map of the LMS landscape. I would like to think that our thirty-minute call saved my colleague from hours of work in attempting to put this information together on her own. In the same way, if you know who within your network can put you in touch with the right information, you can radically increase your learning speed on any new area.

All of this leads to the question of how effective you are when it comes to building a robust social network at work. As I said, forget for a moment how many connections you have on Facebook or LinkedIn. This isn't so much about how many people you know; it is about the extent to which you are knowledgeable of, and well connected to, other parts of your organization. The key to making your network perform for you as a learning tool is to make certain that you have the following types of individuals embedded in your network. As you read through this list, see whether your current network includes people within each of the following categories:

- Those with unique technical expertise
- Those with a solid understanding of your business, competitors, and customer base

- Those who stay at the cutting edge of key trends (technical, market, legal) within your industry
- Those who understand the internal wiring of your organization, who know who within the company is able to influence decisions
- Those who understand the details of key business processes, how to navigate through the IT or financial approval processes, etc.
- Those who sit in the middle of a much broader social network and who can quickly put you in touch with individuals who can help you meet any of the aforementioned needs

Here is a second quick test of your network capability. Think about the most complex project or work problem that you are going to be tackling over the next month. Now sketch out a graphic map of the people whom you would call upon to help you (1) anticipate the kinds of challenges that you might face on this project, (2) identify key risks and opportunities embedded in this project, and (3) identify and prioritize preventive and corrective actions for managing these challenges. Now take a look at the map that you have created. How robust is your map? How many people are included in your map? Do you even know where to go to access help from other areas of your organization not included in your map? How well known, liked, and respected are you by the people on your map?

If you are dissatisfied with your results, here are a few initial steps that you can take to become a better boundary spanner:

1. Begin by seeking out new lunch partners. If you are like most professionals, you probably eat lunch with the same two or three people every week. Vary it a bit. Think about people outside your immediate network in other departments or work functions with whom you'd like to connect; then take the initiative.
2. The same thing goes for conferences, training workshops, sales meetings, and so on. The next time that you are at one of these events, resist the urge to sit next to one of your friends. Instead, check the sign-in roster and identify someone in another functional area whom you'd like to know a bit more.
3. If another work group or function could benefit from your expertise, offer to attend one of their staff meetings and share your ideas.
4. In the same way, the next time that you are stuck on a problem, try to identify at least three people outside of your functional network who could provide you with unique perspectives or support you with specialized skills.

5. Consider taking the initiative to form a volunteer "lunch and learn" group in which you meet regularly with other professionals from around your organization. Each person spends one lunch session bringing everyone else in the group up to speed on a new work process, method, or customer engagement activity.

The key to using networks is not to abuse them. Here are some suggested do's and don'ts in managing your networks:

• Develop your work relationships in advance. Before you ask them for help, make certain that you have already formed a strong trust bond with them.

• When asking for help, provide context that allows the person you are approaching to understand the rationale for your request. This should be a brief, articulate summary that gives the other person the background she needs to understand not only the type of help you are requesting, but also why you are asking for this help and why you are approaching the person for assistance.

• During that same call, it is helpful for you to provide a brief summary of the steps that you have attempted to take up to this point (obtain information, solve a problem, etc.) before reaching out to the person. This keeps him or her from experiencing the frustration of retracing some of steps that you have already taken.

• If there are qualifiers to your request, state these up-front. For example, if you need certain information no later than the tenth of the month because you will be presenting it to your manager on the twelfth, tell this to your helper. If you need to get your hands on the current (and still incomplete) quarterly departmental budget, and last quarter's information is not useful, say this up-front. No one wants to go through the steps of providing assistance only to find that these efforts have been wasted.

• Never make your request sound like a demand, even when the initial request came from a senior executive. Be nice and you will get better results.

• Each time you use your network to tap information, the last question you should ask is: "Who else do you know who might be an additional source of information on this area?" Use your networks not just to tap information, but to continually tap different sources of information.

• After help has been extended, take the time to send out a thank you email and (if it is appropriate) copy the helper's manager on your note.

Help that goes unrecognized will seldom be offered again. If the information is going into a report or presentation, credit this individual as a helpful source.

- Healthy networks thrive on reciprocity. If you fail to respond to a request for help from someone else in your network or you plead that you are too busy to help, you reduce the balance left in your trust account. Remember, you cannot make a withdrawal if there is no money in the bank. If others call for assistance, ask a few questions at the beginning of the conversation to see what steps they have taken to this point and whether they require minimal assistance or extensive support. If you are not able to be of assistance, try to at least take the time to put the requestor in touch with other people within your network who could prove helpful; then take a few minutes to provide the requestor with an introduction through a quick phone call or email.

Make Your Body an Ally

With all of my previous references to physical fitness, I am sure that you knew this moment was coming. Yes, I am talking about making your body your ally in your learning process. Thanks to the legacy of René Descartes (no, I am not going to explain; you will have to look him up) we have grown up in a culture in which mind and body are viewed as two entirely different things. Without belaboring the point, I intend to argue the opposite; that mind and body have a profound interactive effect on one another in the learning process. There are two ways in which this interaction directly affects your ability to learn on the job.

First, there is a rapidly growing body of research that is demonstrating that participating in vigorous, sustained (thirty minutes or more) aerobic exercise directly prior to engaging in any learning activity increases the effectiveness of that learning process. John Ratey and Eric Hagerman, the authors of *Spark: The Revolutionary New Science of Exercise and the Brain*, have produced some very impressive research showing that when you engage in aerobic exercise you boost oxygen levels to your brain. In addition, the longer your workout the greater the effect; with exercise routines of forty minutes practically doubling the oxygen intake produced by thirty minutes of exercise. Sustained aerobic exercise also appears to accelerate learning by stimulating the production of a compound in your brain known as brain-derived neurotrophic factor (BDNF), which helps to stimulate cellular brain growth. In support of their claims, Ratey and Hagerman produce a substantial body of solid research. One study compared freshman students who were placed in a special aerobics class at the start of school each day to a second group that was given the school's regular PE class. While both groups showed improvements in reading and comprehension over the course of the school year, the increase rates were 17 percent for the aerobic group versus 10.7 percent for the traditional group. That is a 65 percent difference! Most parents would kill to obtain that type of jump in their kids' reading and comprehension scores. The bottom line is that, if you are planning to take on a significant learning challenge this year, you might want to consider giving yourself an aerobic exercise boost (and related oxygen infusion) immediately before you tackle your work day. It will make a big difference in your learning capability.

Work with Your Biorhythms

Each of us operates on a different twenty-four-hour cycle. I happen to be a "lark"; that is, I tend to jump out of bed each morning with a fairly high level of energy, which gradually winds down as the day progresses. By ten at night I am not a very exciting person to be around. "Owls" are just the opposite. These are people who have to drag themselves out of bed in the morning but gain their energy and mental focus as the day progresses. I have found over the years that your daily biorhythmic cycle tends to be very regular. If you think about it, there is a two-hour block during the day when you are at your peak. Your energy level is highest during this period, concentration comes easier to you, and tough mental challenges don't seem so overwhelming.

How about you? Let's stop for a minute so that you can take a quick test. First, identify the two hours of the day when you feel that you are typically at your peak. Now go back through your calendar and ask yourself what you were doing during this time period during the past two weeks. Chances are that you treated it just as you would any other period of the day. In short, you used this time to read mail, take a few phone calls, hold meetings, or do whatever else wandered onto your desk. If this sounds like your situation, then I would argue that you are wasting your biological peak time. I would further suggest that you can get at least a 10 percent lift in your learning effectiveness by blocking this time period off on your calendar each day for your most difficult work-related learning challenges.

Another simple step that you can take to make your biorhythms work for you is to take steps to avoid peaks and valleys in your daily energy cycles. Six months ago I shifted away from coffee (I used to drink about six cups a day) to green tea and mate (a South American herb that tastes like tea). Both green tea and mate have a fraction of the caffeine that coffee has, as well as a much higher yield of antioxidants, which are very healthy for your body. In my case, I used to go through cycles of intense energy (and accompanying stress) followed by hours when I would feel tired and drained. Since making this small dietary change, I have noticed that my energy level is far more balanced and my stress level has noticeably decreased.

One final suggestion is to try to avoid meals that are very heavy in carbohydrates (pasta, rice, breads) during the workday. They will make you feel sluggish and will decrease your energy level. As with any commentary on exercise and nutrition, if you are not sure how these suggestions would apply to your own situation, then I would advise you to first seek out the counsel and advice of your family physician before implementing them.

Eliminate Self-Imposed Constraints

Many of us go through life holding onto a belief that severely restricts our ability to learn through experience. The belief is that we are born with a certain degree of intelligence, which gradually diminishes once we hit middle age.

There are two important areas of psychological research that directly challenge this notion. The first deals with the concept of implicit intelligence, an area of research that has been pioneered by Dr. Carol Dweck, a Stanford psychology professor and the author of *Mindset: The New Psychology of Success*. Dr. Dweck's research over the past twenty years suggests that each of us operates from an implicit model of intelligence, that is, an unexamined set of assumptions about what we think intelligence is and how we view the role of new learning experiences in shaping intelligence. *Entity* theorists believe that you have only so much intelligence and you cannot increase it, regardless of learning. People who are entity theorists see intelligence as a relatively fixed and unchangeable part of themselves. *Malleable* theorists, on the other hand, view the brain as being more like a muscle; the more you use it, the more you strengthen your cognitive ability. Dweck refers to these different ways of looking at intelligence as implicit models, since we seldom take them out for examination.

When it comes to workplace learning, the key takeaway from Dweck's research is that entity and malleable theorists tend to respond differently when confronted with learning challenges. Believing that IQ is fixed and unchangeable, entity theorists are more likely to view difficult learning tasks as potentially threatening situations that could expose the limitations of their intelligence. Accordingly, they tend to choose easy learning challenges over tough ones. Malleable theorists, on the other hand, view each tough learning challenge as a way to strengthen their cognitive ability. When stuck on a learning task, instead of giving up they are more likely to put additional effort into their learning. They are also more willing to ask for help or direction when tackling difficult learning challenges, because they don't view such help as an admission of weakness.

In my own doctoral dissertation, I tested Dweck's theory with a unique population of doctoral students in psychology. My initial interest in this research came from studies that I had previously encountered, which suggested that close to 40 percent of doctoral students never graduate. Being a doctoral student myself, I wondered whether there was a relationship between students' implicit self-theories of intelligence and how they dealt with learning setbacks in doctoral study, such as having a dissertation proposal turned down by a dissertation committee. What I found was that those students who were malleable theorists viewed learning setbacks as opportunities for personal and intellectual growth. In contrast, students who were entity theorists viewed such setbacks as personally threatening. Faced with academic setbacks, the entity theorists were more likely to engage in self-doubt and recrimination over their learning "failures." When knocked down, they tended to take much longer to get back up, with the result that they took much longer to complete their doctoral studies. This research study brought home to me the idea that the mental model that each of us carries around in his or her head of intelligence as fixed or fluid operates as a kind of self-fulfilling prophecy. We tend to approach learning challenges differently based on how we construct the concept of intelligence, and the approach we choose directly affects our ability to persevere in the face of tough learning challenges.

The second area of research that challenges the concept of fixed intelligence is the exciting frontier of brain research known as brain plasticity, otherwise referred to as cortical plasticity or neuroplasticity. Until recently, the prevalent assumption was that by the time individuals reach adulthood their brain structure is relatively fixed. Recent studies now suggest that the human brain can continue to reorganize itself throughout adulthood—and actually create new brain cells and neural pathways as the brain encounters learning and cognitive stimulation. The research within this growing field ranges from studies on cab drivers in London to the impact of intensive learning activities on cognitive functioning in late-stage adulthood.

Additional information on this field can be found in two excellent books. I highly recommend *Aging with Grace*, by Dr. David Snowdon, and *The Brain That Changes Itself*, by Dr. Norman Doidge. I also urge you to go online and conduct your own investigation into the field of brain plasticity. I believe that what you find will strongly confirm what I am saying here.

The point is that a critical part of accelerating your learning is to stop setting limits on yourself when it comes to learning. The next time that you are thrown into a difficult and frustrating work situation that temporarily has you stumped, instead of saying to yourself, "I guess this just means that I am not as smart as I thought I was" or "It seems so difficult that I must be too old to learn," try reframing your thinking. Tell yourself, "This is a taxing situation which is going to require a lot more effort, but at the end of it I am only going to get smarter and become more competent."

Become a Mindful Learner

Over the course of the workday, it is easy for us to put our minds on automatic and stop paying close attention to everything that we could extract from new learning experiences. After all, this is a product of our national education system—at an early age we were sold the myth that learning something means memorizing isolated facts and ignoring everything but the "right" answers. Mindful learning is quite different. It emphasizes paying attention to what is happening in the moment—not in a passive, sponge-like way, but in a manner in which we allow ourselves to remain open to new perspectives, to look for patterns in the variations of results we are achieving, and to attack learning in fresh and novel ways. A great source introduction to mindful learning can be found in the book *Mindful Learning* by Dr. Ellen Langer, a Harvard University professor and one of the seminal researchers in this field. Some of the ideas on which mindful learning is based are

1. The mind is designed to pay attention to what is new or unique.
2. It is important to learn in a conditional manner and make ourselves aware of the assumptions on which our thinking is based.
3. We learn best when facts and data-points are presented within a meaningful context.

These findings have a high level of relevance for workplace learning. Consider a situation in which you are about to read a technical or business report. If you want to take away more from this learning experience, before wading into the report try the following:

- Write down on a piece of paper the one decision that the report should be able to help you address.
- Underneath that decision summary, identify three questions that you want to be able to answer in making that decision.
- Examine the context that has shaped the report's conclusions. If the authors of the report represent different sets of expertise and political interests within your organization, how might these factors affect their recommendations?
- To help you view the report from a new perspective, take out a piece of paper and graphically map out the relationships you see between the key ideas that come to mind as you read through it.
- If you are a manager, give it to two different team members; then use a tool like the Plus/Delta Technique to break out the pros and the concerns associated with each suggested course of action (see my book *The Team Troubleshooter* for more details on this and related techniques).

When it comes to understanding data within context, keep in mind that organizational decisions are usually derived from a strong historical context. Every "new" organizational change process, marketing strategy, or product launch has probably been previously attempted (even if only in some misshapen, aborted form) somewhere within your organization. Think about this the next time that you are attempting to evaluate a proposed change within your organization. Ask yourself how the history behind this proposal and the biases that different parties bring to the table are likely to shape the conversation that emerges around it. In the case of reorganizations, I have seen companies move from functional organizational structures to ones that are product- or customer-based, and then (ten years later) shift back to a "brand new" functionally based structure. "So what is new this time around?" you might ask. I believe that this is a legitimate question that helps to put the new change initiative in historical context.

The idea of testing our assumptions can be applied to situations as varied as evaluating someone's business case for supporting a new product introduction or troubleshooting the estimated time and cost projections for a work project. The next time you find yourself in one of these situations, have the author go to the whiteboard and summarize those key assumptions on which his recommendations were based. Now ask the author three questions:

1. Are those assumptions valid?
2. Is the information on which these assumptions were formed still considered to be current and relevant?
3. What are the degrees of freedom within the decision set? In other words, what would happen to the credibility of the business case, given small adjustments to any of those underlying assumptions?

These same three questions can help you conduct a check and balance on your own decisions.

One way to remain open to new perspectives is to get into the habit of expressing your initial ideas in a tentative manner, rather than as absolute truth. The reason for this is based on research involving cognitive dissonance or the human need to think of our beliefs as consistent and congruent. Studies conducted by Dr. Elliot Aronson, a social psychologist and author of *The Social Animal,* and others have shown that the faster we lock into a strong position on a topic in a public setting, the more likely it is that we will be invested in defending that perspective and in dismissing any new, contradictory information that might present itself. Making a few small behavioral changes can make a big difference in how open you remain to new perspectives. Learn to use the words, "Let me tell you what my initial reaction is to that" or "Let me share with you some of the concerns that come to mind as I hear what you are saying," rather than the more common "No, you are wrong." When you find yourself jumping to conclusions, force yourself to construct a list of pros and cons, along with a second list showing what you know/still need to know about the situation. If your work team is trying to think through a difficult problem, invite someone from a totally different function to attend your next team meeting as a guest to ask questions from a very different perspective.

A final suggestion is to consider taking up the practice of "mindful meditation." This is a deceptively simply technique that involves carving out a piece of time each day to allow yourself to be fully aware of, and receptive and open to, whatever comes into your field of awareness. A growing body of research has shown that the extended use of mindful meditation helps to reduce stress and anxiety, focus attention, and even improve cognitive functioning. If that sounds a bit far-fetched, let me refer you to the works of Jon Kabat-Zinn, professor of medicine emeritus at the University of Massachusetts Medical School. Dr. Kabat-Zinn has written several other books on the subject of mindfulness, and his audio book, *Mindfulness for Beginners* is a good starting point for exploring this topic. In addition, several of Dr. Kabat-Zinn's lectures can be found on YouTube.

Conduct After-Action Reviews

During the workday we are sometimes in such a rush to jump from one fire-fighting crisis to another that we miss one of our best opportunities for workplace learning. This occurs immediately after we have tackled a difficult work challenge. This is the best time to stop, while the situation is fresh on our minds, and conduct a review of what happened and why. What I am talking about is similar to the concept of an after-action review (AAR), a formal process that the U.S. Army regularly conducts to help its leaders learn from tough situations. During an AAR a team meets to compare what an event was supposed to accomplish with what actually occurred. They then determine what can be learned from the experience to ensure that it can be accomplished more effectively in the future. The focus here isn't so much on changing resources or work processes, but on examining how the process was managed by those leaders who were in charge.

In my experience, some of the most effective leaders I have encountered in my career are masters of conducting their own AARs. One sales leader I worked with used this approach to examine what transpired after her group failed to successfully bid on a large commercial project. This leader took the responsibility of leading her team in a thorough review of their bid and proposal process. More importantly, she also critically examined the steps that she could take as a leader to up their odds in winning proposals.

A second example involved a leader I worked closely with early in my career who had the responsibility of directing the construction of new nuclear power facilities. This executive was renowned in the field for being one of the few people who had established a good track record for having such facilities built on time and on budget. One day I sat down in his office and asked him what his secret was in being so successful as a project manager. In answer, he took out a weathered-looking three-ring binder. He explained that in the binder he kept a running journal of the lessons learned from each facility design, and he used it to create additional failsafes and contingency plans with each new project. He also used it to periodically review the assumptions that went into his own decisions as a leader.

The AAR concept probably does not seem new to you, as I am sure that you have seen it used as a common practice in sports training. After all, how many times have you seen a high school or college football coach videotape a game and then review it with the team once the game is over? You can take two steps to conduct your own AARs. First, get into the habit of keeping a learning journal. Whenever you find yourself saying, "If I had this to do over again I would… ," write down your thoughts in the journal. If you like to type, keep your journal in electronic form and group your comments according to key categories, such as "dealing with difficult people," "working with senior-level executives," or "managing project planning." Once a month go in and review what you have written; then use the prompting technique discussed earlier to remind yourself of these lessons learned when you find yourself facing a similar situation in the future. In addition, periodically invite your work team or trusted colleagues to help you perform a debriefing on the aftermath of one of your work projects. Try not to treat these discussions as report cards on your performance, but rather as a method for identifying aspects of your leadership style that could be successfully adapted to future work situations.

Make the Best Use of Your Learning Style

Each of us learns in a different way, but we seldom pause to consider how it is that we actually learn. When processing new information, some individuals are very dependent upon visual learning. When they find themselves attempting to understand a problem, they immediately go to the whiteboard and sketch out a picture or graphic. Visual learners need to anchor their thinking in visual models and metaphors that help them draw analogies between those things they already know and those they are attempting to learn. Other people depend on auditory learning. When attempting to master a new technical skill, they would prefer to hear someone verbally explain it before they attempt to read or visually review it. The final group relies a lot on learning through discovery through action-based learning. An action-based learner who was attempting to learn a new software program might prefer to go online to the training site and start her learning process by experimenting with different software commands.

The concept of visual, auditory, and action-based or tactile learning styles isn't new; it has been around for many years. However, many people still don't understand how to fully apply this concept to accelerate their development. If you know how you learn best, you can set up a learning process that increases the efficiency of your learning. In my case I know that I am a lousy auditory learner; I don't always recall in detail what I hear or find it easy to envision another person's verbal description of a situation. I am, however, extremely strong in visual learning, with tactile learning coming in close behind.

There are several ways that I try to put this knowledge to use in my daily life. For example, I frequently am invited to attend webinars on new software systems in the area of talent management. I have found that, rather than allow a software provider to drag me through a webinar at a fixed pace, I learn faster by going through the following steps. First, I go to the provider's website and view any self-directed tutorials that might be available on the new system. When doing this, I like to frequently pause, rewind the tutorial whenever I come to an area that is difficult to understand, and make detailed notes on these points of confusion. As a second step, I may search through my network to see whether I know anyone who is using the new software and find out what that person's experience has been. I will then try to play with the system, jotting down any questions that may come to mind. If I am one of a number of people who will be attending the webinar, I keep these questions in hand and ask them during the Q&A portion of the discussion. However, if the webinar is being run solely for me, I email these questions to the software provider in advance, requesting this person to focus the webinar on these topics of discussion, rather than take me through a canned presentation. While this learning approach might sound a bit cumbersome to you, the fact is that it works very well for me. It enables me to use the limited time that I have available with the software provider to focus on unresolved questions or technical issues that I have difficulty grasping.

How about you? How do you learn most effectively? In attempting to answer this question, think back to the last time you tried to learn something new and found the experience enjoyable and, perhaps, almost effortless. What learning steps did you go through? How does this experience differ from any situation you encountered in which learning was tedious and you found yourself obtaining only a tenuous grasp on new skills or information? If you can identify the differences between these two learning experiences, you can replicate the more effective learning process in future on-the-job learning scenarios and greatly accelerate your learning.

Make Use of Naturally Occurring Events

I have said elsewhere in this book that we have a tendency to regard work and professional development as two separate things, but hopefully by now you have seen that this is a false assumption. One of the best ways to accelerate your learning is to exploit any naturally occurring event in your life. In putting this method into use, you will find that your Outlook calendar is your best friend.

Start by going back to the development goals that you have already identified; then scroll through your Outlook calendar until you see the next event that logically links to these development goals. If you are a manager and your development goal is to become a better managerial coach, then you would look for the next series of events in which you will find yourself attempting to coach or provide feedback to some member of your work team. If you are attempting to develop your skills in influencing others to action, then you would try to identify an upcoming event in which you will be tasked with selling an idea or building a business case for action. You can couple this technique with the prompting technique mentioned earlier by loading into your calendar any suggestions that you want to keep in mind as you tackle these new situations. You can also use this approach with any unanticipated work event that suddenly emerges on the horizon. Keep your development goals posted where you can refer to them as these situations arise to make it easier for you to make use of these impromptu events as learning opportunities.

Employ Prompting and Stimulus Control

Sometime what we are attempting to learn is a totally new behavioral pattern. Whenever we try to change a behavior that has become an ingrained habit, the problem that most of us encounter is that we automatically fall back into that habituated pattern as soon as our attention wanders. It is like the person who wants to stop smoking but automatically reaches for a pack of cigarettes without thinking about it.

If you find yourself in this situation, two tools can really help you. The first of these, *stimulus control*, involves shifting around your work environment to help change your behavior. As an example, if you want to stop smoking then it helps to alter your five-year habit of taking your breaks in your company's outside smoking area. Similarly, if you find yourself coming up with excuses for not working out, you can make it easier to reverse this habit by packing your gym bag and sticking it in the front seat of your car the night before. When you get up in the morning, your gym bag is there, a blatant reminder of your commitment to your fitness program. This technique also takes away the convenient excuse that before you can work out you first need to go home and change (whereupon you will immediately talk yourself into having a beer and sitting in front of your computer, video game, or television, rather than hitting the gym).

So how do stimulus controls operate at work? To answer that let me introduce you to Dora, a brilliant IT director who was having problems selling herself as being a strong, aggressive, take-charge manager. One of the things working against Dora was her very soft voice, which tended to be drowned out in a meeting with her peers, most of whom were very loud and vocal men. The problem was even worse when she had to make a presentation, as executives would strain to hear her from the far end of the conference table. In Dora's case I suggested a few simple changes. First, instead of trying to outtalk her male peers, she learned to allow them to start off the conversation. When she was ready to put across her point, she would take a marker in hand and walk around to the whiteboard, where she would say something like: "Let me sketch out for you a few ideas that I have." The simple act of standing up and moving to the board to visually diagram her ideas served not only to help her get her points across, but also to assume a facilitation role (most meetings wander aimlessly because no one does this) in guiding her peers to resolution on issues. When it came to staff meetings, Dora also discovered how helpful it was to select smaller conference rooms and to position herself in the middle of a long conference table rather than on one end. When giving presentations or briefings, she learned to wear a lavaliere mike. Together these small changes went very far in helping her make significant changes in her leadership behavior.

Stimulus controls can also work when you are managing up. Years ago, when I took on my first leadership position, I reported to a manager (I will call him Jerry) who had a very nasty disposition. Jerry would frequently yell at us and would occasionally launch into angry tirades. One morning I came in a lot earlier than usual and bumped into him by accident in our break room. The change was amazing—Jerry was actually smiling! (It was a little scary at the time.) What I came to realize at that moment was that Jerry would start the morning on a very calm note, but by the time he moved on to his fourth cup of coffee he was impossible to talk with. After that, my strategy was simple. Whenever I had something difficult to discuss with him, I just came in early and handled it first thing.

Prompts are closely related to stimulus controls in that they are visual or auditory reminders that prompt you to action. Being a bit of a Type A person, I use prompts to remind myself when to shift gears. For example, if I have scheduled a meeting that I am afraid could become confrontational, I might put the words "Listen First!" or "invite Jack to lead with his suggestions" on my Outlook calendar as part of my meeting reminder. One of my clients, who tends to get so wrapped up in discussions that he runs over on meetings, has learned to use the alarm feature on his iPhone to give him a reminder five minutes before the start of his next meeting. That way he remembers to wrap up each meeting on time. I have another coaching client who tends to be harshly critical when giving feedback to her direct reports. Early in our coaching sessions, I sent her an electronic copy of a bulleted summary of guidelines for administering feedback in a positive way. Following my suggestion, she now notes, on her Outlook calendar, any upcoming meetings, such as performance appraisals or project reviews, during which she knows that she will be giving out heavy doses of feedback. She then establishes an automatic prompt so that the list of feedback guidelines pops up on her computer screen a few minutes prior to each of those scheduled meetings.

In summary, stimulus controls and prompts are very simple tools you can use to take control of work habits that are keeping you from performing at your best. When I first present these tools to executives, I often hear a skeptical response. "How can anything so simple help change behavior?" they ask. That, however, is exactly the point. It is the simple, easy-to-implement stuff that we are most likely to put into practice. Just ask me. As we speak, my gym bag is packed and in my car, waiting to confront my excuses.

Case in Point: Kirk

Kirk, a coaching client of mine, was a general manager within a mid-size engineering company. One of Kirk's issues was that he tended to become stressed out over the course of a workday and to take this stress out on his work team in the form of critical comments and angry tirades. During our first few sessions, I realized that Kirk was a very private person. This meant that before he attempted to work through tough problems he needed to have time during the day to pull back and think about things. The problem was that Kirk's job left him little time to go "offline." Instead, from the moment he walked in each day he was continually inundated with the demands of other people. During our first meeting, I also noticed that Kirk worked in what I call a "fishbowl," that is, one of those offices that has glass walls on three sides. To make matters worse, his office was in the center of his floor. As a result, people would continually stand outside of his door, motioning that they needed to talk to him. Even when they weren't clamoring for his attention, the visual distractions were driving him nuts.

Following my suggestion, Kirk set up several stimulus controls to address these issues. First, he had his facilities group install blinds on his windows, which he usually kept closed. In addition, he learned how to use his secretary as a palace guard to keep visitors at bay when he needed personal think time. Finally, he shifted his office hours so that he came in an hour earlier in the morning. This not only gave him more quiet time, but he discovered how much he could bring his stress level down just by avoiding rush-hour traffic each morning.

Kirk also made use of prompts by writing down on sticky notes reminders to himself, such as "Listen to the whole thing before you react!" He found it helpful to place these notes on his computer screen before he sat down to engage in difficult conversations with his work team. In addition, Kirk employed the AAR technique to periodically self-audit his progress. Every week or so he would ask selected team members to conduct debriefings with him on the effectiveness of some of the new communication approaches that he was attempting to adopt, both within staff meetings and in one-on-one discussions. By using these simple steps, Kirk was able to bring his stress level down and concentrate more intently on his work, while greatly improving his communication style as a leader.

Your Next Steps

During the next three weeks I would like to see whether you are willing to take three actions to help you accelerate your on-the-job learning. The first two actions will help you determine the degree to which you are learning agile, while the last step is designed to strengthen your learning agility.

1. *Interview others to obtain feedback on your learning agility.* From the list of questions that follow, select three that you think could help you gather valuable information about how others view your learning agility. Then select five people with whom you have worked closely over the past year. Ask each person to select one situation, such as a work task, project, or short job assignment, on which the two of you have worked closely together in the past. (An option is to select people who have weathered a difficult organizational change with you, such as a restructuring, a merger or acquisition, or the installation of a new executive team.) After each person has finished sharing his or her story, use the three questions you have selected to interview the storyteller and get this person's perspective regarding the degree to which he or

she feels that you displayed learning agility in that work situation. After you have completed your interviews, look through your notes and see whether you can identify common themes among all of the stories shared by your five feedback providers. Try to determine what these themes tell you about areas in which you can strengthen your learning agility.

Questions You Can Ask to Evaluate Your Learning Agility

Responding to New Ideas

How receptive do I appear to be when someone else is presenting me with a new idea?

Do I appear willing to hear the idea out completely, or is my first reaction to challenge the idea or to recommend a different course of action?

If an idea has both shortcomings and merits, do I start out by discussing what I like about the idea before discussing my concerns, or do I immediately focus on the part of the idea that I consider to be problematic?

Learning from Many Sources

Do I appear to be able to make a realistic distinction between those work areas in which I have strong expertise and those areas that extend beyond the boundaries of my knowledge and skills? In the latter case, do I present myself as a person who is seeking out the advice and counsel of others?

If one learning route (self-study, observation, etc.) is closed to me, do I take advantage of other avenues for learning (experimenting, learning through others, etc.)?

Do I appear to learn from my mistakes and apply what I have learned to new situations?

Adapting to Change

Do I present myself as being resilient when confronted with stressful change?

Do I bounce back quickly whenever I encounter setbacks?

Do I introduce new perspectives when I am attempting to help others manage organizational changes?

Do I keep my cool when working under stressful conditions, or do I come across as being angry and resentful?

Do I come across as being able to handle the pressure of leading difficult change situations and of dealing with resistance to change from others in our organization?

Being Results-Focused

When I encounter an obstacle to a work goal do I present myself as being tenacious? In other words, do I persevere and show that I can stay focused on results even when the outcome of a project or task is uncertain?

Do I look for alternative, innovative ways to get results when the most obvious solutions have been blocked?

Am I known as someone who keeps commitments (meets deadlines and milestones, returns email or calls, responds to requests for information in a timely manner, etc.)?

Seeking Out Learning Experiences

When it comes to trying to understand our business, do I come across as an enthusiastic, aggressive learner?

Do I seek out new learning opportunities, even when that means taking on more work?

Do I take advantage of formal learning opportunities, such as workshops, conferences, or webinars, as those opportunities become available?

Understanding the Big Picture

Do I appear to keep abreast of emerging trends in our industry and business?

Do I attempt to understand the broader organizational changes that influence a particular work situation?

Do I understand the broader, long-reaching implications of short-term decisions?

Do I frequently check in with others outside of my work group to understand new developments that can affect the outcomes of projects?

Do I appear to stop occasionally to try to make sense of new situations so that I can distill what I am learning from them?

Working with Complexity

Do I effectively manage projects when stakeholders may initially hold very different views regarding the project's desired outcomes or the methods and approach that should be employed?

Do I appear to work with complex data without getting lost in the details?

Can I effectively identify patterns in complex data?

Am I able to consolidate and integrate different ideas or facts into new patterns?

Managing Diversity

Do I work well with different organizational groups in our company, or do I appear to interact effectively only with certain types of people, such as executives, first-line managers, corporate personnel, etc.?

Do I present myself as being adaptable when working with people who are very different from me with respect to their age, ethnicity, and cultural backgrounds?

How effectively do I resolve conflicts and issues?

Do I adapt my communication style to meet the needs of different people?

Do I work effectively with people who approach work issues and problems from very different perspectives?

Do I appear to understand how my actions and communication style affect others?

2. *Conduct the résumé test.* One way to perform a self-evaluation of your learning agility is through what I refer to as "the résumé test." Before you read further, put down this book and pull out a copy of your most current résumé. Using a highlighter, indicate everything in your résumé that reflects something that you have learned and applied during the last six months. Are you satisfied with what you have accomplished? All right, make it easy on yourself. Go back and do this again, only this time look at what you have accomplished over the past twelve months. Based on what you have highlighted, to what degree do you feel that you are an aggressive learner?

As the second part of this exercise, close your eyes and imagine it is a year from now. Now go back to the electronic version of your résumé and rewrite it. This time have some fun with it and fold into your résumé all of the accomplishments that you would like to be able to say that you have achieved twelve months from now. (This part of the exercise makes little sense unless you actually go through the steps and rewrite your résumé.) As you scan through this list of hypothetical accomplishments, take note of those technical and leadership skills and organizational and industry knowledge that you would like to develop over the next twelve months.

3. Match your learning options to your development needs. In the left-hand column of the following chart, list five things that you attempted to learn over the past few months. These areas could include product knowledge, new technical skills, sales techniques, information on your organization or industry, leadership skills, etc. Under the "Development Options" column, check off those options that you recall using to increase your learning for each of these skill areas. If you found that you relied exclusively on only a few learning avenues, ask yourself what new learning approaches you could experiment with to become a more diversified learner.

Development Goals   *Development Options*

_____   Organizational Training

_____   Professional Conferences

_____   Formal Education

_____   Self-Directed Learning

_____   Shadowing and Mentoring

_____   Practice Runs

Additional Reading

Aging with Grace. (2001). David Snowdon. New York: Bantam.

Global Talent Management: Using Learning Agility to Identify High Potentials Around the World. (2008). Kenneth P. De Meuse, Guangrong Dai, George S. Hallenbeck, and King Yu Tang. Chicago: Korn/Ferry Institute.

"High Potentials as High Learners." (2000). Michael M. Lombardo and Robert W. Eichinger, *Human Resource Management, 35*(4), 321–326.

Mindful Learning. (1997). Ellen Langer. Cambridge, MA: Perseus Books.

Mindfulness for Beginners [audio book]. (2006). Jon Kabat-Zinn. New York: Sounds True.

"Mindfulness, Openness, and Transformational Learning." (2011). Robert Barner and Charlotte Barner. In Carol Hoare (Ed.), *Oxford Handbook of Reciprocal Adult Development and Learning.* New York: Oxford University Press.

Mindset: The New Psychology of Success. (2006). Carol Dweck. New York: Random House.

Structural Holes. (1992). Ronald S. Burt. Cambridge, MA: Harvard University Press.

Spark: The Revolutionary New Science of Exercise and the Brain. (2008). John Ratey and Eric Hagerman. New York: Little, Brown.

The Brain That Changes Itself. (2007). Norman Doidge. New York: Penguin.

The Social Animal. (2003). Elliot Aronson. New York: Worth Publishing.

The Team Troubleshooter: How to Find and Fix Team Problems. (2000). Robert Barner. Palo Alto, CA: Davies-Black.

CHAPTER SIX

MANAGING YOUR PERSONAL BRAND

The Importance of Brand Distinction

Whether we are picking out items in a grocery store or deciding what make and model of car to purchase, we tend to base our buying decisions on how we view the comparative strengths of certain brands. A brand can be thought of as the set of overall attributes and features that are called to mind each time we encounter the name, logo, or image that is associated with a particular product or service. When you think of Starbucks, a certain image comes to mind. For many people, that image is associated not only with purchasing a quality beverage, but also the experience of indulging in the guilty pleasure of one's choosing. The name Neiman Marcus has become synonymous with high-end clothing and an upscale shopping experience. When you think of Wal-Mart, a different image comes to mind; namely the ability to choose among an impressive array of products offered at comparatively low prices.

Companies and organizations invest a lot in building and maintaining their brands. This makes sense, because there are several reasons why a good brand is worth a great deal when it comes to obtaining customer loyalty and retention. First of all, the best brands call attention to their unique features. By doing so, brands are able to stand out from their competitors and become more memorable in the minds of their customers, who view them as hard to imitate. Take the case of Cirque du Soleil. In once sense you might be correct in referring to Cirque du Soleil as a circus, but it is also a lot more. Many people regard it as a unique entertainment experience that incorporates the best elements of circus, theater, dance, and even street performance. By positioning itself in a class apart from its competitors, Cirque du Soleil has not only gained a loyal following, but has also been able to sell tickets at a price point that is well beyond what one would expect to pay for a traditional circus experience. Moreover, it does not have to directly compete against circuses or theatrical productions because it has established itself in the minds of its patrons as being something distinctly different from those more traditional forms of entertainment.

Once a product or service establishes a strong, positive brand, the brand begins to operate as a self-fulfilling prophecy. Each time we encounter the brand name or logo, we begin to anticipate the kinds of experiences that we have come to associate with that brand. The Disney brand automatically brings to mind an expectation of "magical," wholesome family entertainment. Over time customers have come to expect those qualities whenever they encounter the Disney logo attached to any entertainment experience—be it a family cruise, a theme park, a movie, or a new toy. Another great corporate brand is Apple, which commands a premium in the marketplace and enjoys profit margins on its products that are far higher than those received by Apple's competitors. Apple is able to do this because of the reputation that it has built for designing "cool" state-of-the art products that are seamlessly integrated into the complete Apple product line.

Not all brands are successful. In order for a brand to be powerful, all of the features associated with it have to come together through what I refer to as "the 3Cs," that is, the brand is *clear* (you clearly understand the value that is being offered), *consistent* (you trust that you will receive the same experience every time), and *compelling* (there is something about the brand that is uniquely attractive). When some aspects of the brand experience don't support the overall brand image, a brand can suffer a certain amount of erosion. As I write this, Toyota is attempting to address problems related to customer complaints regarding alleged unintended acceleration on some of its models. This is an important challenge for Toyota, given that this company had developed a strong brand image that is associated with very high automotive quality and safety standards.

You Have Your Own Personal Brand

So, you may be thinking, what does the subject of brands have to do with my professional development? In attempting to answer that, let me suggest that all of the brand characteristics that we associate with products, services, or organizations also apply to each of us as individuals. Like it or not, over time each of us establishes our own uniquely distinctive personal brand. Your personal brand is that combination of behaviors, appearance, and communication patterns that characterize you in the eyes of other people. It is your unique personal signature, the way that others come to know and define you. Your work brand is forged from more than just your work performance and includes the whole package that you convey to others. In other words, your personal brand is

- What makes you special and unique in the eyes of other people, both as a work professional and a person
- Those qualities and attributes that other people most readily associate with your name
- Those values and beliefs that you believe that you stand for as a work professional
- Those personal idiosyncrasies that make you stand out from other people
- The reputation (good or bad) that you have gained over time with others

It is also important to understand that the value of a personal brand can continually change over time. Brands can be gradually strengthened through conscientious effort or abruptly diminished by a careless unfortunate act. Quite recently, a major sports figure lost millions of dollars in product endorsements. These losses occurred not through any decline in this figure's athletic performance, but rather because certain facts about this celebrity's private life have surfaced in the news media, which has damaged this person's marketable image as a clean-cut, wholesome family man.

The lesson here is that it is important not to underestimate the degree to which your personal brand can significantly impact both your professional development and your career success. On a short-term basis, your brand influences the degree to which others are willing to provide you assistance or support the projects and business initiatives that you are leading. Your personal brand can also affect your chances of growing and learning on the job. People with strong positive brands are more likely to be recommended by their managers to lead important projects or participate in leadership development programs. Your brand position also influences whether your manager and senior leaders view you as being the kind of "good will ambassador" they would choose to represent their function in managing work across departments or negotiating with outside customers or vendors.

Once formed, brands tend to have a life of their own, a phenomenon that is neatly captured by the phrase "your reputation proceeds you." Over time, the organizational reputation you have built travels before you, establishing a positive or negative bias in the minds of individuals you may not yet even have met. This bias influences the degree to which these people are willing to respond to your requests for help in tracking down information, provide needed technical support, or assist you on key projects. Individuals who have developed strong personal brands are able to build up huge trust accounts with others in their organization, based largely on their reputations. At the other end of the spectrum are those leaders who have developed very poor brands. Their reputations spread out before them like tsunami waves advancing in front of an earthquake epicenter— leaving a path of destruction in their wake.

On a long-term basis your brand image can also affect your chances of advancing within your organization. To understand this, keep in mind that promotions are not given out as rewards for past performance. They are, instead, based on the degree to which you are able to instill confidence in others regarding your ability to perform well at higher levels in your organization. An additional, often overlooked factor is whether your co-workers and managers can readily picture you as being the type of person who would "fit in" at a higher leadership role.

Understanding Personal Brand Attributes

All of us have certain brand attributes or features that work for or against our overall personal brands. It is important to keep in mind that the same behaviors that can help us build our brands can also become major brand detractors if they are not carefully managed. Consider the following:

- The professional who is extremely dedicated and hard-working, but at the same time is so driven to reach his goals that he continually finds himself involved in conflict

- The person who is respected for being highly intelligent, but who has difficulty hiding the fact that she regards others as less competent and intelligent
- The leader who is very supportive and friendly, so much so that her manager fears that she has difficulty making hard decisions
- The individual who prides himself on being "all business," to the extent that he fails to show a human side when co-workers find themselves struggling with difficult personal issues, such as the death of a member of the immediate family

In my own case, early in my career my first experience with executive coaching was that of receiving coaching when I came into a company to direct a new HR work function. As part of my coaching process, my coach shared with me feedback that she had gathered about me from my manager, peers, and selected team members. In my debriefing session, I learned that there was a general consensus that I had established a strong reputation as being as a results-focused leader. The people with whom I worked saw me as someone who acted quickly and decisively, spoke in a forthright manner, and aggressively pushed projects to completion. Sounds good, doesn't it? The problem is that when overused or applied incorrectly these same strengths can become weaknesses. In my case, a little further exploration showed me why I wasn't getting the results that I had wanted. Some of the other feedback that I received during the debriefing was that other people felt that I came across as cold and aggressive. I learned that in my efforts to quickly "get down to business" I could be too curt or abrupt and shut other people down during conversations. Furthermore, I could be so concerned about selling my own views that I could fail to listen to other people, and I had a tendency to become very impatient when conversations drifted off track. Over time I learned that these aspects of my "cut to the chase" signature were keeping me from building rapport with others at work and making it more difficult for me to gain their support.

Based on this feedback, I worked hard to strengthen my personal brand. Now let me qualify this by admitting that I didn't attempt to give myself some kind of complete personality makeover. Personalities are rather deep-seated and unchangeable parts of us, which is the reason why I seldom use personality assessments in executive coaching. (Why evaluate something if you cannot change it?) In my case, I will always be a "Type A" personality. However, I can control some aspects of my behavior that get in my way. One small change that has made a big difference is that I have learned to slow down more during the first few minutes that I am engaged in conversations and to hear other people out completely before rushing in with my own ideas. I also think more carefully about how I plan to start discussions when I am going to be meeting with someone who will probably be approaching the discussion from a completely different perspective. Individually, each of these changes is fairly small, but together they have helped me to form stronger relationships with my colleagues and clients and have made me successful in my management consultancy. In the same way, making a few small changes to your own personal brand can go a long way toward helping you accelerate your professional development.

Now it may be that in hearing me talk about changing your personal brand you are concerned that I am asking you to be something that you are not, or to act in a phony way. If that is the case, let me reassure you, once again, that I am not attempting to get you to change who you are as a person. At the same time, when it comes to your personal brand there are a couple of things that you need to keep in mind. First, it would be nice to pretend that you can ignore your brand because your work speaks for itself, but that is not how life works. The fact is that how you come across to other people sets up positive or negative expectations on their part regarding your performance. They respond, not just to your work, but also to who you present yourself to be as a person.

The second important consideration is that you need to take the responsibility for actively managing your brand. If you abdicate this responsibility, you leave it up to other people to speak for you in interpreting your motives and intentions to everyone in your organization. The truth of the matter is that at the end of the day you either manage your brand or someone else will.

In short, I am not telling you to be something other than what you are. I am only suggesting that you try to form a more complete picture of how you currently convey yourself to others. After a little self-reflection, if you think that your brand is working for you, stop there. If not, keep reading to learn how to take steps to create a powerful personal brand.

The Two Layers of Personal Brands

One way of understanding your personal brand is to visualize it as consisting of two layers, as represented by Figure 6.1.

Each of these layers engages a different aspect of your brand image. The outer layer can be thought of as consisting of those *first impressions* that you leave with other people during your initial contacts with them. I use

FIGURE 6.1. Two Brand Layers

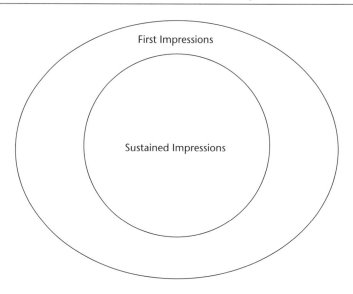

the word "contacts" instead of "conversations" because the first time someone may encounter your brand could be through an email or voice-mail message, rather than through direct discussions. Our first contacts are usually task-focused; that is, they involve giving or receiving information or direction, negotiating expectations or requirements, or addressing work issues. The first impressions that others form of you are highly influenced by those brand attributes that are immediately noticeable; such as your professional appearance, general demeanor, and conversational style. During initial contacts, these elements are highly influential because the people you are meeting for the first time lack the experience and relational context needed to accurately interpret your body language and communi-cation style. Sitting across the table from you, they may be asking them-selves: "Is she totally disinterested in this meeting or just extremely reserved?" or "Does that intense scowl on his face mean that he is upset with me for some reason, or is he always this intense?" Lacking the context to make those kinds of distinctions, these new contacts will tend to accept what they see at face value.

It is easy to underestimate how our behavior during the first few minutes of any new work interaction can substantially shape our work relationships and job performance. Those people who have only sporadic contact with you will tend to base their overall assessment of you on how you come across during those first impression opportunities.

This is especially true for those senior executives who may only come in contact with you for a few minutes each year. Not too long ago, I saw a manager deliver an executive briefing that I knew he had carefully researched and reviewed. Unfortunately, the presenter didn't know how to provide his audience, two members of his company's executive team, with a concise, hard-hitting presentation. Instead, he tended to belabor small points and went into far too much detail. More importantly, this leader wasn't attentive to the non-verbal clues that he was getting from his audience; clues that should have warned him that they were becoming increasingly impatient. Over the course of the next few minutes, I watched helplessly as a lot of hard work quickly evaporated, with an accompanying diminishment of a large part of the presenter's personal brand. It is sad, but this sort of thing happens all of the time.

At the other end of the spectrum, I am currently working with a high-potential leader who is extraordinarily strong in managing first impressions. Having observed this leader in several first encounter meetings, I find that her high energy level and warm smile are contagious. She always presents herself as being enthusiastic about her work, and when she approaches other people she takes the time to listen carefully, occasionally stopping to summarize the speaker's perspective before presenting her own views. These two situations represent leaders who have either been ineffective or successful in managing first impressions.

Your second, inner brand layer involves those *sustained impressions* that you forge over time with those who work closely with you. There are several factors that differentiate this inner branding layer from the outer layer. First, as people begin to work with us they learn to read us a bit better. This means that they are less swayed by thirty-second sound bites and are more influenced by those behavioral habits that we have developed over several years; habits that we may not even be aware of. Take the person who pops into your office unannounced to ask whether you can drop what you are doing and help her meet one of her work requirements. This type of thing can be a bit irritating, but when working with someone for the first time we may decide to overlook it for the sake of maintaining good work relationships. On the other hand, if this person works closely with us and displays a consistent pattern of communicating that "my work is more important than yours," we will be less willing to tolerate this kind of behavior. In the same way, we may choose to ignore a sarcastic comment made during a work meeting by someone we hardly know, but it is a different story if we come in contact with these kinds of comments on a daily basis. The point here is that, over time, as we continue to work with the same set of people, our communication habits and work styles begin to become a lot more visible to them.

In addition, the focus for these brand layers is very different. As I said earlier, our outer brand layer typically involves interactions that are depersonalized and task-focused. In contrast, when we work with people over an extended period of time, brand management becomes less about managing tasks and more about managing relationships. These "inner layer" interactions are more likely to be personal and emotional, given that they involve negotiating expectations, priorities, resources, and leadership roles with work associates on whom we are highly interdependent.

Quite often it is a combination of all of the little things that we do that shape how effectively we manage sustained impressions. I once coached a leader who was viewed by her co-workers as being unresponsive to their requests for assistance. Upon receiving this feedback, this leader expressed surprise and concern. She then went on to share several examples of situations in which she felt that she had worked extra hours or gone well beyond her functional role to aid and assist other people. As we continued to talk, the disconnection between what this leader was saying and what I had been hearing from her co-workers became clearer. I realized that when she received a request she would often immediately begin working on it. However, if she encountered delays or problems along the way she seldom took the time to immediately circle back to the person who had made the request to explain the situation and provide a revised response time. Instead, she felt that it was more professional to wait until the situation was completely resolved before contacting the other party. From the perspective of the requesting party, she appeared to be ignoring the request for help and lacking the professional courtesy of responding in a timely manner.

Understanding Where You Fit in the Brand Matrix

Another way to learn more about your personal brand is through the use of the Personal Brand Matrix, which is presented in Figure 6.2. The matrix is based on the assumption our personal brand attributes can be charted in terms of two dimensions. The horizontal axis identifies certain brand attributes that can either have a positive or negative impact on the strength of our personal brands. The vertical axis divides brand attributes into two dimensions; those *task-based attributes* that are associated with the degree

FIGURE 6.2. The Personal Brand Matrix

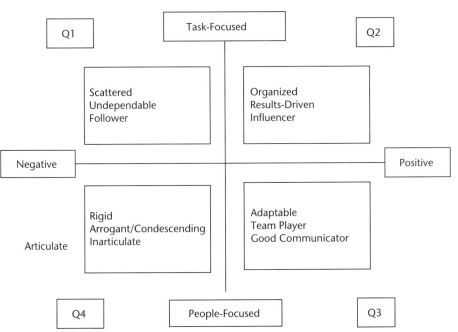

that we are viewed as being competent performers and those *people-based attributes* that speak to how others view us as a person.

Together these two dimensions yield four quadrants that can tell us a lot about our overall brands. Inside each quadrant I have identified three brand attributes that, in my experience as a talent management executive and coach, appear to be particularly important to career success. This is not an exhaustive list, and certainly you could make a good case for adding several other brand attributes to each quadrant, but I believe that it provides a good starting place for review.

Later on in this chapter, I will introduce you to some of the steps that you can take to strengthen each of these brand attributes. For now, let me just say that people seldom find that all of their brand attributes are neatly bundled under one of these quadrants. The more common scenario is that we discover that we have some attributes that work for us professionally and personally—and others that can erode our brand. You are also likely to find that some of these attributes play a critical role in defining your brand image during first encounters with others at work, while others play a greater role in shaping the success of your long-term work relationships. The value of the matrix is that it can aid you in answering four questions:

1. Are you stronger in the personal (people-focused) or professional (task-focused) aspects of your brand?
2. Are you equally effective in how you manage first impressions and build long-term relationships?
3. What few brand attributes represent your strong suit?
4. What single brand attribute, if strengthened, would help you achieve your career goals?

Discovering Your Personal Brand

On Overcoming Image-Lag and Myopic Perspectives

So how do you go about strengthening your personal brand? Let's start with the assumption that we don't always understand how we come across to other people. To correct for this shortcoming, we periodically need to perform a self-audit of our brand. Taking this action helps us understand how we are coming across to others NOW, in our current work situation.

While self-reflection is a critical ingredient in the brand-changing process, there are two reasons why we cannot completely rely on it. The first reason is that we all suffer from image lag. To understand this, you only have to think back to the last high school reunion that you attended. Weren't you just a little shocked by how much other people had changed, while you yourself had remained the same? Well, the sad thing is that I am sure that everyone else at that event went home comforted by the same delusions. You see, the image that we hold of ourselves is usually somewhat dated. For that reason, trying to develop a personal brand strategy based solely on self-reflection is about as effective as trying to drive a car by staring into your rear-view mirror.

This point comes across strong to me whenever I perform outplacement coaching with displaced executives. Anyone who has worked for several years within the same position and organization tends to develop certain habits in his communication and leadership style that may not serve him well. Unfortunately, over time all of these little habits become so ingrained that we may stop paying attention to them. When we are faced with a dramatic change, such as losing our job, these events force us to hold a mirror up to ourselves and obtain a clearer, real-time view of everything that is baked into our personal brand.

The second obstacle we enter in self-assessment is that, when it comes to assessing our own personal brands, it is easy to become myopic and see ourselves from a single, limited perspective. Remember the last time that you saw yourself on video? Chances are that there were certain aspects of your communication style that surprised you. After all, you don't really look and sound like that, do you? There is a reason why you have difficulty recognizing yourself on video. Whenever you look at yourself in a mirror you are typically viewing yourself from a single perspective. When you hear yourself talk, the sound of your voice is distorted as it reverberates though your ear canal. Seeing ourselves on video forces us to see and hear ourselves from different perspectives, which is what makes videotaping such an important developmental tool. In the same way, the most effective brand managers try to step out of their own heads to see themselves from the perspectives held by their work colleagues.

We could, of course, passively wait for our work associates to keep us informed of how we are coming across to them. The only problem with this approach is that they may be reluctant to comment on those things about us that may irritate them or that impede our relationships. I am sure that at some point or another you had a co-worker or a car pool partner who tended to do things that really bothered you but which, for the sake of keeping peace in the office (or your carpool), you tried to ignore. In addition, the more you advance in management, the less likely it is that you will find people who will be courageous enough to give you candid, unsolicited feedback about your brand.

For all of these reasons, our self-image always tends to be a little out of kilter with the face that we present to other people. Since we don't always know the extent to which these two images are aligned, an important first step in managing your brand is to form a more complete, objective picture of those brand attributes that are working for or against you. Once you do, you can make decisions regarding any changes you want to make to your personal brand. Often these changes, although relatively minor, can strengthen our work relationships and performance in profound ways. I once coached an executive who didn't like using a smart phone or cell phone. Given this manager's travel schedule, he was unreachable by phone, email, or text during large chunks of the day. It wasn't until I began to share with him the feedback that I had received from other members of his team that he began to realize how much this simple idiosyncrasy was bottlenecking his team's workflow. More importantly, it made him look like a modern-day Luddite—not the type of image that a leader who works within an innovative high-tech company wants to encourage. After following my advice and purchasing a smart phone, he was pleased how much this small change contributed to his work performance. More importantly, this small decision sent an important signal to this leader's work team that he was trying to be more responsive to them.

How to Discover Your Personal Brand

Here are a few steps you can take to gain a more accurate and complete picture of your personal brand:

Start by performing a simple self-audit. What is it about yourself that makes you extremely proud? If, during a promotional interview, you were asked to identify your key personal strengthens and weaknesses, what few adjectives would come to mind? What brand attributes, if strengthened, would make you more successful in your career? With those thoughts in mind, take a few minutes to complete the following (Table 6.1).

In the top half of the left-hand column, list three work events (meetings, projects, critical conversations, etc.) that you think you managed very

TABLE 6.1. Personal Brand Matrix

Work Successes	Associated Brand Attributes
Work Problems	Associated Brand Attributes

successfully during the past twelve months. Next to each event, in the right-hand column, describe the personal quality or attribute that you think enabled you to perform so successfully. Now take a look at what you have written. Do any patterns come to mind?

Next, under the header Work Problems see whether you can identify at least one work situation that wasn't that wasn't received well by your manager, peers, or senior stakeholders. Again, what consistent themes appear to emerge?

After completing this exercise, give some thought as to how you are coming across to others in your workplace. The next time you are in an important conversation, build in "pause points" where you force yourself to stop and focus completely on the other party's reaction to what you are saying. Occasionally stop and ask, "How is that working for you?" or "How comfortable do you feel with what I am suggesting?" As you ask these questions, listen carefully to how the other party appears to respond to your communication style.

In addition, pay close attention when you hear your work associates introduce you to other people. Comments such as, "You will like working with Sara; she always keeps on top of things" tell you a lot about what is most noticeable about your personal brand. Your personal brand can also be revealed through the humorous comments that your friends at work make about you. Sometimes these comments are disguised ways of trying to communicate aspects of your brand that can be irritating or bothersome to them. As you take these steps, try to identify the major brand themes that you hear emerging from these discussions. Over time you will probably hear the same four or five words used to describe you. What picture comes to mind when you hear these words?

Take every opportunity to observe yourself on audio- or videotape. Some team leaders find it convenient to audiotape certain phone conferences or webinars as a means of archiving these sessions for those people who weren't able to attend. If you find yourself in one of these situations, wait a day and then listen to the audiotape again, paying close attention to your personal communication style. In the same way, if you are preparing for a difficult meeting or presentation, consider making an audio- or videotape of your practice run to hear how you set up a conversation or present key points. Some of the smart phones, such as the iPhone, come equipped with built-in audio-recording capabilities that make this technique easy to implement. Once again, watch and listen not only for content, but also your overall tone and demeanor.

Another suggestion is to ask someone whom you trust to tell you how she would describe the brand image that you have formed in your organization. The trick here is not to put this person on the spot by asking for a personal evaluation. Instead, ask for an impartial assessment regarding the impressions that she believes you leave in the minds of your work associates. A way of soliciting this feedback would be to say something like: "I am not asking you for a personal evaluation of me, but rather an objective picture of how you think that I come across when I am interacting with other people. If you were walking around this organization, what are the six words, both positive and negative, that you most often hear used to describe me?"

Another brand discovery opportunity presents itself whenever you find yourself being asked to lead new projects, take on temporary assignments with other work teams, or move into broader leadership roles in your organization. Before you attempt to tackle these work challenges, try to solicit brand feedback from your co-workers, manager, or the members of your new project team. You might consider saying something like: "This project is very important to me and I want to succeed in it. I know that an important part of being successful is establishing a level-setting process for determining how I come across when I am working with other people. Tell me, if I were a product, what words would you use to describe my personal brand? What aspects of my personal brand do you think will help me succeed in my new role? What aspects of my brand could get in my way? What suggestions do you have for strengthening my personal brand?"

How to Strengthen Your Brand

The following suggestions can help you strengthen the six brand attributes that were identified in the Personal Brand Matrix. As you read through each list, give special attention to those attributes that you would like to develop, and check off those action items that you think might be particularly applicable to your own brand improvement goals.

Improving Your Brand Image as a Good Communicator

First impressions are strongly impacted by how effectively you communicate verbally and in writing. When your manager receives a report that contains minor errors, omissions, or misspelled words, she is going to be worried about whether she can trust you to effectively represent her to senior management. Here are a few suggestions for improving your communications skills:

In General

❏ Make it a point to eliminate all non-words from your vocabulary. Statements such as, "Well, it is like … the problem appears to be with the vendor … and, uh, he's like, not responding to my emails, so what I kind of want to do is…" sound sloppy and incoherent. Using a lot of non-words can easily make you lose 20 IQ points in the eyes of your listener.

❏ Before undertaking any communication, take a minute to clearly define your objectives. In planning a presentation, for example, you first need to determine your intent and decide whether you are trying to inform your audience, sell a plan of action, or solicit good ideas.

❏ Proof your work. Plan additional time into your work schedule to provide the time needed to spell-check and review your writing before sending it out. If you are not a detailed person, ask a co-worker to provide a second pair of eyes in reviewing your work before you send it out.

❏ If your communication style tends to be quiet and reserved, work on communicating in a high-energy, confident manner. Other people find it hard to tell whether a monotone voice and deadpan expression convey shyness or disinterest.

❏ If you are the kind of person who becomes nervous when asked to present ideas in a meeting, then use a whiteboard to illustrate your ideas.

❏ When communicating with senior executives, keep it brief, focused, and to the point. If you have difficulty figuring out how to compress complicated business or technical issues into a few sentences, try writing your summary statements in short, bulleted phrases before presenting them.

Managing Meetings

❏ Manage your meetings like you do your project plans. Write down, and send out to all attendees in advance of the meeting, an agenda and outcome statement. Once your agenda is set, stick to it and honor the time limits you published for the meeting. Arrive a few minutes early during those instances when you will need to set up for conference calls or videoconferences, and always have on hand the number of your local tech support person. It is also helpful to have on hand the email addresses and cell phone numbers of all attendees so that you can send out a quick reminder to those no-shows who may have forgotten about the meeting.

❐ Attendees are often asked to complete certain action items. If you want meeting attendees to honor these commitments, review them at the end of the meeting (what will be done, by whom, and by when).

❐ For critical meetings I connect my laptop to an LCD display and project the team's action items onto a wall screen for everyone to view. There is something about seeing your name up next to an action item and promised delivery date on a large screen that helps to seal a commitment. This is also an excellent way to give the entire team one last opportunity to jointly review their action plan before they disperse.

❐ In addition, before the meeting concludes, email the agreed-on action plan to all participants; then immediately confirm that everyone has received the action plans on their BlackBerrys, iPhones, or laptops and that they concur with the plan. In addition, before leaving the meeting make certain that you set the time, date, place, and agenda for the next meeting.

Directing Phone Conferences

❐ Consider sending all team members, in advance of the meeting, a simple one-page graphic or summary that can make it easier for virtual meeting members to follow the flow of the team's conversation.

❐ At the start of the meeting, perform a quick verbal check-in with everyone to confirm who is on the call. Next, perform a quick level-setting step by making certain that all attendees have received and reviewed any materials that were sent out in advance of the session. If they have not done this, have your laptop set up so that you can immediately correct the situation without leaving the room.

❐ During phone conferences it is not unusual to find that those participants who are on the phone cannot be heard over the conversations that are taking place between those who are in the room. To compensate for this, periodically use your attendance roster to check in with, and obtain input from, those participants who are calling in.

Managing Email and Social Networks

❐ Always assume that whatever you write in an email will be passed on to other people. Never send something in an email that you would be embarrassed to have intercepted by third-party readers.

❐ Similarly, when using social media, such as MySpace, Facebook, or LinkedIn, keep in mind that what you say can get back to others. For this reason, use common sense when discussing work events. If you have your own blog, don't use it as a forum to make critical comments about your co-workers, managers, or company.

❏ The average work professional suffers from information overload. Avoid copying everyone on all of your emails; use your judgment to determine who really needs to receive certain information.

❏ No one is willing to read a four-page email. Sending out very long email messages will make you appear either dense or egotistical. Hit the high notes and provide the rest as attachments, should your readers be interested.

❏ Never use your company's email system to send out cute or funny jokes, news, or personal stories. Apart from being a violation of most companies' internal policies regarding the appropriate use of email, generating a lot of internal spam coveys the impression that you have a lot of empty time on your hands.

Improving Your Brand Image as an Organized Professional

The brand attribute of "being organized" goes beyond whether other people view you as being neat and tidy. It has more to do with whether or not you are viewed as someone who can manage complexity and juggle a number of assignments—characteristics that are typically expected of leaders able to take on broader responsibilities. Here are some suggestions for becoming more organized:

Organize Your Work Space

❏ Keep your desk organized. If this is extremely difficult for you to do, keep one section of your desk reserved for paperwork related to key projects.

❏ If you are a project team member who has difficulty organizing your work, find someone else on the team who is very organized. Next, find out whether that person would be willing to take on the responsibility of loading your team's data and reports into a common groupware file. This way your team does not have to wait for you while you struggle to remember where you buried critical information in your hard files or software folders. This approach is particularly important if you are likely to be out of touch with your team for several days and they will require access to certain project information. Finally, since the information that everyone needs resides in a common repository, it eliminates problems created when team members claim that they never received information via email.

Leverage Technology

❐ If you are currently using a traditional phone, you may want to consider switching to a smart phone. This can help you to stay connected with other people in a variety of ways. Both my personal and consulting email messages are routed to my iPhone, which also keeps me connected by text, phone, and mobile Facebook and Twitter accounts. My iPhone also gives me instant access to the web and holds my complete contact list, as well as a calendar that is synchronized to the one on my laptop.

❐ Mobile technology can also increase your efficiency in other simple ways. One of the apps that I use is Dragon Dictation (DD), which automatically translates my voice into text. Without leaving the app I can immediately email the text to myself or someone else. I use this technique to remind myself of key events or to capture ideas in real time. Some of the ideas included in this chapter came to me while I was driving along one day. Within a few seconds I was able to dictate what I wanted to say and immediately email the text to my laptop for a cut-and-paste insertion into this chapter. The same approach works well as a meeting action organizer. After leaving a meeting or one-on-one discussion, I often use my DD app to send myself quick notes about decisions or actions that have emerged out of those sessions.

Improving Your Brand Image as a Team Player

This brand attribute represents you as being the type of "low maintenance" work professional who can build good relationships with others. It also conveys the degree to which you are willing to put your team's interests ahead of your own and demonstrates that you can be relied on to function as a goodwill ambassador when representing your team to other work functions. Here are some suggestions for becoming a stronger team player:

Building Relationships

❐ Don't be stingy about sharing credit for projects. If you are representing a group of people on a formal presentation, make sure that all of their names are listed on the cover sheet. If you build on someone else's idea, then make sure that you acknowledge the person's input when presenting the idea.

❐ Take time for the little things. Even if you are not a chatty kind of person, try to take small steps to build relationships. Examples include starting off the work-week by asking people whether they had a nice weekend or joining your co-workers in your office's monthly birthday celebration.

❑ Avoid gossiping about other people in the office. Word gets around eventually and, although no one may ever confront you about it, being a gossip-monger will quickly erode your trust level with others. After all, if they see that you are nice to someone else to his face but talk about that person behind his back, they are bound to wonder what you might be saying about them.

Managing Difficult Conversations

❑ If you are going to be engaging in a discussion that you fear could become confrontational, prior to the start of the discussion jot down on a notepad both some of the key points that you want to cover and some of the concerns that you feel may be presented by the other party. Treat those concerns as valid in the eyes of the other party and be prepared to address them. By checking off each point as you cover it during the conversation, you can use your list as a kind of emotional anchor to ensure that the discussion does not become volatile or go off track.

❑ When you are in a difficult discussion, start by inviting the other party to share his or her concerns and take a moment to summarize the other person's position. Doing so will let the person know that you are trying to understand things from his or her perspective. In addition, this slight pause will give you a few seconds to regain emotional control before you attempt to respond.

❑ Try to take steps to avoid escalating issues up respective chains of command. Each time you raise a dispute to a higher management level, the bigger it gets, the less control you have over it and the more that you are likely to be viewed as someone who has difficulty managing issues through your own skills.

Avoiding Email and Voicemail Wars

❑ If someone upsets you, resist the urge to immediately fire off an angry email or voicemail message. No matter how upset you are, always keep your tone civil when leaving someone a voicemail message. Given that your voicemail could be forwarded on to other people in your organization, always present yourself in a way that will not cause you to be embarrassed should this occur.

PARTICIPANT'S GUIDE

❐ If you receive a nasty email or voicemail from someone, wait a while before responding. Remind yourself that when you lose your temper you lose control of the situation. When you feel ready, pick up the phone and tell the other person the following: "I received your email and it is easy to tell that you have some strong feelings about this situation. I want to hear more about how you feel about it. Do you have a moment to talk?"

Responding to Requests

❐ Whenever you approach someone for help or to resolve a problem, start by asking the person whether she would like you to provide a little background information. A simple introductory statement might be something like: "I am calling because Jeff mentioned that you might be willing to assume a sponsor role in the leadership development executive advisory council that we are forming. Has Jeff filled you in on that, or would it be helpful for you to have me take a minute and provide you with a brief overview?"

❐ When you receive an unanticipated request, avoid immediately responding with a "yes" or "no." Instead, take a few minutes to ask a few questions of the person making the request so that you can obtain a little context and background about the situation and evaluate your current time commitments.

❐ If someone gives you what you feel is an impossible task, it is understandable that your first response may be to interrupt the person or come back immediately with a negative statement such as, "That's impossible!" or "No, I can't do that." Once again, try to avoid making "No!" your first response to any request. If you know that there are certain aspects of the request that you won't be able to meet, always start by explaining what you *will* be able to do and direct the requester to other sources of help. Then move on to discuss any concerns and reservations you might have regarding the request.

When Meeting with Senior-Level Executives

❐ Keep in mind that senior-level executives find themselves bombarded daily by meetings, phone calls, and emails. As a result, it is quite possible that you may walk into your meeting only to find that the executive in question has forgotten the purpose of your discussion or hasn't prepared for it. To prevent this from happening, take the following steps:
  ❐ Call the executive's administrative assistant in advance of the meeting to confirm that your meeting time hasn't slipped.

❐ In addition, let the assistant know of any documents that the executive may need to have in front of her during your discussion. A suggested face-saving statement might be: "I know that Jana had wanted to have a copy of the budget report in hand during our discussion today so I emailed it to her last night. With all of the emails that she receives each day, I didn't know whether she had the opportunity to review mine. Would you like me to email you a copy of the budget report so that you can print out a copy for her?"

❐ As you enter the office, begin your conversation by saying something like: "Thanks for meeting with me today to discuss [subject]. You had mentioned that you had thirty minutes to discuss this. Is that time frame still good? [Pause to confirm.]

❐ This approach will save the executive from the embarrassment of walking into your discussion unprepared and will save you the frustration of having to spend the first part of your meeting waiting while the executive reviews your documentation.

❐ When preparing documents for senior-level meetings, get into the habit of generating a single-page executive overview that summarizes the project or issue on which you have been working, the key steps that have been taken to this point, and decisions that are still outstanding. In your executive overview, flag any urgent decisions that you want during your meeting. Provide all other information as an addendum.

Improving Your Brand Image as an Adaptable Leader

In the previous chapter I mentioned that adaptability is a key component of learning agility as it shows that you can readily adjust to new situations and respond well to changing circumstances. It is also important to note that the opposite attribute, being viewed by others as being rigid or inflexible, has been shown to contribute to leadership failure and derailment. It is especially important to display the attribute of adaptability if you are working within the kind of high-change environment that requires leaders to perform as strong change agents. The following suggestions can help you become a more adaptable leader:

Managing Stress

❐ One of the most important steps you can take to manage your stress is to develop the ability to remain calm under pressure. Doing so will portray you as being someone who can deal effectively with stress. One technique that can greatly help in this area is to practice mindful meditation, which involves being able to focus your attention for a prolonged period of time in the present moment without distractions. The audio book *Mindfulness for Beginners* by Jon Kabat-Zinn, which was referenced in the last chapter, is a good starting place for learning more about this technique.

❐ If you have a stressful commute to work, try to vary your work schedule. Leave home an hour early, avoid rush-hour traffic, and find a place to have breakfast next to your office. You will start the day feeling more in control of your schedule.

❐ Everyone needs some time each day offline, away from other people and distractions, to focus on his or her most difficult projects. Look for ways to balance your need for personal concentration with the time requirements imposed by others. This could involve finding some spot away from your work area, such as a vacant conference room, to spend some time each day on those projects that require your full, sustained attention.

❐ Learn to muzzle your complaints. If you have a habit of complaining aloud to your co-workers, then exercise a little impulse control. Continued complaining between team members tends to create a negative energy spiral, one that keeps everyone focused on the most dismal aspects of the situation. Moreover, complaining serves as a magnet for non-performers; if you continually complain, at some point you will find yourself surrounded by a circle of friends and associates who are probably generally regarded as the least successful members of your work team. Being viewed as a close confidant of a group of complainers can cause serious damage to your professional brand.

Establishing Your Reputation as a Change Agent

❐ We find it easier to take the lead in directing change whenever we are able to stay ahead of it. Over 30 years ago a psychological study was done involving patients who were about to undergo surgery. The first group received only the cursory pre-surgery briefing that was typically given to patients, while the second group received more detailed information pertaining to what the surgery entailed and the probable outcomes of the surgery. Post-surgical comparisons of these two groups revealed that the second (well-informed) group tended to have a much faster recovery time and require less pain medication. This experimental result has been since replicated consistently since it was first published (references are provided at the end of this chapter). The moral is that having good information in advance of any change event reduces our stress and anxiety and make us feel more confident about our ability to manage the situation.

❐ To stay ahead of broad-scale changes within your own organization, keep abreast of what is happening in your organization and industry. Periodically review your company's press releases, investment conferences, and quarterly briefings. Check your organization's website occasionally to see whether any of your senior managers have posted podcasts, videos, or webinars describing changes in the business picture. Use your social network (more on this later in this chapter) to pull together any information that you have gathered that points to impending changes. Then go back and review Chapter 1 of this book, giving some special consideration to how these changes are likely to impact both you and your work team.

❐ When confronted with a major change, don't become so preoccupied with worrying about possible threats that you overlook potential opportunities. The best change managers show that they can extract some opportunities from any difficult situation. Consider using a SWOT (Strengths, Weaknesses, Opportunities, and Threats) matrix to help your team map out potential strengths, weaknesses, opportunities, and threats. (An adapted version of this type of matrix is presented in my book, *The Team Troubleshooter.*

❐ Choose your battles. There are bound to be several aspects of any complex, large-scale change process that you find difficult to deal with. If you attempt to fight everything, you will gain nothing. Learn the wisdom of being accommodating on small points in disputes so that you can gain some traction on the larger ones. To put this in practice, create a list of all of the change issues that are causing you grief. Now rank them from top to bottom in order of importance, then divide the list into three chunks. Consider the bottom group as those relatively minor irritations that you should choose to ignore. The middle chunk includes more serious issues that might require some minor adjustments on your part. Try to focus most of your energy on the two most important items at the top of your list. These are the change issues that are worth your time and attention.

❐ One of the ways that others gauge your adaptability is to see how well you roll with the punches whenever you are faced with unanticipated, challenging, new work situations. Examples include reporting to a new manager, coping with a reorganization, or adjusting to a major change

PARTICIPANT'S GUIDE

in your work responsibilities. Your first reactions to these changes will determine whether you gain a reputation as a change agent or are viewed as someone who is locked into the past. (Read this chapter's Case in Point to hear an example of this.) When confronted with an unexpected change, develop the habit of holding back on expressing your views until you have had an opportunity to gather your facts.

❏ A simple technique for gathering such information is to facilitate a discussion on the change event with others in your work team. Use a whiteboard to create a list of what is currently known or unknown about the change event. (Are you sure, for example, that an impending reorganization will result in budget cuts within your group, or is this an unverified assumption?) Now take a look at all of the unknowns that you have listed. Of these, which are the most important pieces of information that you need to gather? Who on your team could take the lead in going out and gathering this information? By progressing through this discussion you can shift your perspective from that of a helpless victim of change to a take-charge change agent.

❏ Another simple tool involves drawing three overlapping circles on a whiteboard, like the ones in Figure 6.3, with the first circle representing the current state of affairs and the last circle representing how your work environment will look after the change. The middle circle that connects to the first and third represents the transition state, in other words that confusing time period during which you will be attempting to make the transition between the "before" and "after" states. Use this model to capture the most important things that need to be considered before, during, and after the conclusion of the organizational change.

FIGURE 6.3. The Three Change Perspectives

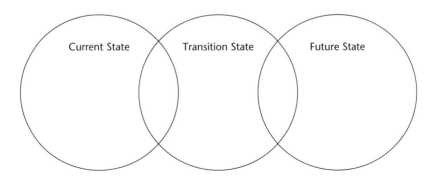

❐ Spend sufficient time developing ideas for helping your team manage the transition phase. Years ago, when I helped direct a reorganization of a sales department, part of our transition planning process involved determining how and when customer accounts would be managed as sales managers were slotted into new jobs. At another company, due to our department's rapid organizational growth we feared taxing the ability of our training department to keep up with the demand for training. An important part of our transition planning involved determining how we could make creative use of contract labor and vendor support during the six-month period that it would take to hire and orient new staff members.

❐ A number of simple change tools are available to help you manage change events more effectively. One of my previous books, *The Team Troubleshooter*, provides detailed instructions for tools and methods, such as the Stakeholder Analysis Chart, Threats and Opportunities Analysis, Change Management Grid, Scenario Forecasting, and the Run the Gauntlet technique, which have been created to help you more effectively manage organizational change.

Conveying Your Receptiveness to New Ideas

❐ Before attempting to drive forward a new plan of action, make certain that you begin by "socializing" your plan with your key stakeholders. Schedule individual meetings with senior leaders and key support personnel to gain their perspectives and to show them that you are open to their ideas. Take detailed notes both on their concerns and on what they like about the plan, and after each meeting summarize these conclusions in confirmation emails back to each stakeholder. Fold into your project plan the steps you intend to take to address concerns, and finally, circle back to your stakeholders to let them know that their concerns are being addressed.

❐ If you are in a meeting and someone takes a stand that you don't agree with, resist the urge to immediately attack the speaker's logic. Instead, draw the speaker out before you react. I have learned that one of the most valuable comments in the English language is "Tell me more about that." As you listen, take notes of the main points that you are hearing and summarize these points for the speaker. Before presenting your own views, focus on the part of the speaker's idea that you feel is valid or salvageable. An example would be: "What I like about what you have said about the sales model is…" or "I agree with you that

PARTICIPANT'S GUIDE

lack of staff could be a big constraint in getting this project approved and. ..."

❑ You are now ready to discuss your concerns. Avoid presenting your position in absolute terms, such as "Based on my experience, there is no way this will work." Instead, present your concerns in a tentative way by saying something such as "The part that I need to understand better..." or "The part of what you have said that I am a bit concerned about is. ..."

❑ Whenever possible, make use of a whiteboard or flip chart to sketch out your ideas. Whenever people see an issue laid out visually, particularly with graphic models, the discussion becomes less emotional and confrontational. Before you attempt to react to what a speaker has said, go to the board and try to sketch out a rough graphic that captures the speaker's point of view.

❑ As an alternative option, hand a marker to the speaker and ask this person to build on your drawing or to sketch out a different graphic that represents her ideas. As you do this, position your chairs side-by-side with both of you facing the whiteboard. This simple shift in posture creates a strong shift in perspective—instead of confronting each other as adversaries you jointly view the problem from the perspective of a partnership.

Strengthening Your Brand Image as a Results-Driven Performer

I had mentioned earlier that a powerful brand is consistent; that is, it provides a guarantee that each time you encounter it you will provide the same experience. For a personal brand, this means that an individual is viewed as someone who can be consistently counted on to meet deadlines, deliver on promises, and keep commitments. Here are some steps that you can take to become viewed as a results-driven performer:

Managing Expectations on Assignments

❑ Start by explaining what portion of the assignment you feel confident you will be able to accomplish. If there are aspects of the assignment or request that are outside of your control or for which you lack the necessary resources, explain how these elements are likely to affect the outcome of your work. If getting the job done is contingent upon your ability to obtain information or approvals from other people, be clear about how these contingencies may influence your ability to meet project milestones.

❐ Give assurances. Avoid "I will try" in favor of "Here is what I will do." Never over-promise; it is always better to under-promise and over-deliver. Never make commitments on behalf of people whom you don't directly manage until you have confirmed with them that they are willing to invest their time or resources.

Set and Act on Priorities

❐ In establishing work priorities, keep the broader picture in mind. To test what priority you should assign to a work project or task, ask yourself four questions: (1) If this is not completed, will anyone care? (2) How does this particular work item fit into the broader goals for our work group and organization? In other words, is it a work area that is closely linked to higher-level business objectives? (3) Six months from now, will anyone remember the work that was done on this project? and (4) Does this project or task have visibility to, or is being sponsored by, a senior-level stakeholder in our company? Items that don't fit these criteria should be moved to the bottom of your to-do list.

❐ Rigorously prune your to-do list on a daily and weekly basis.

❐ If you are a manager, make sure that the people on your team know what constitutes critical email messages and set up a coding system that they will be expected to use to visually flag such emails. Let your direct reports know that the decisions they make in determining what to flag as being "critically important" directly reflect on their decision-making ability.

❐ Arrive at your work area thirty minutes early each day and post a visible list of actions that must be completed for the day. Assume that unexpected events (calls, impromptu staff meetings, emails, etc.) will clog up at least 20 percent of your day and plan accordingly by building buffer zones into your schedule to meet your most critical work priorities.

❐ Set tough performance goals for yourself. If you tend to evaluate your own work performance in terms of the hours you work or the amount of effort that you put into a project, develop a new set of goals that are based entirely around measurable results.

❐ When it comes to negotiating performance expectations with your manager, make certain that the two of you reach agreement on what deliverables will be expected at the conclusion of a work assignment and on how success will be measured. Consider the example of being assigned to lead a process improvement team. In this situation, your responsibilities and associated deliverables could be viewed in three different ways: (1) you could be expected to just evaluate the process,

PARTICIPANT'S GUIDE

in which case the end deliverable would be a process map that pinpoints the glitch areas (points in the process in which errors occur, redundant work is performed, or bottlenecks exist); (2) in addition you might be expected to work with your team to recommend improvements for strengthening the process, in which case your additional end deliverables would include a list of recommended actions for each process problem, along with associated costs and estimated ROI; or (3) if your boss also expects you to implement those solutions, your deliverables would include the implementation and testing of those recommended process changes, including a final analysis of achieved ROI.

Improving Project Planning

❐ Establish systems to track how you are performing against your plans and to alert you to milestone slippage. It does not matter whether you use sophisticated project management software or a simple "red light, yellow light, green light" color-coded system to distinguish between project deliverables that are on track, those that are experiencing some difficulties, or those on which you are encountering significant delays or problems. Just make sure that the method you choose provides your organizational stakeholders with a quick, graphic method for gauging your progress.

❐ Always assume that something will go wrong at some stage of project planning. The trick is to anticipate your weak spots and build in contingency plans for dealing with these weak points should they arise. Ask a co-worker to help you troubleshoot your plan; then jointly "red flag" those project steps that appear to be most vulnerable to delays or obstacles. Once you have charted the critical path for a project, build in safety buffers (extra time, the option for contract support, etc.) for those steps that represent areas of greatest vulnerability.

❐ When you are working on a project, it is easy to get into the habit of sending a series of small "micro-bite" emails out to people, with each email posing some small question as these questions enter your mind. This approach can make you look a little scattered and impulsive. As an alternative, write down all questions as they come to you; then consolidate them into a single concise response that hits the high notes.

Improving Your Brand Image as an Influencer

Influencers are people who can get things done in organizations by moving agendas forward, making an effective business case for new initiatives, or persuading others to courses of action. They have the respect and support of a wide range of organizational stakeholders. Here are some suggestions for becoming a stronger influencer:

☐ Know how frequently you need to be communicating with your manager and how much detail your manager expects from you when it comes to providing status updates. Your objective is to keep your manager in the communication loop, while at the same time not spending so much time checking in that you appear needy and dependent. When you first receive an assignment, try to reach an understanding with your manager on how often you should provide progress updates and the method your manager would like you to use to provide those updates.

☐ An important skill for working with senior executives involves learning how to strike the right balance between being appropriately differential and respectful and knowing when and how to push back and present a strong point of view. This is an area in which obtaining feedback from your manager or another organizational leader could be very helpful.

☐ Influencers effectively "manage the white space." By this I mean that they are willing to go beyond a narrow definition of their jobs to extend help to their co-workers and other departments. Taking this action not only strengthens your brand as an influencer, but also helps you build a robust group of allies and stakeholders. Finally, it makes you more knowledgeable about the broader operation of your department. This brand attribute is particularly important for new employees or for those professionals who are attempting to establish themselves with a new manager or work team.

☐ If you find it difficult to speak up in staff meetings or find that other people tend to talk over you, there are a few steps you can take to stand out. Offer to take over the role of the meeting facilitator to make sure that ideas are fully discussed and that everyone at the meeting has an opportunity to voice concerns. [One of my previous books, *The Team Troubleshooter*, outlines several techniques to support meeting facilitation.] A simple approach is to simply stand up from the meeting table at some point and begin to graphically sketch out your ideas on the whiteboard. As you do this, summarize and confirm what you have heard from other team members and fold their ideas into your graphic. This approach will automatically begin to place you in the role of meeting facilitator.

☐ When taking on an assignment or responding to a request, take the time to ask questions that can help you understand why this work is important and how it will be used. This is particularly important when you are responding to a request from another department. Knowing the "why" can help you continually adjust priorities if the underlying reasons for the request or assignment change.

❒ Influencers take the time to understand how their organizations are wired. They know which senior stakeholders are most likely to weigh in on certain decisions and which direct reports are most listened to by those stakeholders. The next time you are involved in a major project, develop a simple graphic that maps out the key stakeholders (and potential blockers) for that initiative.

❒ Strong influencers are sensitive to adapting communication strategies to the needs of different audiences. I know of some executives who like to have someone present a quick verbal briefing on a situation before they are asked to read a detailed report and others who like to have a day or so to digest the report before they sit down to talk. Some individuals are very visual and respond well to having someone go to the whiteboard to sketch out their ideas, while others respond better to seeing quantitative data organized on Excel spreadsheets. The key here is to watch closely to how well each of your key stakeholders appears to respond to different forms of communication and then follow suit.

❒ Never fall so in love with your own ideas that you aren't willing to adapt or adjust them in small ways to meet the needs and expectations of your stakeholders. When these adjustments are made, make certain that the originators of these ideas are credited for their contributions.

❒ Part of becoming an influencer is to be seen as someone who can easily fit in and socialize with senior leaders in your organization. Take your cues for how to dress from observing those leaders who hold higher-level leadership positions. In addition, make certain that you have a clear understanding of the types of social behaviors that your senior leaders consider to be representative of work professionals. As an example, do your senior managers communicate in a outgoing, informal manner, or do they appear to feel more comfortable with people who are more reserved and formal in their communication style?

❒ Influencers tend to associate with other influencers. Start becoming aware of those individuals within your own professional or leadership level who have developed especially strong personal brands as influencers. Take the opportunity to reach out and network with these individuals, and use them as role models. The next time you have an opportunity to observe one of them selling an idea or debating a point, try to identify what that person does that appears to help him or her be successful in influencing others and take a few notes for later review.

Create Opportunities to Leverage Your Brand

So far I have discussed the importance of taking steps to strengthen your brand. It is equally important to be able to determine the kinds of situations in which your particular brand profile provides the best "value-add" to your organization and then work to create those situations in your work experience. Take a minute to review Table 6.2, the Brand Application Table. The left-hand column provides descriptions of the six strong brand profiles that I have covered in this chapter that could support the career development of any professional. The middle column suggests the types of work situations in which each profile could be applied for maximum advantage. The right-hand column provides caveats or cautionary notes that need to be considered when leveraging a particular brand profile. As you review this chart, try to determine which of these six brand profiles most closely matches your greatest strength as a work professional. Then ask yourself whether you are currently taking full advantage of how you could apply your brand to help your organization while supporting your own career goals. Finally, try to identify any steps that you could take to address the caveats noted for your brand profile.

Case in Point: Sandra

One of my coaching clients was Sandra, an incredibly productive woman who had just made the move into the role of vice president of operations. With an extensive background in finance, Sandra had seen a promotional opportunity open up in operations and jumped at it, even though it required her to quickly get up to speed on business processes with which she had little familiarity. During our coaching sessions, I explained that one of the things that could keep her from continuing to advance was her personal brand. Specifically, several managers were of the opinion that she was change-resistant. Sandra had a difficult time understanding this and took the time to tell me about several change initiatives that she had successfully led.

My cautionary note to her was that in each of these situations it was true that she had eventually come around to supporting the change

TABLE 6.2. Brand Application Table

Brand Profile	Areas for Application	Caveats
Organized: I don't become overwhelmed when faced with complex projects that have a number of moving pieces. I can juggle a number of assignments, am able to carefully think through and formulate project plans, track time and resources, and anticipate obstacles that could emerge in project planning.	Look for opportunities to manage the overall planning process for complex projects, such as facility moves or reorganizations. As an option, volunteer to help other team members or your manager formulate their project plans, troubleshoot potential vulnerabilities in those plans, and/or develop solutions for overcoming these obstacles.	Recognize that others have different work styles, and be patient with people who may not think through work projects to your level of detail. To avoid burnout, recognize that not all work projects warrant the same level of detailed attention. Learn to identify situations in which it makes more sense to spend less time organizing certain aspects of your work or when you need to be delegating the details of work to others.
Adaptable: I am readily adaptable to new and difficult situations and respond well to changing circumstances. I don't get thrown whenever I am tossed into new work settings, and I work well with a variety of people. I am very flexible when it comes to taking on new leadership roles or learning new work skills.	Look for opportunities to lead organizational change initiatives or to support other professionals or work teams in developing strategies for planning for impending changes. Volunteer to step into new job roles, such as being temporarily assigned to another work team. Consider taking on the responsibility of being the first in your team to learn new technical or business skills, and then train other team members in those skills.	Try not to be dismissive of others in your organization who are more change-resistant and who require some time and persuasion to come on board with new ideas. Be careful not to be so enamored with new ideas or concepts that you fail to sustain prolonged effort on more tedious and routine tasks.

Results-driven: I find creative ways to work around obstacles, such as insufficient resources or time, to get things accomplished. I generally exceed performance expectations and am extremely tenacious when it comes to pushing ideas through to implementation.

Look for opportunities to lead teams in resolving a tough business or technical issues, such as difficult process improvement challenges. Work with your manager to establish stretch goals for your work team. Consider finding a work area in which the return on investment has not been clearly defined, then use your unique skills for recommending a method for evaluating progress. If you are not a manager, jump into the lead role for a project or assignment and solicit feedback from others on the team on your team leadership style.

People who are extremely results-driven can be rather unforgiving when others don't meet their expectations or fail to display a high level of enthusiasm for projects. Try to not to appear dismissive of people who may not appear to have your drive for results. Also, look for ways to balance your emphasis on results with the need to build and sustain relationships.

Team player: I can form good relationships with a variety of people and can often find a way for people with very different perspectives to discover common ground for reaching agreement on issues. I can be counted on to perform well as a goodwill ambassador when representing my team to other work functions.

Volunteer to negotiate disputes between your team and other departments or to take on the challenge of resolving long-standing disputes with customers or suppliers. Use your team-building skills to direct a cross-functional team. As another option, consider volunteering to take over the role of team facilitator should your manager want to conduct a strategic planning or team-building session with your work group.

Solicit feedback from others regarding your ability to balance your focus on group harmony and interpersonal relationships with the ability to make difficult decisions and push for results. Be careful of being so quick to acquiesce to others, lest you let other people steamroll over you when it comes to pushing their own decisions or taking over the leadership of a work project.

TABLE 6.2. *Continued*

Brand Profile	Areas for Application	Caveats
Good communicator: I am able to convey complex ideas or difficult concepts in a way that makes it easy for others to understand. I express myself exceptionally well in writing or when presenting on a topic, and I know how to match my communication style to the varying needs of different audiences.	Companies are always looking for "organizational translators"—people who can translate the goals and intentions of senior managers into a communication form that is easily understood by, and is sensitive to the concerns of, different organizational members. Volunteer your services when you encounter situations in which the senior leaders of your organization are looking for ways to communicate important organizational changes or changes in policy to others in your organization.	When volunteering to take over a communication assignment, be selective. There is a difference between being involved in projects that showcase your talents and those thankless, low-level assignments that should be delegated to an administrative assistant. When volunteering to take over communication projects for senior leaders, make certain that your manager understands and supports your use of time.
Influencer: I can speak persuasively and compellingly. I understand how our organization is "wired," know which stakeholders will weigh in on different business decisions, and the best way of approaching those stakeholders to gain their support. I am able to think from the perspective of other people and build a strong business case to sell a business decision.	Represent your team when they are attempting to solicit support and buy-in from stakeholders for key initiatives. Volunteer your assistance the next time your manager is attempting to develop and present a business case for a new proposal to your executive team. When the other members of your team are given the responsibility of directing major projects, offer to assist them in mapping out key stakeholders and in determining the most effective approach for reaching out to these senior leaders.	Know when it is to your best interest and the interest of your company to take a lead role in driving change or to work behind the scenes in a less-conspicuous support role. In your efforts to influence others, don't be so invested in selling people about your point of view that you fail to give their views an honest appraisal.

initiative that was underway. At the same time, her *first response* when each of these new organizational or business changes was announced was to assume what I call the "Chicken Little" stance. This meant throwing up her hands and telling everyone that the sky was falling.

"Don't they [the corporate office] know," she'd plead, "that we don't have enough advance notice, staff, resources to pull this off?" She'd then drag her heels on getting behind the change process. Instead of using her business smarts to take a leadership role in guiding the change wave, she would invest her time trying to convince her senior managers that their performance expectations were unreasonable. As her stress increased, her behavior tended to become more erratic, including emotional outbursts in staff meetings and sarcastic comments made about "those idiots at corporate."

Ironically, in each case once she accepted the fact that the new change was not going away, she would climb on board the change bus and provide strong leadership. Unfortunately, by this point she would suffer some brand erosion, and what stuck in the minds of her senior stakeholders was her entrenched resistance to change. While they were willing to accept her behavior in her current role, what they were looking for at the next level was a leader who could not only acclimate to change, but also sell her department on the value of moving forward. After a few coaching sessions, Sandra began to fully accept responsibility for managing her brand, and over the remaining six months of her coaching assignment she was able to make a remarkable change in how she was viewed in her organization. The moral of this story is that it is not enough to get great results. Given a choice between two leaders who are both great performers, an organization will always choose the one with the strongest brand.

Your Next Steps

Your next steps involve identifying your brand, strengthening it, and seeking out organizational challenges that give you the opportunity to showcase your brand.

1. Start by identifying your overall brand profile. Based on everything that you have reviewed in this chapter on brand attributes, which of the following six brand profiles comes closest to representing your strong suit as an organizational leader?

❒ Organized
❒ Results-driven
❒ Influencer
❒ Team player
❒ Adaptable
❒ Good communicator

2. Identify the behaviors that comprise your personal brand. To perform a more granular review of your brand, start out by considering all of the informal feedback on your personal brand that you may have received from others over the past few weeks. What three words are most used by your manager, peers, and direct reports to describe you? Add to that any comments that have appeared on your last two performance reviews, which would shed some light on how your manager views your brand. In addition, if you received a 360-degree feedback report during the past year, the same technique can be used to flag any brand strengths and weaknesses that are noted on the comments section of the report. For the purpose of this exercise, ignore any comments that may refer to your technical skills or weaknesses. Focus only on those comments that say something about your personal brand. Now take a careful look at all of this feedback. Does it paint a picture of a professional who truly stands out from others through the application of certain brand attributes?

3. Make use of the 3Cs. I have mentioned that a strong brand is characterized by the 3Cs: that is, a strong brand is *clear* (you clearly understand the value that is being offered), *consistent* (you trust that you will receive the same experience every time), and *compelling* (there is something about the brand that is uniquely attractive). Consider what you could do to improve in these three areas:

   a. Make your brand more clear: What steps could you take over the next few weeks to more clearly convey your brand profile to other people in your organization? What opportunities could you create to let key stakeholders see you exercise your strongest brand attributes?

   b. Make your brand more consistent: How consistent are you in presenting your brand? If you pride yourself on being results-driven, are you getting feedback that you are viewed as consistently meeting commitments? If you see yourself as being a good team player, do you collaborate well with other people, even when you have limited control over the work situation that you are in or when you are forced to work with difficult people?

c. Make your brand more compelling: Over the next few weeks, take another look at the last two annual performance reviews that you received. Use a highlighter to flag those positive brand attributes that were consistently noted by your manager and co-workers and a different color marker to flag areas for improvement.

4. Commit yourself to improving your brand. Of all of the brand improvement actions listed in this chapter, what three actions are you willing to commit to taking over the next three weeks? Write your answers in the space below.

Additional Reading

"Altering patients' responses to surgery: An extension and replication." Jean E. Johnson, Sarah S. Fuller, M. Patricia Endress, and Virginia H. Rice. (1978). *Research in Nursing and Health, 1*(1), 111–121.

Psychological Approaches to Pain Management: A Practitioner's Handbook (2nd ed.). (2000). Dennis C. Turk and Robert J. Gatchel (Eds.). New York: Guilford Press.

"Sensory information, instruction in a coping strategy, and recovery from surgery." (1978). Jean E. Johnson, Virginia H. Rice, Sarah S. Fuller, and M. Patricia Endress. *Research in Nursing and Health, 1*(2), 4–17.

PART II

LEADER'S GUIDE

LEADER'S PREFACE

How to Make the Best Use of This Book

Before you read any further, let's discuss some of the steps you can take to get the most out of the coaching process that is outlined in this book.

First, if you haven't already done so, I would strongly recommend that you read through the participant's text. Taking this step will provide you with a better understanding of the development approach that your team members will be following. It will also put you in a better position to determine how you can best adapt this generic development approach to the unique requirements of your work setting. Finally, by taking the time to complete this program as a participant, you send a strong message to your team members about your commitment to your own professional development.

Second, before attempting to implement anything in this book, take the time to tell your team members about how you view the coaching process, why you think its important, and how you view your role in it. This is especially important if the concept of developmental coaching is new to you and your team and represents a relatively new area of discussion.

Third, give each of your direct reports his or her own copy of this book. Encourage them to read it and work through the exercises and let them know that, while you support their development, they need to take the responsibility for being self-directed learners. A few weeks after you have given out the book, ask each person to share with you the progress that he or she has made in implementing what was learned. Taking this simple step can tell you a lot about the importance that each team member places on his or her development.

As you and your team members continue to read through your respective guides, there are several ways that you can choose to apply this book as a coaching tool. The most common approach is to conduct regularly scheduled individual coaching sessions with those direct reports who have an interest in, and who are appropriate candidates for, developmental coaching. A second option is to see whether some of the members of your work team would like to work together as peer coaches. A peer coach is a work associate who can function as a good listener and devil's advocate to help a coaching partner troubleshoot his or her proposed development plan. A third option is to make use of a team coaching model in which you set aside one meeting a month for a team development discussion, with each discussion focusing on a different chapter in the Participant's Guide. A final option involves using this text as an integral part of a workshop on accelerated leadership development. Additional information on workshops offered by the author on this subject can be found on page 241.

CHAPTER ONE

THE WHAT AND THE WHY OF MANAGERIAL COACHING

The Business Case for Accelerated Development

The premise behind this book is relatively simple. It is that, with careful planning and some serious effort, it is possible for work professionals to substantially reduce the time that it would otherwise take for them to develop professionally in their careers. Part I of this book, the Participant's Guide, was created to provide professionals with a comprehensive, systematic development framework for becoming stronger performers and more effectively reaching their career goals. This second part of the book supports that text by providing you, the career planner's manager, with several guidelines and tools that you can use to foster the development of your team members.

Before going further, let's make certain that you have picked up the right book. You see, whenever a manager performs coaching it is usually with the intention of achieving one of three things. *Performance coaching*, otherwise known as remedial coaching, is directed toward those professionals who need to turn around their performance in some critical area. Often such coaching has to address not only technical skill deficiencies, but also serious problem areas related to leadership style or communication issues. *Transitional coaching* is very different in that it is concerned with helping employees who are new to an organization make a successful adjustment to a new work culture, a different set of work norms, and/or a very different set of performance expectations. In this book I focus on a third form of coaching known as *developmental coaching*. This area of coaching application is specifically designed to help good performers fully develop and grow on the job and to be better prepared to take on broader and more demanding organizational responsibilities.

The preface to Part I makes the claim that professional and leadership development can be greatly accelerated. For now, let me simply say that one of the reasons why I make this claim is that professional development is one leadership area that holds the potential for significant improvement. The reason is that development planning, as it is typically practiced today, is seldom treated with the discipline and rigor that one would expect from any other business process. That is, typically individuals don't approach their professional development in a systematic and detailed way, one that includes a targeted set of goals, a written plan, a clear assessment of priorities, and measures for assessing progress. In this book, I introduce a disciplined and effective developmental coaching approach that can help you extract the greatest benefit from your coaching efforts as a manager. In adopting this approach, you will find that the professionals whom you are coaching will be able to make faster progress on their development goals.

Why You Should Make Development a Top Priority

At this point you may be having a few doubts about how much time and effort you can afford to devote to the area of leadership development. From my perspective, there are several pragmatic reasons that you may want to assign this area a top priority.

Reason One: Your Time Is Too Precious to Waste. Yet your time is wasted if your team members fail to carefully think through their development priorities. The result of this kind of sloppy thinking shows up when direct reports inundate you with requests for a variety of training courses, when only a few of these courses help move them down the "critical path" of their development goals. Another symptom of sloppy development planning is when employees attempt to tackle work projects or assignments that have little payoff to either themselves or your organization.

Your time is also wasted if a year from now you are managing a group of people who have exactly the same skill sets and expertise that they have now. If you are typical of managers who have survived during the past few lean years, I am sure that you are operating with a very lean staff structure.

To make do, you may be requiring people to take on work responsibilities that they haven't previously managed or to stretch their efforts over a much wider range of work responsibilities. You simply can't do this effectively unless your people are able to step up to the plate and find ways to accelerate their on-the-job learning.

Reason Two: Your People Are a Reflection of Your Leadership Ability. As someone who has conducted leadership talent reviews for more than twenty years, I find that when senior executives attempt to evaluate the leadership potential of a manager, one of the most common questions that they ask is, "Is this someone who knows how to grow talent?" In attempting to answer that, your senior executives will take a look at how much the members of your team have grown during the past year under your coaching and direction. It says a lot for a manager when the people who report to him or her are asked to support key work projects or are able to demonstrate that over time they are becoming more knowledgeable and competent on a wide range of work functions. In addition, your ability to advance is directly dependent on your ability to groom exceptional successors for your own role. Finally, consider the fact that the talent management judgment calls that you make as a leader, such as determining who to recommend for a limited-seating executive development workshop or who to assign to a cross-functional team, say a lot about your ability to assess talent. In other words, in order to make good talent management decisions, you need to be able to understand and speak knowledgeably about the development needs and leadership potential of your people.

Reason Three: It Pays to Use the White Space. The traditional apprenticeship model of leadership development places almost all of the responsibility for development on you, the individual manager. The truth is that today many of the most important opportunities for professional development actually occur within your organization's white space, the term used to described those functional areas and projects that span organizational silos. I am talking here about such avenues as cross-functional project teams, having people temporarily loaned out to other work teams, encouraging them to assist second-level managers on selected initiatives, or making use of social networking tools such as online forums. The point is that professional development takes a lot longer and is less effective if we limit our concept of development to those opportunities that exist within our immediate work teams. In addition, we overlook excellent opportunities for matching professionals' development needs to organization-wide business challenges. Without your direction and guidance, the members of your work team are more likely to miss out on these opportunities because they lack your knowledge of organizational white-space opportunities.

Reason Four: Incremental Development No Longer Works. Most organizations can no longer afford to live with wasteful and protracted professional development cycles. Take the case of succession planning. When it comes to succession planning, many companies find it difficult to identify two or three exceptional successor candidates who are ready now to move into key roles. By exceptional candidates I am not talking here about people who, in a pinch, could serve as so-so replacement candidates. Instead, I am talking about identifying professionals who, should a promotional opportunity arise, you feel confident could successfully compete against the best external candidates who could be obtained from a major search firm.

If you are not sure whether this is an issue for your own department, put it to a test. Take out a red pen and mark all mission-critical positions within your department's succession plan. These are positions that, were an incumbent to suddenly leave, would create a serious problem for your organization. Now make a guess at what your estimated time-to-fill would be if you were forced to go out on the street and locate, screen, hire, and train top-notch replacements. I am willing to bet that in many cases you would have to wait about nine to twelve months for those positions to be filled. When you add to these risks the increasingly rapid churn in leadership positions that frequently accompanies organizational restructurings, then the problem gets stickier. The bottom line is that we are living in a period in which agile companies have the advantage, and this means having access to a broader number of talented individuals who can be quickly deployed on key projects and accountabilities. Accelerated development is the key to increasing organizational agility.

Reason Five: The Sink-or-Swim Approach to Development Results in Unwanted Risk. It is not uncommon for a manager to try to plug a hole in a key function by throwing in the best (not-yet-ready-for-primetime) promotional candidate and, in the process, placing that person in a sink-or-swim role. A more reasonable plan of action is to begin to test people against responsibilities that are somewhat beyond their current skills and experience levels, well before we are forced to place a big bet on their leadership potential. In other words, accelerated development does not just mean getting people through the pipeline faster. It also means helping people to be better prepared to deal with any new development opportunities that may come their way. Using development opportunities to test an individual's leadership capacity and business savvy also helps your organization perform a more accurate assessment on that person's readiness for advancement.

Reason Six: Your Best People Won't Wait. The last, and possibly most important, reason for investing in the development of your team members is that doing so provides you with the most effective tool for retaining them and encouraging them to give their best performance. The old apprentice model, with its slow and protracted approach to development, tends to be very attractive to mediocre performers. It offers them a safe, gradual learning curve that doesn't push them out of their comfort zones. At the same time, your best people are likely to become impatient with this same slow-growth approach to professional development. The result is that they may begin to look around to other areas within, or outside of, your company that can provide greater challenge and fulfillment. For these same reasons it is difficult to attract top-notch people into a work function if that work function has developed the reputation of being the organizational "elephant graveyard" where people go to plateau, stagnate, and die.

Together, these six reasons suggest that it is to your best interest, and the benefit of your company, to make a solid investment in developmental coaching. Having said that, let me assure you that it is possible for you to encourage the development of your team members without feeling you have to take over the responsibility for managing their careers. You will find within this Leader's Guide a managerial coaching model that provides a good balance between management support and professional accountability.

Understanding Your Role as a Coach

Some Common Misconceptions About Coaching

Having talked about the importance of coaching, I would now like to shift gears and talk about what it takes to succeed as a coach. Perhaps the best way to start is to take a careful look at five of the more common misconceptions that people have regarding the coaching process:

LEADER'S GUIDE

Misconception 1: Coaching Is Therapy. To perform as a therapist, an individual needs to possess very specialized skills, applied training, and appropriate academic credentials in the areas of clinical or counseling psychology. A therapist takes on a completely non-directive role when helping clients address important emotional or adjustment issues. Another characteristic of therapy is that therapeutic conversations tend to intrude into a variety of areas across a client's entire life, including family and marital issues, and clients feel safe in disclosing very intimate details of their lives to their therapists. Finally, the goal of therapy is to help individuals make substantial changes in the way that they feel about themselves and their lives.

In point of fact, no one expects you to have the background to address problems of drug or alcohol abuse, martial discord, or personal anxiety. If you encounter these types of issues in any management conversation with an employee you need to refer the employee to your company's employee assistance program (EAP) for counseling by a qualified third-party. As a managerial coach, the balancing act that you strive for is to respect your team member's work/life priorities, while at the same time having a strong say in ensuring that a team member's development plan is directed tied to the performance goals of your company. The scope for managerial coaching is the workplace; discussions that extend into a direct report's personal and family life are typically considered unwelcome and intrusive. In short, as a managerial coach the focus for your discussion are those skills, knowledge areas, and professional behaviors that are likely to either support or impede an individual's career success within your organization.

Misconception 2: Coaching Is the Same Thing as Performance Management. Throughout the year I am sure that you set performance goals and expectations, establish success measures and metrics, and provide employees with feedback and performance coaching. Once a year all of this is capped off with the formal feedback and evaluation process that you provide as part of your company's annual performance review. It is important to understand, however, that the focus for performance management is an evaluation of current and past business results and identifying short-term actions that can help get sub-standard performance back on line. It's true that during the last few minutes of a performance review you may get into discussions about setting "improvement goals." The problem is that these discussions tend to be very cursory and task-oriented and are largely overshadowed by the employee's concerns regarding performance ratings and compensation.

Throughout this book, when I use the term "developmental coaching," I am talking about a very different kind of manager-employee discussion. First of all, a developmental coaching discussion is, by definition, future-focused. It is intended not to help mediocre performers correct performance issues, but to help good job performers prepare to take on broader leadership roles within your company. Preparation for next-level assignments often requires individuals to develop and acquire very different kinds of skills and abilities than they currently have in their professional arsenals. As a result, a person's past performance may not always provide a definitive indicator of future leadership potential, or a clear guide for how the professional can best prepare for broader leadership roles.

Misconception 3: Good Coaches Should Have All the Answers. Managers are sometimes reluctant to take on coaching roles because they are concerned that, when it comes to advising their direct reports on questions such as what it takes to advance up a certain leadership ladder, they won't have all of the answers. The truth is that coaching is not about having the right answers; it is about asking the kinds of insightful questions that can encourage a person to reflect more carefully on his or her career plans and undertake a more in-depth review of development needs.

Misconception 4: Coaching Involves Taking Responsibility for Another Person's Career Success. If coaching is performed correctly, there should be no doubt in the mind of your team members that they have the lion's share of responsibility for their own professional development. No one expects you to be a crystal ball gazer and predict a team member's chances of advancing within your organization, or lay out a detailed blueprint to ensure that person's career success. The content and the format of the Participant's Guide reinforces the concept of self-accountability, by directing career planners to focus their efforts on those development actions that are directly within their control. The coach's role is to help career planners think more clearly about their career goals and plans and to provide information and assistance that can assist them in implementing these plans.

Misconception 5: Coaching Raises False Expectations on the Part of Employees. I have heard this one many times. It usually comes across in a statement such as, "We have limited promotional opportunities here. If I ask my people about their development and career goals, aren't I simply raising expectations that I can't possibly meet?" While this is a valid

LEADER'S GUIDE

concern and is certainly understandable, stop and think about it for a moment. First, for a lot of people "developing on the job" simply means knowing how to make a bigger contribution to their organizations, while gaining recognition for the efforts they are making to grow as professionals. It can involve something as simple as getting one of your performers selected for a cross-functional project, helping someone develop new technical skills, or giving someone more visibility to your senior managers. In addition, you may discover that there may be ways to formally expand the scope of a team member's current job, either by broadening that person's existing roles or by talking to your HR manager about the option of revising the person's formal job description. Finally, if few advancement positions are available in your organization, I would argue that this is even more reason why you should push professional development. Without your support, the members of your work group will find themselves at a serious disadvantage when competing for those limited positions. Should your direct reports decide to apply for promotional positions, you don't want them to feel that they are unable to compete because they haven't received the right training, development support, or career assistance.

What Good Managerial Coaches Do

If coaching isn't therapy, performance management, or employee caretaking, then what is it? The answer is that coaches help employees think more carefully and critically about their development and career choices, while leaving it up to those employees to be accountable for both making and acting on those choices. As a coach, there are nine steps you can take to accomplish this. As you read through the following list, take a second to check off those areas where it might be helpful for you, as a coach, to invest greater time and attention.

❏ First, you can give your people needed encouragement by urging them to move out of their comfort zones and experiment with new work challenges, by recognizing their unique skill sets and strengths, and by helping them identify those incremental actions they can take to close skill gaps.

❏ The second thing you can do as a coach is to encourage career planners to engage in critical self-reflection. This means helping them take a candid look, not only at how they perform within different work situations, but also how they professionally present themselves to key stakeholders in those situations. It also means using probing, open-ended questions to help career planners turn fuzzy thinking into ideas that are clearly delineated. In the next chapter I will provide a few examples of some of the questions that you can use to encourage team members to perform a deeper, more substantive self-critique of their career goals and development needs.

☐ Coaches also help develop people by encouraging big-picture thinking. Compared to your direct reports, you probably have a broader, more complete idea of what it takes to advance in your organization. As a result, you can provide career planners with realistic previews of what it takes to succeed in next-level assignments or the different work conditions and performance expectations that characterize different departments or work locations. Finally, you probably are able to look further out on the horizon to detect the onset of large organizational changes, such as new product launches or reorganizations, that could directly affect the success of their development plans.

☐ Other developmental coaching roles that managers take on are those of impartial sounding board and devil's advocate. A person who uses a "shotgun" approach to career planning (blasting blindly against the target in the hope that something hits) is likely to find himself attempting to take on too many development activities. By simply taking the time to listen and ask reasonable questions, a coach encourages individuals to more critically explore their career decisions. A coach can also help professionals understand the tradeoffs (in time, money, and personal investment) that need to be taken into consideration when choosing among different development options.

☐ Good coaches also help their people think carefully about the long-term consequences of different development actions. An individual may, for example, consider turning down a promotional offer because she feels that the offer doesn't come with a large enough compensation increase. At the same time, this individual may not realize that your executives view that position as a necessary stepping-stone to long-term advancement within her chosen career path.

☐ A manager also fulfills an important coaching role in providing employees with feedback on their skills and development needs. Equally important, they help career planners make sense of and consolidate this feedback with that they receive from other managers, co-workers, internal customers, and through formal channels such as 360-degree surveys.

☐ Coaches also support career planning by requiring their direct reports to treat their development and career plans with the same professional consideration that they would any other aspect of business planning.

LEADER'S GUIDE

This means getting plans in writing, translating "fuzzy" intentions into concrete, time-limited actions, establishing metrics for periodically assessing their own progress on their plans, and giving their best when presented with development opportunities.

☐ Managerial coaches know that they can't possibly be all things to all people. For this reason, they also take the time to direct their people toward other resources that can help, including the company's leadership development department, outside professional and trade organizations, or other managers who might be willing to provide useful information and guidance.

☐ Finally, managers fulfill an important coaching role whenever they model continual development for their team members. You do this whenever you open up to your people and share your own development goals, show them that you are willing to take on new work challenges, or invite their feedback regarding any actions they feel that you could take to become a stronger leader.

CHAPTER TWO

HOW TO IMPLEMENT COACHING

How to Build a Strong Coaching Relationship

Framing the Dialogue

Even after you have explained the purpose of developmental coaching and discussed the approach that you will be using, you will find that some of your team members might be hesitant to seek out your advice as a developmental coach. There are several reasons why people are sometimes reluctant to approach their managers for help on their careers. Some of your direct reports may feel that if they ask you for help, you may view them as weak and indecisive. For others, if their only experience with "coaching" is the heavy-handed feedback that typically accompanies a performance review, then they will naturally view the development discussion as just another situation in which they will be placed under a microscope and minutely evaluated. In addition, if you are buried in work, your team members may be reluctant to impose upon your busy schedule. Finally, some of your best and brightest direct reports may be considering career and development goals that would eventually move them out of your work group or department. These individuals may be concerned that you might view their career choices as a sign of disloyalty.

175

You can take a few simple steps to nullify these concerns. First, put people at ease by explaining to them the difference between performance coaching and developmental coaching. Also, emphasize that you are extending the offer of coaching assistance because you feel that they have leadership potential. In addition, present coaching as an optional, rather than a mandatory process. Let them know that, while you are extending the invitation to meet with them, you will leave it up to them to determine if, or when, they decide to follow through on this invitation.

To put career planners more at ease, try to hold your initial coaching discussions at a location other than your office. A private, quiet area, such as a conference room, can provide a more relaxed meeting place. If you are worried about being distracted by walk-in visitors or other interruptions, consider conducting the discussion over lunch. If your schedule is too hectic to accommodate an hour for lunch, invite your team member to come in early one morning so that the two of you can conduct your first coaching discussion over breakfast. I strongly advise not to conduct your first discussion at the very end of the day, with both of you are more likely to feel stressed out and fatigued, and particularly not on a Friday afternoon.

The Most Important Thing: Listening

Over the next few chapters I will share some suggestions for managing each phase of the development process, but for now let me suggest that the most important thing that you can do during the first session is to *listen in a non-judgmental way*. Unfortunately, sometimes managers feel that they have to come up with the "right" answers or be able to immediately provide solutions to all of the questions and concerns that are presented by the career planner. As a result, a well-intended coach may end up jumping in prematurely with advice giving and action planning, even before a career planner has had the opportunity to do in-depth thinking about her career goals and development needs. The result is a development plan that ends up looking like a simple "check-in-the-box" exercise and which soon degenerates into a set of very superficial development activities.

The best way to safeguard against these misgivings is to use a lead-in that frames the discussion in a positive, comfortable way and encourages the career planner to do most of the initial talking. Three examples are described below.

- "Dave, last week you mentioned that you were having a difficult time choosing between a couple of career targets. Could you tell me a little bit more about that? I would be interesting in hearing your thoughts."

- "Keri, I want you to know that I think that you are an excellent performer who has the potential to do a lot more in our company. Before now we haven't really had the chance to pull back and talk about your development plans. I would really like to hear more about what you are looking for, both in terms of your long-term career goals and some of the development actions that you would like to complete over the next year."
- "Tina, you had mentioned that working through the Participant's Guide forced you to stop and reexamine some of the assumptions that you had previously held about your career. It sounds as if you have really given this subject some serious thought. I'd like to hear more about that."

How to Make the Best Use of Questions

Managers sometimes view the initial development discussion as a data extraction process in which they have the responsibility for pulling out isolated pieces of information that they feel are particularly important. When this happens, they tend to present career questions in a rapid-fire sequence and end up taking over the discussion:

Coach: "You mentioned that at some point you would be interested in shifting from a role in product development to sales. Exactly what position are you looking for?"

Client: "I'm not exactly sure, I guess that. . . ."

Coach: "Well, I know of only three sales positions that would represent promotional opportunities for you—the Sales Support Director, the Field Sales Director, and Director of Large Account Management, so it's got to be one of those. So which is it?"

Client: "Umm. … I don't know. Field Sales Director, perhaps?" (As he looks to his manager for confirmation.)

Coach: "That might make sense. How many years of product development experience do you have again?"

Client: "Five."

Coach: "But no direct sales experience or background in field operations, is that right?"

Client: "Right."

Coach: "So let me ask you another question. …"

While this kind of rapid-fire, interrogational interview approach might be appropriate for a fraud or murder investigation, it works against the goals of the development coaching process. It will not only put a career planner on the defensive, but it will also discourage that person from taking accountability for his own development. If you were to watch this type of conversation through a one-way mirror, you would see that as the discussion progressed the career planner would become more and more quiet and passive. In contrast, the manager would appear to take on more and more of the responsibility for thinking ahead to the next set of questions, digesting all of the data bits, and regurgitating this information back as advice and counsel.

A more effective approach is to think of the career discussion as part of a life story that is slowly woven together by the career planner. Like any good story, it has a start ("where I've been in my career"), a middle ("how I view my current job situation"), and an ending ("where I envision myself headed in the future"). It is in the telling of the story that the storyteller is able to piece it together in a thoughtful way, extract personal meaning from it, and use it to construct his chosen future. Seen from this perspective, the coach's objective is to encourage the story to unfold. To accomplish this, it is more effective to make use of a few very general open-ended questions that encourage a career planner to pull together his thoughts in a coherent whole. These types of questions tend to be very simple:

- (To a person who throws out a one-word response) "Could you tell me a little more about that?"
- (To a person who suddenly stops talking or who stumbles over his words) "That's OK. We are not in any rush here. Take the time you need to put your thoughts in order."
- (To a person who uses nebulous words to describe her situation) "When you say … what exactly do you mean? What kind of picture comes to mind for you as you hear those words?"

The Why and How of Unpacking Terms

During developmental coaching conversations, team members may use terms that are rather vague and can be interpreted in very different ways. Consider the following statements:

- "I want to develop more *executive presence*."
- "I feel that I am very *strategic* as a leader."
- "It's important for me to move into a job area that fully *engages* me."

In each statement the italicized words are rather nebulous and don't convey a clear picture of what the individual is thinking. As a coach you can help bring more precision into your coaching conversation by encouraging career planners to "unpack" their terms. This means clarifying what this term truly means to them. Examples would be:

- "When you say that you want to develop more executive presence, tell me what you mean by that."
- "You mention that it is important for you to be seen as being a strategic leader. What does being 'strategic' look like for you?"
- "You mentioned that it is important to you to move into a job area that fully engages you. When you think about that, what kind of picture comes to mind?"

Getting employees to unpack their terms helps you to see more clearly the thoughts and feelings that lie behind the words. Having performed coaching for many years, I have discovered one other interesting thing about this technique: it can also force the speaker to reflect more deeply on her own words. In doing so, quite often the person generates a much more vivid and useful picture of the future that she is attempting to create.

How to Clarify Roles

I had mentioned before that some of your team members may assume that, as their coach, you will assume the responsibility for laying out a detailed, step-by-step career path for them or that you will guide them in making the "right" career choices. If the members of your work team have read the Participant's Guide, this situation will be less likely to occur, since the guide clearly places the primary accountability for development planning back on the career planner. Having said that, during the first career session it is always useful to clarify how far your responsibility extends as a coach, and what the coaching role entails. One way to do this is to make use of the Career Accountability Model shown in Figure 2.1.

At the start of your first career discussion with someone, draw this figure on a whiteboard and use it as a framework for discussing your role as a coach. During the early part of your discussion, list under each circle those development actions that you feel are the responsibility of the coachee, versus those that you will assume as the coach. You can also use this graphic to indicate those factors that are beyond the control of either

LEADER'S GUIDE

FIGURE 2.1. The Career Accountability Model

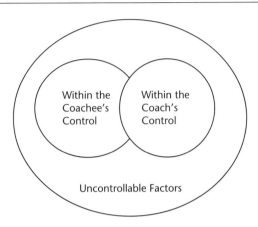

Within the Coachee's Control

Within the Coach's Control

Uncontrollable Factors

of you and are, by definition, outside the scope of a developmental coaching session. For the coachee, typical responsibilities may involve:

- Reading through the Participant's Guide and completing the exercises
- Creating a written development plan
- Identifying short-term and long-term career goals
- Performing a self-assessment of leadership and professional strengths and development gaps
- Evaluating the strength of his professional network
- Performing a self-assessment of her personal brand (see Chapter 6 in the Participant's Guide)

For you as a coach, these responsibilities may involve:

- Reading through the Leader's Guide and completing the exercises
- Helping the career planner review and troubleshoot his development goals
- Working with the career planner to identify development actions that support her career goals while providing some benefit to your organization
- Providing the career planner with information that can be used to weigh the tradeoffs between alternative development options
- Sharing information you might have regarding the changing expectations that your organization holds for leaders at different management levels

- Mapping key stakeholders who could directly influence the career planner's development goals and discussing the most effective ways of working with each of these stakeholders

  Factors that lie outside of either of your control might include:

- Current staffing restrictions imposed by your organization
- HR policies regarding positions, titles, or grade levels
- Mandatory educational requirements for certain positions in your organization
- Compensation guidelines

By taking a few minutes to clarify respective roles and accountabilities, you can make certain that the career planner has a realistic set of expectations regarding the work that she will have to put into the development process and the degree of support that can reasonably be expected from you.

How to Give Developmental Feedback

At different times in the coaching process you will need to give the career planner developmental feedback. This is especially important when you want to help the career planner:

- Perform a realistic assessment of his most important strengths and development needs
- Accurately gauge the extent of those skill gaps that need to be addressed to meet short- and long-term career goals
- Understand those aspects of her communication style and leadership behavior that work for or against her personal brand
- Learn more about the roles that interpersonal style and leadership approach played in the outcomes of a key work project

One of the coaching challenges that we face is that most of the feedback that we give as managers usually occurs immediately after an employee's performance has gone off track or as part of an employee's annual performance review. As a result, team members are sometimes concerned that the coaching discussion will take the form of other feedback sessions; that is, it will be highly evaluative and judgmental and focus primarily on their weaknesses.

LEADER'S GUIDE

As a managerial coach, here are a couple of guidelines you can follow to encourage career planners to make the best use of feedback:

1. *Don't overdo it.* Instead of overwhelming the career planner with developmental feedback on every small task that the person performs, ask the individual to tell you the one thing that he would like to learn about his leadership or interpersonal style, business skills or technical skills, or project management expertise. Suggest that the two of you focus your discussion on jointly identifying one aspect of the selected area that works well for this person and another area that could benefit from improvement.

2. *Ask before you tell.* An important part of coaching is to encourage professionals to be more self-reflective, which involves the ability to periodically step back and objectively assess their performance from the perspective of their organizational stakeholders. The way to encourage this habit is to ask the career planner to describe his or her performance, before you offer your own observations. This also encourages self-accountability by sending the message that "You are an intelligent person who has some insight into your own behavior. You don't need me to explain you to you."

3. *Provide feedback that is descriptive rather than evaluative.* When providing feedback, describe what you observed or what you heard others observe about the individual's performance, and say why you think that it may or may not have been effective in that particular situation. Refrain from making comments that are personally evaluative; they come across as hostile, encourage defensiveness on the part of the listener, and don't provide a lot of informational value. Consider the following:
   Evaluative Feedback: "Your presentation didn't go over well."
   Descriptive Feedback: "I think you did a good job of gathering all of your facts together and you certainly knew the subject. The problem was that when your one-hour meeting was suddenly cut to twenty minutes you didn't condense your presentation and hit the high points. As a result, a few of the executives in that room told me that they were drowning in detail."

4. *Focus on the future rather than the past.* The problem with focusing on the past is that the past is over and done with. When we focus on the past in coaching, the career planner is likely to engage in a game of revisionist history and focus energy on justifying what has happened rather than move forward. Talking about the future forces the listener to learn

from his or her mistakes while preparing for similar upcoming events. An example is presented below:

Focus on the Past: "So, can you tell me why you missed the last two project milestones?"

Focus on the Future: "We agree that you missed the last two project milestones. Let's look ahead to next month when you are probably going to be working on the new software upgrade. Based on what you know now, what are a few things that you might do differently, both to keep the same situation from occurring and to keep close track of milestone slippage?"

Focusing on the future also means getting professionals to understand that, when you are providing them with feedback, you are taking into consideration not only their current jobs, but also the skills and competencies that they will need to display to succeed within future career targets. A first-line supervisor who reports to you may not understand why you are placing so much emphasis on the ability to work effectively across organizational silos, when the work group operates largely independent of other work functions. A future-focused feedback session would highlight how important these types of political negotiation skills are if the supervisor wants to convince others that she could perform well within the more politically challenging role of a middle manager. When providing feedback to a career planner, some future-focused questions that you might ask include:

- "Six months from now, if you are still [describe what the employee is doing that isn't working for her], how do you see the situation? What is likely to happen?"
- "What's the trend line? Left unchanged, is this area likely to resolve itself, stay the same, or get worse over time?"
- "When you look back to this situation six months from now, what do you want to be able to say to yourself about how you handled it?"

5. *Whenever possible, try to provide feedback in a learning situation rather than wait until performance consequences are on the line.* One of the ways that airlines mitigate risks is to expose pilots to a lot of nasty problems in flight simulators. In the same way, police departments try to minimize the injury rate of citizens and their officers by putting their officers through training that mimics the kinds of situations that they are likely to encounter when they respond to complaints involving domestic disputes. In the same way, you can accelerate learning and perform your

own risk mitigation by identifying learning situations that give the career planner a chance to try out skills in a safe environment. Examples include asking the individual to take you through a trial run of how he intends to approach an important sales call, asking her to meet with co-workers to conduct a walk-through of an upcoming presentation, or suggesting to him that he audio- or videotape himself practicing an upcoming negotiation session with a vendor. These types of learning situations don't have to be limited to the development of interpersonal skills. You could, as an example, have a career planner set up one-on-one meetings with influential leaders to obtain their feedback and advice on a proposed change management plan, before the person attempts to get a group of senior leaders to sign off on the plan.

6. *Break large feedback chunks down into bite-size bits.* For large projects that involve a complex series of steps that will extend over several months, don't wait three months to provide feedback. Instead, jointly agree on more frequent review points that will be linked to the completion of key milestones.

7. *Keep the feedback targeted and precise.* It is easy to be a little sloppy in our language, with the result that we may make comments that imply a blanket criticism of a team member's performance. A more useful approach is to provide targeted feedback that paints a clear and detailed picture of what you observed within a specific situation. The comment, "You need to be a little less argumentative when you are dealing with people" is fairly sweeping and suggests that an individual is consistently hostile and confrontational. This is probably not what the speaker is implying and provides little in the way of useful information that can help someone improve. A more targeted and precise version of this feedback might be to say:

"I notice that when you are working through issues with me or other managers or senior executives you can be very tactful in presenting your position, even when you strongly disagree with what the other person is saying. I am seeing something different happening when you are working with people at your own level. You try to force your views on them, and when they disagree with you your attacks can quickly become personal. Could you tell me how you see this situation?"

8. *Don't make yourself judge and jury.* If a team member seems reluctant to believe what you are saying about the need to improve in a given performance area, rather than argue the point see whether the two of you can identify a third individual who can provide an objective, dispassionate perspective on the situation. Chapter 7 describes the different

types of useful information that can be gained by having a career planner obtain feedback from you, another manager, an internal customer, or a co-worker.

Addressing Blind Spots

You are more likely to get in a car accident during those moments when another driver suddenly moves out of your field of vision. It is in those few seconds that you run the risk of crashing into something that you didn't know was there. In the same way, as work professionals, all of us have certain blind spots, areas in which we are completely ignorant of the impact that we are having on others, that make it difficult for us to successfully navigate through our workplaces. An important aspect of the coaching process involves helping career planners identify situations in which they are relatively unaware of how their behavior is viewed by and directly affects others. Let's take an example. Suppose that during a coaching session, Lisa, one of your team members, proudly describes how she directed a recent staff meeting.

"I did a great job of maintaining control," she says. "A couple of times during the meeting a few people started to go off track, but I quickly corralled them back in."

The problem that Lisa has neglected to mention, and that has been brought to your attention, is that in attempting to maintain control she continually interrupted and aggressively challenged some of the other people at that meeting.

Does Lisa have a blind spot when it comes to understanding whether she's competent to direct a team and help them work through difficult issues? The answer is that you won't really know until you have given her a chance to react to the feedback that you received about her behavior. If you find that Lisa didn't understand how she was coming across to other people at the meeting and wants to make certain that this kind of situation doesn't happen again, then your coaching efforts will focus on suggesting some other ways that she might handle those types of meeting facilitation issues.

You face a very different coaching challenge if, in response to your comments, Lisa tells you that what you are saying isn't a surprise to her, but that she doesn't believe that her performance is creating a problem for her. The coaching scenario now shifts to helping her understand how being perceived as a team leader and collaborator is essential to meeting her career goals. You face still another type of issue if Lisa agrees that her meeting facilitation style is creating problems for her, but also firmly believes that managing a team in a forceful and confrontational way is the only way that she can get results. In this situation, your coaching challenge is to help her test some assumptions about how to lead that will, if left unchecked, eventually blow up in her face.

The moral of this story is that, before you can begin to help someone strengthen a performance area, you first need to determine whether the area in question is a blind spot for the person. Your answer to this question will help you determine the type of coaching challenge that you are addressing and the steps you could take to provide coaching support and assistance.

Applying the Five Steps of the Coaching Process

The Participant's Guide takes career planners through a five-step process for accelerating their professional development. The next five chapters provide you with coaching tools for supporting your team members within each of these steps. Each chapter identifies those challenges that career planners face in completing that step, introduces actions that coaches can take to help career planners address these challenges, and explains how to avoid some of the most common pitfalls that you are likely to encounter in implementing these coaching actions.

The Five Steps to Accelerating Development

Identify the Gap: The first step involves identifying the most critical skill and knowledge gaps that the career planner need to close to achieve set development goals and to be prepared to assume broader organizational leadership responsibilities.

Build the Plan: The second step requires the career planner to build a targeted, highly efficient plan for meeting development needs, while helping the organization achieve solid business results.

Leverage Developmental Assignments: The third step is that the career planner applies guidelines for selecting, staging, self-managing, and tracking progress on important job assignments to obtain the greatest developmental advantage from those assignments.

Accelerate On-the-Job Learning: In the fourth step the career planner looks for ways to reduce the time required for learning by taking full advantage of alternative options for learning and using techniques for improving the efficiency of learning.

Manage Your Personal Brand: During the last step the career planner performs a self-audit on her personal brand to determine how this personal brand may be supporting, or working against, her professional reputation and those actions that can be taken to strengthen her personal brand.

LEADER'S GUIDE

CHAPTER THREE

HELPING OTHERS TO IDENTIFY DEVELOPMENTAL GAPS

The Challenges Faced by Career Professionals

During the last few years, many organizations have been forced to undergo a number of quick adaptations as they try to keep pace with changing customer requirements and competitive moves. These adaptations show up in a number of efforts to reorganize and build new organizational structures, including:

- The shift from decentralized to centralized structures (or the reverse)
- The shift from functional to brand-centric structures (or the reverse)
- The elimination or reduction of certain high-cost, back-end functions
- The attempted use of mergers and acquisitions to achieve larger market mass or vertical integration
- The whole-scale outsourcing or off-shoring of selected functions or entire product units

Many organizations have concluded that the success of such adaptive changes depends upon their ability to quickly develop or hire professionals who have the technical skill sets, work experiences, and leadership competencies needed to perform well in volatile business environments. For professionals who work in such fast-change work settings and who want to advance and grow on the job, the first challenge involves knowing where to start. This requires the ability to scan the business horizon and anticipate the types of skills and competencies that are going to become increasingly important to their organizations. It also means determining how these changing talent requirements are likely to translate into emerging opportunities for professional growth and advancement.

They then use this consolidated information to select a career target, that is, a position or leadership role and organizational setting that represents the next stage for their professional development. A career target could involve moving into a different job, but it could just as easily mean looking for ways to take on broader responsibilities within one's current job. To assess development gaps, effective career planners take a hard look at the skills, organizational knowledge, and job demands that characterize their career targets. They compare those factors with the set of skills and experiences that they bring to their current positions. They then attempt to define any development gaps as precisely as possible to allow themselves to set well-delineated developmental priorities.

How You Can Help

Some individuals have difficulty formulating well-defined career targets. While the goal of "moving into a broader leadership position" may sound reasonable, it is simply not detailed enough to provide a good anchor point for a professional development plan. By making use of a few open-ended questions (for additional guidelines, refer back to the examples provided in Chapter 2), you can encourage a career planner to put more thought into her gap analysis, to allow her to focus energy on a few key value-laden development actions.

Sometimes career planners undermine their development efforts by performing only a cursory review of potential career targets. They may, for example, automatically define a career target in terms of a job title, because that job is somewhat familiar to them and because it provides a readily assessable model. As a coach, you can help your team members perform a more in-depth gap assessment by encouraging them to reflect on what they think lies underneath a given job title. Some of the questions that you could ask might be:

- "Forgetting about job titles for a moment, what is it about this particular job that really excites you?"

LEADER'S GUIDE

- "Have you taken the time to look at other positions in our organization that would make similar use of your skills and experience?"
- "What comes to mind when you think of this job? Tell me a bit about what you have learned about it."

A related issue is that people tend to make career decisions in the abstract. During developmental coaching conversations I often hear my clients describe their career goals in vague terms such as wanting to "take on a more strategic leadership role in the company." Part of getting people to be more insightful about their own career needs is to encourage them to describe what they have encountered over the past few years in terms of job assignments, leadership roles, or work settings that, upon reflection, they recall as having been the most enjoyable and rewarding work experiences. The flip side of this is to be honest about those aspects of work that have proved to be the most tedious, stressful, and unfulfilling. One of my clients who held a leadership role within a non-profit organization had initially set her sights on a senior-level executive position in her organization. However, during our second discussion she reflected on the fact that the promotional opportunity would require her to spend most of her time in fund-raising activities and community outreach, job functions that she really didn't enjoy. Eventually, she decided to aim for a lateral position that would allow her to expand her skill base while giving her a lot more free time to pursue her personal lifestyle.

A related problem involves what I call career myopia, or the failure to look beyond short-term gains to carefully consider whether a proposed development activity or job move will support the individual's long-term career goals. As a developmental coach, look for opportunities to explore this area without directly challenging the career planner's development decisions, as I've illustrated in the following example:

- "I am interested in how you see this [proposed job move or development action] supporting your long-term career goals. Ten years down the road, where do you hope that this move will take you?"

Career planners may also fail to perform an effective gap assessment because they lack an accurate understanding of what it takes to succeed within certain organizational positions. They may, for example, underestimate the political finesse required to succeed within a chosen leadership role or be unaware that another position requires the ability to meet the contradictory priorities and expectations set by different senior stakeholders. Similarly, they may fail to realize that certain technical skills are beginning to emerge as "must haves" for anyone who hopes to progress down a certain organizational career path. You can be a big help here, both by sharing any information you might have regarding what it takes to succeed in different positions and by referring the career planner to others in your company who may be able to provide additional information.

Another valuable coaching action is to make certain that career planners are basing their conclusions about what it takes to succeed within certain positions on valid and timely information. They may, for example, be basing all of their conclusions on discussions with a single manager. If this manager has worked within the same function for many years and hasn't kept pace with changing job requirements, his career advice may be obsolete. In the same way, if your team members would like to interview other managers about what it takes to succeed within a certain leadership role, you can provide good coaching support by directing them to leaders who are respected as exceptional performers and strong career models.

A mistake that individuals frequently make during this first step is to define development gaps in terms of the types of technical skills or knowledge areas that they need to develop, while ignoring how they may need to develop in terms of leadership competencies and interpersonal skills. As a coach, you can help career planners broaden their investigation. Encourage them to take a hard look at how certain organizational moves require them to build new leadership skills or demonstrate their ability to perform within very different types of work settings. An excellent model to use in guiding this discussion is the leadership pipeline model developed by Ram Charan, Steve Drotter, and Jim Noel. In *The Leadership Pipeline,* the authors describe how leadership requirements change as one advances along major leadership moves, such as the move from middle manager to functional manager. More information on the pipeline model can be found in Chapter 2 of the Participant's Guide.

Another useful technique for helping career planners identify development gaps is the crucible model described in Chapter 2 of the Participant's Guide. This model shows professionals how to construct a composite profile of a career target by describing: (1) the leadership behaviors and technical skills required to perform well in a given job area, (2) the work context in which that job is performed, and (3) the performance measures against which success in that position is measured.

As a development coach, you can be a big help by encouraging career planners to weigh the respective tradeoffs associated with pursuing alternative career targets. The challenge here is that sometimes team members focus their attention on the most obvious features of a job move, such as status, a bigger office, an impressive title, or additional compensation. In doing so they are less likely to consider what they need to be willing to give up in making a move, such as the opportunity to work independently, greater flexibility in scheduling work, being able to perform work that is intrinsically rewarding, or the fact that the move requires the transition from working within a technical area that they love to investing more time on managerial and administrative duties.

One way to encourage a career planner to review the types of tradeoffs associated with different development options is to have him create a two-column sheet, listing the respective pros and cons of pursuing a particular development option. You can take this exercise a step further by challenging the person to highlight in green marker those pros and cons that are based on solid information and to mark in red those data points that reflect "best guesses" or untested assumptions. The career planner's immediate development action is to determine any steps that can be taken to transform unknowns into knowns.

Finally, keep in mind that a person cannot accurately gauge the size of a development gap unless she is able to form an accurate assessment of her current skills and abilities. In some cases, having overestimated the development gap that needs to be closed to reach a career target, your team member may falsely conclude that the challenge of bridging the gap is insurmountable. The more common scenario is that people tend to underestimate the amount of work and effort that they will need to invest in their own development to close certain gaps. In both cases, you can perform a valuable coaching role by providing career planners with detailed behavioral feedback on their current skills and on how they are viewed by key stakeholders in your organization.

Avoid These Coaching Pitfalls

When attempting to coach your people, be alert to the following pitfalls, and take the recommended steps to address them:

Making Your Career Priorities Their Career Priorities

Any development plan requires professionals to be able to weigh the potential tradeoffs between alternative career options. Examples include:

- Determining whether to pursue a job that provides a great promotional opportunity, but at the price of an undesirable relocation
- Determining whether to make the move from a relatively autonomous business unit to the political hotbed of the corporate office
- Determining whether to take on an exciting development project that would also require adding on a lot of hours to an already crowded workday

In all of these situations, most of us would tend to provide advice based on those tradeoffs that have worked for us in the past. We make these decisions based on what is most important to us—our unique set of personal needs and career aspirations. Unfortunately, this is one of the reasons why individuals are sometimes reluctant to approach their managers for career coaching. Career planners want support and assistance, but they don't want to be directed or pressured into making certain career choices.

In my own case, until recently I have tended to be a big risk taker. This has been reflected in such career decisions as leaving a Fortune 100 corporation to form my own consulting company, being willing to build out totally new work functions, and signing on with business units that were undergoing difficult turnaround situations. In each of these cases, I willingly gave up security and comfort to go after job opportunities that were incredibly challenging and intellectually stimulating. This consistent theme in my life—of risk and challenge over security—has worked well for me, but whenever I am coaching I am very much aware that if I am not careful I can easily direct my clients based on this personal value perspective.

As a managerial coach you face the same pitfall. To avoid it, hold back on giving your team member strong recommendations regarding the career choices that you would make if you were in that person's situation. Instead, help the individual identify the questions that he or she has to ask to more carefully consider all of the long-term implications of career choices. One tool that can prove helpful here is to make use of some of the open-ended questions that were introduced to you in the previous chapter.

A second technique involves graphically mapping career tradeoffs. Ask the career planner to talk about some of the most important tradeoffs that she has identified in framing her career choices; then place those as a split sheet on a whiteboard, with one side representing the "pros" for a decision and the other side the "cons."

As the person creates the list, make note of any tradeoff factors that you can identify that the career planner hasn't considered. For example, a team member may be excited about the idea of moving toward one career path because that option would give him a chance to be working with state-of-the-art technology. He lists the factor "opportunity to work with cutting-edge tech" on the "pro" side of his ledger. At the same time, he may not be considering the fact that professionals who work within this area have to spend a lot of their time and energy resolving conflicts between internal customer groups. Knowing that your team member dislikes dealing with conflict, you might call his attention to this factor and suggest that he add it to the "con" side of his list.

Jumping into Development Planning Prematurely

When helping others identify development gaps, the second pitfall that you should avoid is the temptation to jump into development planning prematurely. After engaging in a thirty-minute career discussion, it is easy to think that you have captured the essence of someone's development needs. You will certainly be able to put a few ideas down on paper, but at the cost of rushing into development planning and discouraging the career planner from engaging in a thorough self-review of her career needs and goals. An unintended by-product of moving to developing planning too quickly is that during this type of rapid-fire brainstorming coaches are more likely to take over too much of the responsibility for career planning.

To avoid this pitfall, suggest to your team member that the two of you restrict your first discussion to a review of key development gaps, as discussed previously in this chapter and Chapter 2 of the Participant's Guide. You can then devote your second coaching session to the construction of a development plan. By spacing these two discussions two to three weeks apart, you give the career planner an opportunity to revise her gap analysis and, if desired, to conduct interviews with organizational stakeholders.

The Golden Child Syndrome

A final coaching pitfall is something that I have termed the "Golden Child Syndrome." To help you to understand this pitfall, let me start by acknowledging that it is understandable that managers can sometimes be a little protective and even experience total denial when other organizational leaders give them critical feedback on their best performers. As an executive coach, I have seen many instances when, upon hearing that a star performer has acted in an insensitive or arrogant fashion, a manager's first reaction is to either deny the feedback ("There must have been some legitimate reason why she acted that way") or attempt to minimize its importance ("In the big picture, this is not a big deal. Overall, she's my strongest player"). When managers fall into this pitfall, the result is that they ignore vital feedback on leadership issues that could, if ignored, eventually derail a performer's success. Another damaging by-product of this pitfall is that it can cause other managers to be antagonistic toward the performer in question, because they fail to see that individual making an effort to alter behavior based on feedback. The final, most damaging outcome of the Golden Child Syndrome is that your star performer may subtly pick up on your protectiveness and interpret it as meaning that she is beyond the need for professional development. When this happens, it is easy for a professional to lapse into arrogance and insensitivity, two leadership traits that have been shown to be highly correlated with leadership derailment.

LEADER'S GUIDE

CHAPTER FOUR

HELPING OTHERS BUILD THEIR PLANS

Accelerated Development Starts with a Solid Plan

The second step for accelerating development involves constructing a written plan for closing identified development gaps. Chapter 3 of the Participant's Guide provides participants with details on how to work through this process, and in this chapter I'll provide suggestions for coaching your team members on the development planning process.

Before an individual can create a development plan, he first has to be able to clearly define his intended development outcomes or what he hopes to take away from those development actions. Ideally, he should select development options that help him to grow, while at the same time helping your company to achieve solid business results. In other words, if carried out effectively a professional's development plan should be fully integrated with, and supportive of, your team's annual performance objectives.

Along with defining development outcomes during this step, career planners also must apply some discipline to their planning process. This means being able to convert what typically starts out as a few vague and nebulous development goals into detailed, behaviorally detailed plans of action.

LEADER'S GUIDE

Because it is easy to come up with an extensive list of development actions and many of these actions may require substantial time and resource commitments on the part of the career professional and/or your organization, it is very important during this step to set developmental priorities.

We all know that planning is relatively easy; the tricky part is being able to effectively execute against plans. This means identifying concrete actions that will move development goals forward and determining the most effective sequence and timing for implementing selected development actions. Effective execution also involves having career planners develop methods for tracking progress against their plans and developing methods to calibrate their progress.

Finally, career planners must identify to whom within their organizations they can reach out for additional help and to determine which of their development actions can be initiated at their level and which will require assistance from you or other organizational stakeholders.

The Challenges Faced by Career Professionals

Several challenges typically emerge during this phase of the development process. Quite often career planners mistakenly assume that the development planning process begins with identifying the competencies or skill sets that they need to develop in order to move ahead. Every organization has its own special wish list of core leadership competencies, and while these lists are useful in supporting development planning, career planners should refer to them only after they have first identified the key demand features of next-level assignments. Simply put, a development plan should spell out how a leader needs to grow and develop in order to successfully meet more complex job roles or next-level positions. Examples would include the ability to develop an annual budget forecast, to negotiate multi-product sales with key corporate clients, or to develop HR plans that encompass multiple business units and geographic locations.

With this focus in mind, career planners should set their development goals. It's at this point that they often make a second mistake, creating development goals that are no more than a list of isolated learning activities (take a training program, read a book on leadership, attend a conference, etc.). A related problem is the tendency to want to quickly throw together a rather disconnected set of vague and intangible development goal statements, such as "I want to become a stronger, more influential leader." The challenge that career planners face is being able to translate these vague intentions into detailed development objectives. These objectives should focus not on activities, but on development outcomes. The test of an outcome-focused development objective is (1) it clearly explains what new skills and learning you will be able to apply to your current job or totally different work setting upon its completion and (2) the objective can actually be evaluated. In the case of the previous example, a more tightly defined development objective might read as follows:

- "I want to be able to develop a solid business case for any business initiative that I undertake, understand the best way to approach stakeholders to gain their support, and anticipate and develop plans for minimizing potential objections. If I am successful with this goal, I should be able to gain approval and signoff for those business initiatives that I undertake, while gaining the respect of key stakeholders."

The third challenge that career planners face at this point is being able to successfully execute on their plans. Let me borrow an analogy from the area of dieting and healthcare. Each year the publishing market is flooded with a potpourri of new books describing the latest and greatest diet fads. Well-intended people continue to buy these books in the hope that eventually they will stumble across some magic bullet that will enable them to effortlessly drop several pounds. I'm willing to bet that for many people who have failed to lose weight despite the array of dieting books on their shelves, the problem isn't the diet but the lack of a disciplined approach that supports sustained healthy lifestyle changes over an extended period of time. The bottom line is that anyone can create a plan, but the true artistry is developing a process for translating that plan into execution. In the case of development planning, this involves being able to create a realistic plan that takes into consideration one's time and resource constraints, while keeping development activities at the top of one's work agenda.

How You Can Help

Work professionals don't always know how to link their development plans back to the performance requirements of their organization. You can provide a lot of assistance here by helping team members to identify work challenges and projects that can serve as great developmental opportunities. This is particularly the case for development opportunities that are unknown to your team because they involve assisting a different department, working on a cross-functional project that spans functional silos, or providing project support to senior-level executives.

You can also challenge your team members to demonstrate the organizational payoffs that they feel will result from implementing their proposed development actions. I have seen many leaders gain the reputation of being corporate "lightweights" because they are seen by their senior executives as wasting their time (and the company's money) on development activities that don't appear to be even remotely connected to their ability to perform more capably in their jobs. As a coach, it can be helpful for you to point out to your team members how different development options may be regarded by their senior stakeholders.

Let's take the case of a sales leader who would like to develop skills in negotiating complex, large-revenue contracts with corporate clients. Given a choice, would the leader develop more from attending a sales conference or from assisting a more senior sales leader in the preparation of an actual contract negotiation?

In addition, quite often career planners make the mistake of attempting to pack too much into their development plans, with the result that they try to take on an unrealistic and unachievable wish list of development activities. As a coach, you can serve as a sounding board for them, by listening to their plans and encouraging them to identify those potential development actions most likely to yield a strong payoff for both themselves and your organization. The paradox here is that, while individuals have no trouble picking fifty small development activities, they tend to shy away from taking the risk of going after a major development objective that forces them well out of their comfort zones. A number of research studies, such as those cited in *The Lessons of Experience* (published by the Center for Creative Leadership), have shown that the work experiences that leaders say pushed their development the most were dealing with tough, complex situations, such as working with a struggling operation, building a work function or business from scratch, or directing a distributed work team. My point here is that, as a coach, you should encourage your team members to set their sights high. Whenever feasible, recommend that they address a big, complex, and difficult work challenge, rather than disperse their energy among small-risk, small-payoff activities that don't really test the limits of their abilities.

Still another coaching action is helping career planners assess the robustness of their development plans. This could mean helping them obtain greater yield from their development activities by rethinking the sequencing or timing of those activities. It could also mean helping them think through steps they could take to ensure that a few weeks after your discussion their development plans are not languishing in a file drawer somewhere, completely forgotten.

You can also help career planners identify those individuals they should approach for feedback on their leadership and communication styles. Quite often, exceptional performers focus so much on how they are regarded by their senior executives that they fail to solicit feedback from co-workers and internal customers. A career planner's co-workers are in a better position to observe how he or she collaborates on projects or resolves workplace conflicts, while internal customers have a lot to say about the degree to which performers work effectively across silos and build inter-departmental teamwork. As a coach, you can play a helpful role here by identifying five to ten people who can provide very different perspectives on the individual's performance.

A related coaching function is helping an individual make sense of any third-party feedback received if he or she has difficulty interpreting it. Take the following example:

Coachee: "I don't get it. You are saying that some of the managers in the other departments are telling you that I'm not being a team player. How can they say that when I put more effort into my work than anyone else on our team? I'm working seventy hours a week right now trying to get their deliverables to them on time. What more do they expect?!"

Coach: "I think the confusion here is that you are equating effort with teamwork. No one has a problem with your level of work effort and commitment, which everyone agrees is exceptional. From what I can piece together, I think that they are talking more about how you go about working through differences with other people on the team. Examples include sending out nasty emails or voicemails to people when you are upset with their unwillingness to meet their commitments or when you make comments to other people during meetings that could be taken as personal attacks."

A final role that you can play is to encourage your team members to leverage their strengths. It is easy for people to become so caught up in wanting to improve skill areas or behaviors in which they are deficient that they fail to consider those skills, abilities, and knowledge areas that set them apart from other people. As a starting point for exploring this issue, ask yourself:

1. "What is it that this person does that sets him apart from other people in his work area and that is highly valued by my organization?"
2. "Is he making full use of that capability in his current role? If not, how could his job be redesigned or what other leadership roles could he fill in our company that would take full advantage of these unique capabilities?"

Case in Point: Charlotte

Let's consider the case of Charlotte, which illustrates how coaches can encourage career planners to leverage their strengths. Charlotte was a first-line leader who had identified as a weak area in need of improvement the difficulty she had in creative problem solving. As part of her development plan, Charlotte expressed an interest in taking part in a process improvement team that would be working over the course of a year to test and implement a new enterprise-wide software system across her company's several businesses. With this "weak area" in mind, Charlotte approached her manager and suggested that they explore ways in which she could contribute to the improvement team during its initial brainstorming stage. While Charlotte's manager was supportive of this idea, he also pointed out that the project gave her the perfect platform for showcasing her strong suit, which was the ability to anticipate potential roadblocks to projects and plan effective work-around strategies.

He suggested that, while there were some techniques that they could explore to strengthen her ability to contribute to the team's problem-solving efforts, she could play a major role during later project stages when the team would be faced with difficult project milestone reviews. During those project tollgate sessions, team members were expected to assess the impact of unanticipated project roadblocks and establish risk-mitigation procedures for keeping the project on track and on cost. This was Charlotte's forte. Once she shifted her attention to becoming a more creative problem solver, it helped establish her reputation in her company as being a results-focused project leader.

LEADER'S GUIDE

Avoid These Coaching Pitfalls

When attempting to implement coaching during this step, be alert to the following pitfalls and take the recommended steps for addressing them:

Fuzzy Communication

At the start of their planning process individuals tend to describe their development goals and plans in vague and fuzzy ways. As coaches we can unintentionally exacerbate this problem when we take the same verbal shortcuts. The result is that, as we engage in a coaching dialogue, we run the risk of drifting further away from understanding the person we are coaching, because we make assumptions about what the coachee is thinking that are untested and unfounded. Here is an example:

Coachee: "One of the ways that I want to develop is to become a stronger leader." [Unknown to the coach, when the coachee uses the term "stronger leader" she is talking about her desire to come across more skillfully when presenting ideas or negotiating issues with her co-workers.]

Coach: "I'm glad you brought that up. I agree with you completely. If you want to be able to move into a middle management role, becoming a stronger leader is probably the one area that would provide the greatest payoff to your development." [Unknown to the coachee, when the coach uses the term "stronger leader" he is referring to the fact that the coachee needs to be able to set more challenging performance standards for people in her work team and to hold them more accountable for their performance.]

Left unchecked, it is quite possible that the career planner and her manager could agree that "becoming a stronger leader" is a valid development goal, with neither of them realizing how very differently they interpret this goal statement. To avoid this pitfall you should follow the guidelines that were introduced in Chapter 2 of this Leader's Guide for unpacking language during coaching discussions, so that career planners specifically describe what it is that they are attempting to accomplish through their development plans.

The Heir Apparent Syndrome

Another pitfall is falling into the "heir apparent syndrome." In this situation a manager makes statements to a team member that imply that this individuals is the inevitable replacement candidate for the manager's job or for another promotional opportunity within the organization. The heir apparent syndrome creates several problems for both the manager and the direct reports. It creates false expectations on the part of employees, since in most situations a number of people, including one's senior managers and the company's HR leadership, weigh in on these types of promotional decisions.

Most importantly, however, this situation will stunt the development of even the best employee. At times in my coaching career, I have heard managers indicate that little more in the way of development is required of a particular team member because that person is "fully developed" or "has the complete package." Generally, these types of statements signal the employee that he has gone as far as he needs to in his professional development and is ready to advance in position. Apart from engendering an unhealthy arrogance on the part of the employee, people who receive these kinds of messages tend to place themselves on cruise control and become more complacent in their work. Their attitude—that they are simply waiting for a promotional opportunity that they fully deserve and which has been promised to them—is fairly transparent to others who work with them and tends to create resentment from co-workers, who can typically discern when someone in the group is receiving preferential treatment and attention.

Not Taking a Systems Approach

The last pitfall I want to mention is the failure to take a systems approach in development planning. Throughout this book the focus is on how you can maximize your coaching efficiency with individual team members. In real life you have a number of people who report to you, and you can often leverage developmental planning by looking for a single action that can simultaneously support the development of two or more team members. Here are three examples:

1. You can pair more experienced people with less experienced people on the same project, giving the more experienced team members opportunities to build leadership and development skills as they guide

their co-workers on the project. At the same time, their less experienced counterparts accelerate their own development by observing exemplar models who can provide them with immediate feedback and coaching on their work.

2. If several of your team members are working together on a project, you can ask them to conduct peer reviews in which they rotate presenting their portions of the project responsibilities to their co-workers, who help them troubleshoot their work.

3. If you send one of your team members to an outside conference or seminar, make that person responsible for conducting lunch-and-learn sessions during which she debriefs the rest of your team on those conference presentations that are most applicable to your work team. The same approach can be applied when you send one team member away to conduct a best-practice review at another organization.

Reference

The Lessons of Experience: How Successful Executives Develop on the Job. (1988). Morgan McCall, Michael Lombardo, and Ann Morrison. New York: The Free Press.

LEADER'S GUIDE

CHAPTER FIVE

HELPING OTHERS LEVERAGE DEVELOPMENTAL ASSIGNMENTS

The Challenges Faced by Career Professionals

A major part of any professional's development occurs when that person takes on a job assignment that provides sufficient challenge, while exposing him or her to totally new aspects of the organization's operation. In addition, a well-considered job assignment provides an individual with a "taste test" of what it might be like to work within a totally different job context or leadership role. If they are challenging enough, job assignments can also provide professionals with methods for testing the upper limits of their leadership and technical skills and for forcing the accelerated development of those skills.

At the same time, large job assignments are inevitably accompanied by certain risks. Big assignments may represent the first time that one of your team members comes to the attention of senior managers. Since the most important job assignments are associated with significant performance expectations, your team member will be closely observed by many people in your organization. Success or failure on these assignments can strongly shape your team member's professional reputation. These project outcomes can also reflect directly on you as that individual's manager.

Another consideration is that, since many assignments require people to manage work efforts across different departments or divisions or with outside customers or vendors, the way in which your team members handle

LEADER'S GUIDE

these projects can directly affect organizational work relationships. In other words, when a member of your team steps up to take on a major job assignment, you need to be able to count on that person to act as a goodwill ambassador to those other work groups on which you depend for support and assistance.

Unfortunately, occasionally individuals invest a lot of time and energy undertaking job assignments without showing any substantial professional growth or learning. At times this is because the job assignee and the manager have become so focused on the instrumental value of the assignment that they completely overlook its power as a developmental vehicle. At other times, although the intent for learning is there, the assignment is managed so poorly as to waste a great developmental opportunity. Poor project management can decrease an individual's standing with others in the organization and leave that person feeling less confident in his abilities.

When we ask ourselves what it is about a job assignment that determines whether it is truly developmental, the answers lie in examining how professionals handle the four steps of the job assignment process. The first step is selecting an assignment that provides an appropriate level of developmental stretch and that represents a good balance between the individual's baseline skill level and development needs. The second step is effectively staging that assignment so that the assignee and the manager are in alignment about the assignment's purpose and intended outcomes as well as the resources needed to support it. Since professionals often have to figure out ways for taking on job assignments while maintaining their other work responsibilities and large assignments may extend over a period of several months, individuals also must be adept at managing assignments. Finally, one of the most significant opportunities for development occurs after an individual has concluded a job assignment and has the opportunity to reflect on what he has taken away from the experience. For this reason, an important part of turning a job assignment into a development vehicle is how a professional and his manager use debriefing sessions to follow up on the assignment.

How You Can Help

In the following sections I have listed several steps you can take to coach your team members as they progress through selecting, staging, managing, and following up on a job assignment.

LEADER'S GUIDE

Selecting the Assignment

Sometimes people are attracted to job assignments for the wrong reasons. They may hear of a major work project that is being personally sponsored by a senior executive and automatically decide that this is their big opportunity. They can also become so infatuated with the challenge of working on an interesting technical problem that they don't stop to consider the extensive time commitments that will be required of them. Finally, they may not consider whether the project is the best match to their development needs.

As a coach there are several actions you can take to ensure that your team members select the most relevant and applicable assignments. First, you can use your knowledge of your team members' work experience, skills, and additional work commitments to help them select assignments that are of a reasonable scope, that is, big enough to be challenging but not so large as to be overwhelming. You are also in a good position to help your career planners identify projects that extend beyond the boundaries of your own work team. Finally, you have a realistic appraisal of each of your team member's workload, so you can advise them about the feasible scope and timing of potential job assignments.

Occasionally, individuals volunteer for major projects without fully understanding the commitments that will be involved. I know of one individual who completely underestimated the degree of international travel that would be required to support a temporary project in the UK. Two months into the project, she was placed in the embarrassing position of requesting that she be allowed to back out of the project and turn her responsibilities over to someone else on her team. I have also witnessed a number of situations in which professionals have erroneously assumed that their managers would make significant reductions to their normal workloads to accommodate their involvement in large, time-consuming projects.

The key to avoiding these roadblocks is to engage in a serious discussion with your team member about these factors before he makes a commitment to take on a major job assignment. A great way to prepare for this discussion is to review the seven criteria for selecting developmental assignments, which are discussed in detail in Chapter 4 of the Participant's Guide.

LEADER'S GUIDE

The Seven Criteria for Selecting Developmental Assignments

1. The assignment fosters new skill development.
2. The assignment involves a high, but realistic, degree of stretch.
3. The assignment extends the professional's organizational knowledge.
4. The assignment requires the individual to perform without a safety net (it involves some risk).
5. The assignment provides a realistic job preview of a work setting or job challenge that is closely related to the individual's chosen career target.
6. The assignment expands the sources of feedback that are typically available to the individual (the assignee will have the opportunity to see how different people within the organization view their performance).
7. The assignment includes effective mentoring (it will give the assignee an opportunity to learn from a strong performer in your organization).

You can use these seven criteria as a selection grid for screening potential job assignments. If the person has more than one developmental assignment in mind, see whether the two of you can arrive at a relative weighting (5 to 1, with 5 being the highest) on each assignment, in terms of the assignment's ability to fulfill each of these criteria. If you rate the assignment on each of the seven criteria, all potential job assignments would score anywhere from 7 to 35. As a general rule of thumb, discourage your team member from taking on any job assignment that doesn't score at least a 25.

In Chapter 4 of the Participant's Guide, I identify the following eight types of leadership experiences that really push development. You can refer to this list when helping your team member identify a job assignment that is right for her.

Eight Key Leadership Development Experiences

- Working with messy problems
- Influencing without authority
- Thinking strategically
- Working with diverse groups of people
- Working across silos and functions
- Developing expertise beyond your function
- Managing through to execution
- Taking a broader perspective

In Chapter 4 of the Participant's Guide you will also find four tables that provide examples of how these eight different work experiences can assume different forms, depending on their scope of impact. Thus, we can classify job assignments into those that:

- Will be carried out within the scope of an individual's current job
- Involve coordinating efforts through other work groups or business units
- Extend across your entire organization
- Take place beyond the boundaries of your company (with outside customers, vendors, franchise groups, directing boards, professional associations, etc.)

Working through these four tables with your team member, you can brainstorm a variety of job assignments and select the one that provides the most appropriate degree of job scope and challenge.

As a final consideration, it is important to note that large, complex projects may require the efforts of a number of people over several months, with some members contributing more at different stages of the project. You can use this feature to help your team member determine that stage of a project that is most likely to represent a strong development opportunity for him. The list titled Leadership Competencies That Could Be Developed Through a BPO Process in Chapter 4 of the Participant's Guide provides several examples of the different types of development experiences that might be obtained by having a team member involved in different stages of planning and implementation for a business process outsourcing project.

Staging the Assignment

Once you have helped the career planner select an appropriate job assignment, your next coaching role involves working with her to stage and plan for the assignment. A good starting point is to make sure that you understand what your team member hopes to gain from participating in the assignment. If the assignment involves an extensive project, this is also your opportunity to share your views regarding what the career planner needs to focus on most throughout the course of the assignment:

Coachee: "So one thing that I hope to take away from this experience is working more diligently on my organizational skills so that I don't miss project milestones."

Coach: "Sounds good. Tell me a little more about what that means to you."

LEADER'S GUIDE

Coachee: "I guess it means being able to look more carefully at the time requirements for different project actions and determining how unanticipated roadblocks or obstacles could disrupt our project schedule."

Coach: "Kim, I agree that you are looking at a key element here, but I think that there are a couple of more important things that you may be missing. Until now most of the work that you have performed has been limited to our work function. Everyone on our team works together in the same office, and we know each other very well. That means that we all tend to be rather informal when it comes to restaging our project plans. If something slips, we simply pop into the next office and quickly renegotiate workarounds for correcting it. In contrast, the project that you want to work on is going to involve coordinating project steps across three countries, with time zone differences that extend up to fourteen hours. The other thing that you have to remember is that the other five members of the project team represent three corporate functions and two other operating units. This means that it is going to be very important for you to give the other project members early alerts on milestone changes or obstacles that could make it difficult to complete certain project steps. Otherwise, the other people on your team will find themselves in the embarrassing situation of making project commitments to their managers, only to find out later that the schedule has slipped. For that reason, it will be very important for you to be more disciplined in tracking all milestone changes, risks, and risk mitigation steps and immediately noting these events in the project plan that will be loaded into the share folder. You are also going to have to stretch quite a bit to keep everyone personally informed. At times, this may mean being willing to conduct a Skype or phone meeting at six in the morning or at ten at night to accommodate such a wide range of individual schedules.

"I know that this is a lot to think about, but if you really want to grow through your involvement in this project, you need to think it all the way through. How do you feel about what I've said?"

The other major coaching action you can take during the staging process is to work with your team member to negotiate the parameters for the assignment. The starting point for this discussion should be reaching agreement regarding both the amount of time that he or she will need to invest in the project and the project duration. Then discuss any adjustments that you would be willing to make to the career planner's workload in order to offset the additional time that will be needed to complete the job assignment. As I previously mentioned, one important project parameter concerns the timing of the assignment. As an example, the annual corporate closing period in December is probably not the best time for a finance or accounting manager to volunteer to be temporarily loaned out to another department.

A final consideration concerns identifying any travel costs, or other related costs, that would have to be assumed by your work group as a condition for participation in the project. For this purpose, if the project owner resides outside of your work function, reach out to this person to confirm the accuracy of the team member's understanding of the project scope and commitment. As an example, one of your team members may tell you that she wants to participate in a process improvement team. She assumes that the team will only be involved in mapping out trouble spots in the process and in suggesting recommended improvement actions for correcting those problems. The project's senior sponsors, however, may be expecting the team to obtain comparative benchmark data from other companies and to investigate industry best practices related to this work process. In addition, those senior sponsors may be expecting the project team to not only formulate recommendations, but also implement those recommendations and track their results. With the addition of each new step, the project will grow in duration, complexity, and in the time expected of team members.

Similarly, with projects that require the orchestrated efforts of several people, it is reasonable to clarify the role that the career planner will be playing on the project team. Alternative roles are those of project leader, meeting facilitator, project team member, subject-matter expert, or technical support.

Managing the Assignment

As your team member begins to manage the assignment, you can provide coaching support by helping him clarify aspects of the process that are likely to shape how the project will be used as a developmental vehicle.

To start with, ask your team member how he plans to gauge his developmental progress during the assignment. In the example shown earlier in this chapter, an important part of Kim's development plan involves strengthening her ability to track project status and to coordinate project

LEADER'S GUIDE

changes with her counterparts who are scattered around the world. If Kim is a strong performer, she will not wait until the project is over to discover how the other members of her team are reacting to her. Instead, she will look for ways to approach those team members for feedback on her performance throughout the course of the project. Also explain to the career planner how often you would like to meet with him to discuss project updates and to share how he is progressing on his development goals.

If the job assignment requires your team member to be temporarily assigned to another work group, you should discuss with the manager of that team the role that each of you will play in providing direction and management to your team member. This includes managing HR issues, such as leaves of absence, and whether the other manager will be expected to provide input to your team member's yearly performance review.

For temporary reassignments, a related coaching role you can play is to provide the career planner with guidance regarding the leadership and communication style of the manager she will be supporting. For example, it could be that your team member tends to struggle with presenting information in a crisp and concise way. At the same time you know that the manager she will be supporting has little patience with people who communicate in a cumbersome and convoluted manner. Knowing these two data points, you are in a position to coach your team member on how to streamline her communications to gain the support of the receiving manager.

For large projects that might extend over several months, you can provide great coaching assistance by helping the career planner identify those particular phases of the assignment that serve as a good test point of the skills and competencies that he is attempting to develop. Going back to our previous example, since Kim is attempting to build skills in managing and tracking project plans for a globally dispersed team, a good test point would be having her focus in on that project phase that is most likely to expose the team to the risks associated with milestone slippage or project setbacks. Knowing when this project phase is due to occur would enable you to put it on your calendar and set aside time during this period to provide Kim with a coaching and feedback session.

Following Up on the Assignment

Most organizations work at such a hectic pace that people tend to drop one project and immediately pick up another without pausing for reflection. This is unfortunate, since one of the most important learning points for any development assignment occurs during that brief period immediately following the completion of the job assignment when that experience is still fresh in our minds. For this reason it is really important for you to schedule a debriefing session with your team member. Without some guidance, the career planner is likely to walk into this session mentally focused on the project outcomes. While its important to discuss performance outcomes, you can help your team member learn more from this session by reflecting on the role that she played on the job assignment and how she was viewed by other people. In preparing for this discussion, you may want to ask your team member to think about the following questions:

- "What worked for you in this project in terms of how you presented yourself as a problem solver, influencer, team leader, and team partner?"
- "What did not work as you had hoped? Why didn't it?"
- "How do you feel the other people on this project felt about your interactions with them? What kind of impression did you leave with them?"
- "What were the greatest lessons you took away from this experience? How would you apply these lessons if you were placed in a similar situation in the future? What might you do differently?"

As you and your team members discuss his answers to the questions and develop a clearer picture of how he experienced the recent assignment, help him place the experience in context. It's a fact of life that some people will come away from a challenging work experience focusing only on what they did right, while others tend to worry excessively about relatively small problem points. Part of your job is to help the person achieve a more balanced perspective, particularly if the project in question required him to step up and address entirely new work challenges or to quickly develop new leadership or technical skills.

Before providing a career planner with feedback on a job assignment, you might find it helpful to go back to Chapter 2 of this Leader's Guide and review the differences between evaluative and descriptive feedback. Keep your feedback descriptive, and keep the focus of the discussion on what your team member has learned from the experience that could be applied to other work situations. You might also encourage your team member to discuss what she thinks she has learned from this experience related to both development goals and the chosen career target.

One way of ensuring that you provide your team members with a balanced perspective on their project outcomes is to encourage them to

LEADER'S GUIDE

solicit feedback from others who worked with them on the assignment. If you feel that it would be inappropriate for them to directly solicit feedback from any senior-level project sponsors, you can provide additional help by obtaining feedback from these individuals on your team member's performance. When doing this, try to direct the conversation so that you learn how the senior person viewed the end performance of your team member, as well as any general impressions that the senior leader had of the team member. This may include information on the following:

- Your team member's communication style
- Whether the team member gained the reputation of being supportive of the team
- The degree to which the person came across as being organized and knowledgeable about the details of the project
- Whether he was viewed as a passive follower or an active leader
- How much effort she extended on the project
- How he appeared to cope to project setbacks
- How flexible and adaptable she was when faced with project changes in scope, timing, or unanticipated obstacles

Avoid These Coaching Pitfalls

When coaching during this step, be alert to the following pitfalls and take the recommended steps for addressing them:

Sink-or-Swim Scenarios

Sometimes managers feel that the best learning comes when people are thrown into almost overwhelming situations and left to fend for themselves. To some point, stretch is good, but there is a difference between taking on a stretch objective and feeling as if you are being stretched on the rack. When selecting challenging work projects for your team members, think carefully about how far the proposed project assignment is from the person's baseline skill level. The greater the level of challenge, the more likely it is that the career planner will need a little encouragement and support from you at some stage in the process. A simple: "I have confidence in you; I know you can do this" goes a long way toward encouraging someone to tackle something that he has never before attempted.

Chewing Their Food for Them

The flip side of the first pitfall is placing yourself in a situation in which you decide to take any steps necessary to ensure that your team member doesn't fail on the project. The most effective coaching approach is to ask a lot of questions that push the career planner's thinking, bring his attention to project management issues that he may have overlooked, and advise him on how to manage and approach key stakeholders. Try to avoid making key decisions about how to proceed on the project or wading so far into the details of the job assignment that he finds that most of his thinking has already been done for him. In addition, don't run interference for your people by attempting to rationalize or explain away their poor performance or ineffective behavior to other senior managers. Accept all feedback and file it away for later discussion with your team members. If you feel that during a job assignment a team member is acting in a way that is harming her professional reputation in your organization or is damaging important work relationships, then tell her that you expect her to take immediate actions to correct the situation. Feel free to use techniques such as practice or role-play sessions to help the person feel comfortable with experimenting with different approaches to issues, but leave the final accountability for correcting situations with him or her.

Making Assumptions

Whenever a team member volunteers for a cross-functional project or to be loaned out to another team or senior leader, it is always wise to discuss the assignment with the manager who will be leading that project assignment. In particular, confirm everyone's understanding of the team member's role, project time commitments, duration of the project, outcomes, and success measures.

Death by Project Overload

Having been an internal OD/LD executive for several companies, I have found that every company has its "short list" of a few key high-potential leaders they would like to sign up for every conceivable committee, project, and business initiative. Quite often, those superheroes, who are the center of attention, feel strong commitments to their managers and organizations, and they don't want to feel as if they are letting people down by turning away project assignments. This is where you come in. As your team members add challenging work projects to their plates, realistically assess how much work they can put on their plates at any one time. Keep in mind that if you want them to treat job assignments as learning experiences, they need to be able to pull back occasionally to reflect on their own performance and leadership style, and they can't take the time to do this if they are frantically jumping from project to project. You may also have to run interference for them by letting other organizational leaders know when one of your team members is overextended and simply can't take on any additional projects.

Pushing Too Much

At times you will be frustrated because one of your team members just doesn't seem motivated to take on a job assignment that you view as an incredible development opportunity. If the bottom line is that you need to get a job done and he is the person to do it, then your decision is very simple. He is in the game, regardless of how he feels about it. But if the job assignment goes beyond the typical boundaries of the employee's job, I recommend that you put the potential assignment on the table and leave it up to him whether to act on it. This book is based on my assumption that you are focusing your development efforts on your strongest players—people who feel that they have the potential to move ahead and grow on the job. So treat this situation as a test—if you find that certain team members continue to shy away from taking advantage of development opportunities because those opportunities are too risky or require too much effort, then you may draw the conclusion that perhaps you were wrong in your original assessment of their leadership potential.

CHAPTER SIX

HELPING OTHERS ACCELERATE ON-THE-JOB LEARNING

Building Learning-Agile Leaders

So far we have discussed how career professionals can build a solid framework for accelerating their development by identifying development gaps, constructing a development plan, and leveraging developmental assignments. With this framework in place, they can look for ways to accelerate learning on the job. Chapter 5 of the Participant's Guide shows career professionals how to accelerate learning by (1) performing an honest self-assessment of their learning agility, (2) taking advantage of all possible avenues for learning, and (3) increasing the efficiency of their learning process. In the remainder of this chapter we will review the challenges that career planners face in implementing each of these actions and how you, as a coach, can help your team members effectively address these challenges.

As a starting point for discussion, it might be helpful to start by defining the term "learning agility." The construct of learning agility should not be confused with that of general intelligence. I am sure that you know people who, although very smart, nevertheless continue to act and perform in ways that serve neither themselves nor their employers. In contrast to this, *learning agility* can be defined as an individual's ability to quickly adapt to new situations and to learn and profit from experience. While I won't provide a detailed explanation of learning agility in this chapter (a thorough overview can be found in the first section of Chapter 5 of the Participant's Guide), research from one management consulting group, Lominger Limited, suggests that learning agility can be broken down into the following four key components:

The Four Components of Learning Agility

Mental Agility—The degree to which individuals examine problems from innovative perspectives, work well with problem complexity and ambiguity, and are able to discern meaningful patterns in information.

People Agility—The degree to which individuals work well with diverse groups of people, remain calm and composed when confronted with volatile situations, exhibit a high degree of self-knowledge, and are flexible in their willingness to assume a variety of work-related roles.

Results Agility—The degree to which individuals exhibit a high degree of drive, deliver on results when placed within challenging situations, and inspire confidence in others.

Change Agility—The degree to which individuals exhibit a high degree of curiosity, enjoy experimenting with innovative ideas, and are able to introduce new perspectives to work challenges.

The Challenges Faced by Career Professionals

While the starting point for accelerating on-the-job learning is forming a clearer picture of one's learning agility, several factors make this first step particularly difficult. The first is simply the speed at which we work. During the day I am sure that you have your hands full attempting to juggle conflicting priorities, wrestle with sticky problems, and stay one step ahead of your jammed Outlook calendar and overloaded email account. For people who are operating within this type of fast-paced work environment, it can be difficult to step back from the work and reflect on how they are going to achieve results and the degree to which they are actually adapting to, and learning from, new work experiences.

The second challenge we face is being able to objectively and dispassionately self-assess our own learning agility. Such objectively is hard to achieve because learning agility has less to do with how we process and synthesize information and far more to do with how we apply what we learn to behavioral adaptations to our workplace. In other words, the real measure of our learning agility is not how effectively we acquire new information and skills, but rather the degree to which we change as professionals and leaders as a result of these learning experiences. Seen from this perspective, our degree of learning agility is revealed through such things as our ability to bounce back from setbacks, adapt to new work situations, experiment with new ways to resolve conflicts, examine problems from fresh perspectives, and incorporate others' views into our decisions, all of which are difficult to objectively evaluate.

The third challenge we face is selecting from the wide array of things we could potentially learn on the job those few areas that are absolutely essential to our continued development. Simply put, at the end of the day we have to be able to make hard decisions about how much expertise we truly need to build within different work areas and skill sets.

A related problem involves not knowing where to focus our attention when looking for ways to strengthen our performance as learners. I sometimes find that coaching clients can be locked into learning approaches that, while perhaps useful in their past, aren't well suited to new job challenges or next-level job assignments. The case at the end of this section about Carol, one of my coaching clients, provides a good illustration of this problem.

When it comes to exploring avenues to learning, another challenge is getting stuck in a rut. Over time each of us finds that certain learning approaches, such as self-study or modeling, work particularly well for us. The trick is to know when we are in a situation that requires a new avenue for learning. As an example, as middle managers advance into functional leadership roles, they are suddenly three or four levels from much of the ground-floor work of their operations, much of which is totally new to them and outside their areas of expertise. Faced with this situation, some new functional leaders attempt to become overnight experts in all areas of their operations. Others take the more pragmatic approach of focusing on how to interpret certain key performance indicators that can keep them alerted to how their business is performing and how to evaluate the quality of the key outputs and deliverables generated by their function. In the latter case (which is the only realistic path to success), they have to shift away from being knowledge experts to figuring out the best way to learn from, and leverage, the collected knowledge of those who report to them.

LEADER'S GUIDE

Chapter 5 of the Participant's Guide introduces career planners to six different learning approaches: organizational training, professional conferences, formal education, self-directed learning, shadowing and modeling, and the use of practice runs. A quick review of this information can help you determine which of these approaches might be most applicable to your team members' development needs.

The final challenge professionals face in attempting to accelerate their on-the-job learning is to look for ways to increase the efficiency of their learning process. Chapter 5 of the Participant's Guide introduces participants to nine techniques for increasing learning efficiency. While several of these techniques can be implemented directly by the career planner, three of them—calibrating learning requirements, conducting after-action reviews, and making use of naturally occurring events—require your assistance, and for that reason they are discussed in the following section.

Case in Point: Carol

Carol was a VP of operations within a major healthcare company. Seen from one perspective, Carol was a strong learner. During her fifteen-year journey through finance and operations, Carol had established the ability to develop the people within her work team. During the eight years that she had been with her current employer, she had gained a reputation for being incredibly adept at identifying and quickly attacking any process and business problem that emerged in her work function. She was also respected for having the ability to quickly acquire the new technical skills and functional knowledge that she needed to step into new leadership roles. Carol prided herself on being a strong self-directed learner. She was extremely intelligent and when confronted with a difficult learning challenge would lock herself in her office surrounded by reports, technical manuals, and spreadsheets until she had mastered what she needed to learn.

The issue that brought Carol to executive coaching first came to the attention of her CEO after her company had decided to consolidate operational processes from their existing operating units and from two small business acquisitions. The company had in place a three-year plan for bringing all operations functions under a single structural umbrella. During the interim period, they were counting on Carol to work with their small business acquisitions to arrive at agreed-on procedures for how to manage those operational processes that directly touched the company's patient base.

It was at this point that Carol's problems became apparent. While she could easily master learning when she was working within any situation in which she held final control, she found it extremely frustrating to orchestrate and negotiate process changes in situations in which she lacked authority. When working through complex issues with the other businesses, she tended to forcibly state her position concerning the "right way" to resolve those issues. If the other business unit leaders didn't immediately accede to her views, she quickly found herself embroiled in conflict.

When I explored this situation with Carol, it was easy to see that one of the problems she faced was her record of success up to this point. After all, in this new situation she was simply applying the leadership approaches that had worked so well for her before. My first challenge was getting her to understand that the operations manager who would eventually emerge as the head of the new consolidated organization would need to be a leader who could build a coherent team out of the current patchwork of operational functions. That, in turn, required the ability to manage through conflict, to look for ways to collaborate on reaching common objectives, and to communicate effectively with different people (all of whom had a great deal of pride in their own operations groups).

When examined from the perspective of learning agility, one could say that, while Carol was high in mental agility and results agility, her big challenges lay in strengthening her people and change agility. She was a strong learner as long as she controlled the flow of information and could take the time to go offline and master things by herself. On the other hand, she had a more difficult time when she was dependent upon others to share information and jointly explore solutions to problems.

How You Can Help

Help Calibrate Learning Requirements

The first step you can take to help your team members accelerate their on-the-job learning involves helping them calibrate their learning requirements. People sometimes have difficulty estimating how skillful or knowledgeable they will need to become within certain areas to succeed. Chapter 5 of the Participant's Guide lists four different skill levels, from novice to master. As a coach you can provide valuable developmental coaching assistance by helping your team members use this list to set learning priorities that best support their development and career goals.

Another way to help your team members calibrate their learning requirements is to encourage them to focus on learning outcomes rather than learning activities. If, for example, a team member will be attending a professional conference, require that person to set learning goals for the event. What two things will he bring back from the conference that he will attempt to apply to his work? Is he willing to conduct a lunch-and-learn with the rest of the team to share what he's pulled out of a conference session?

Help Assess Learning Agility

You can also provide coaching assistance by pointing out to team members how certain work-related behaviors can be interpreted as reflecting a high or low degree of learning agility. To prepare for this discussion, first familiarize yourself with the section entitled "Questions You Can Ask to Evaluate Your Learning Agility" in Chapter 5 of the Participant's Guide. During your discussion, ask your team members to tell you how they answered these questions, then share your own responses.

Chapter 5 also includes a description of the CHOICES® multi-rater assessment that can be purchased through Lominger Limited. This 360-degree assessment instrument has been specifically developed to help professionals self-assess their learning agility in terms of a wide range of behaviors. It also allows them to compare their self-assessment with feedback provided by their peers, internal customers, and you, their manager. The instrument can be very useful if you want to provide your team members with targeted feedback on their approaches to learning.

You will sometimes encounter situations in which team members appear resistant to any feedback you provide on their learning agility. This type of resistance may come out in such comments as:

- "That may be how they see me, but it's not valid because they really don't know me."
- "If they really understood me, their views would be different."
- "How can someone else comment on my learning agility when he can't look into my mind and know how I think?"

If you encounter this situation, remind your coachee that an important part of her professional brand—the reputation she forms with others—has to do with the degree to which others view her as being learning agile. Lacking the ability to read her thoughts, other people are forced to draw conclusions based solely on what they observe in terms of the individual's behavior. If a team member's first response to difficult organizational changes is to complain about how those changes are being managed or to make cynical comments about why he thinks those changes will not be successful, then he isn't going to be seen as being adaptable. In the same way, if he walks into a problem-solving meeting and refuses to listen to others' views or he jumps to conclusions before he has gathered all of the facts, then he is not going to be viewed as open to new ideas. In summary, as a coach it is important to point out to your team members how their leadership and interpersonal behaviors either support or get in the way of their learning agility.

Provide Shadowing and Modeling

Try to identify situations in which you could help team members accelerate their learning by having them shadow you as you perform a work function or by watching you model certain work skills. You can increase the effectiveness of shadowing or modeling by targeting in on the particular skill or knowledge component on which an individual needs to focus. For example, if you are a sales executive and the learning area in question is large account management, you might decide to select only one of the following areas for modeling:

- How to qualify large accounts
- How to develop a multi-year plan for managing a large account across multiple customer locations
- Large account proposal development
- How to sell to multiple decision-makers within a complex organizational structure
- How to extend and strengthen client relationships within large accounts

Another important point about modeling is that the most effective managerial models think aloud. To better understand this, consider a magic act. With a sudden hand movement or the flourish of a cape, an object seems to disappear from the stage or to mysteriously transform into something else. It is impressive, largely because at the end of the show you still don't know how the magician pulled off the tricks. Unfortunately some managers operate the same way. When a crisis occurs or a complex problem emerges, they disappear behind their office to emerge later with the solution in hand. The problem is that, while this kind of magic act is

LEADER'S GUIDE

impressive, those managers are not acting in ways that develop the competencies of their teams.

The next time that you want to model something for someone, don't just show her the rabbit that you have pulled out of your hat. Slow down and walk her through the logic that you use to troubleshoot a project, analyze a problem, or evaluate alternatives to reach a decision. If possible, don't do this after the fact because you will probably remember only a small part of the thought process you used. Instead, call her into your office as you are about to wade into a difficult work challenge and sketch out your thinking in real time on a whiteboard. I have found that this technique can be a very potent tool for helping direct reports grasp the complexities of broader organizational issues.

Engage in Thought Experiments

A related technique for accelerating on-the-job learning is the use of thought experiments. In these "what if" scenarios, you encourage team members to talk aloud as they think through how they intend to approach upcoming work situations. For example, it may be that one of your team members is planning to meet with your senior leaders to gain commitment for a large dollar request for technical training support. Given this situation, your thought experiment might look like this:

Coach: "Why don't you go to the whiteboard and map out everyone who will be in the meeting on Wednesday. Then use a 1-to-5 scale to tell me how supportive you think each person is likely to be of this project, with "5" indicating complete support and a "1" meaning active resistance. Also talk to me a bit about what you think each person's primary concerns will be and the kinds of bottom-line payoffs you think that each person will be expecting to see from this project."

Coachee: [Maps project stakeholders who will be attending the meeting.]

Coach: "Good. Now why don't you walk me through how you think this meeting will progress and how you plan to address each stakeholder's expectations and concerns?"

Coachee: [Describes the situation.]

Coach: "Great. Now I am sure that your audience is going to challenge you to explain how you came up with the data on which you based your conclusions, such as how you came up with your ROI estimates. Tell me a bit about where you think you might be challenged and the information that you are ready to put on the table to support your recommendations."

You can see from this situation that the manager is going beyond being a passive audience as her direct report provides a walk-through of his upcoming presentation. Instead, the manager generates questions designed to push the team member's thinking. I have seen this same approach applied effectively for entire work groups. The SVP of an international sales team within the hospitality industry worked with me to construct a hypothetical future scenario to push the thinking of his team. During an offsite session, we distributed to his team a mock news clipping stating that a major hotel competitor had just completed the acquisition of a U.S. brand, an action that would more than double the competitor's customer base. We then divided the group into teams and gave them several hours to (1) determine the immediate and long-term impact that this competitive move would have on their company's market position and (2) reach agreement on the most important steps that would have to be taken to combat this situation. The exercise proved very valuable to the team for, ironically, a year later when that scenario actually became a reality, the sales team found themselves in a very good position to address it.

Conduct After-Action Reviews

An after-action review (AAR) is a formal process that the U.S. Army regularly uses to help its leaders learn from tough situations. When applying this technique to coaching, meet with a team member immediately after he has encountered a critical work situation, such as dealing with a work-related conflict or negotiating with another work function. The purpose of the AAR is to have your team member compare what he wanted to accomplish with what actually occurred and to the determine what he can learn from the experience to be more effective in the future.

When applying the AAR technique, the point is to lead a learning discussion, rather than a blame-casting session. Make use of questions that keep team members from becoming defensive while encouraging them to take the initiative in objectively reviewing their performance. Some questions that might be helpful in leading this discussion include:

- "What did you want to see happen in this situation?"
- "How does that compare with what actually happened? What outcomes met your expectations?"

LEADER'S GUIDE

- "How would you objectively describe the approach you took to obtaining those outcomes? How did that approach work for you?"
- "What did you take away from the situation? If you were coaching someone else on our team who was about to encounter a similar situation, what advice would you give her?"

Make Use of Naturally Occurring Events

The most effective workplace learning is integrated with business requirements. The technique of using naturally occurring events involves using your Outlook calendar to identify upcoming work situations that could provide your team members with great learning experiences. Accordingly, if one of your team members is attempting to learn how to manage conflicts more effectively, you might troll through your calendar for situations that would require him to negotiate project steps or resources with co-workers or people within other work functions. You can also use this technique whenever you consider how to convert unanticipated work challenges into team learning experiences.

Four steps can transform scheduled or unanticipated work challenges into learning events:

1. Quickly determine the aspect of the selected work challenge that is the most difficult or demanding, such as the ability to negotiate priorities with an internal customer or to perform long-term strategic planning.
2. Determine who within your team could benefit most from developing this ability.
3. Conduct a brief staging meeting with the team member to let her know what you want her to take away from her involvement in the work situation in terms of skill development, behavioral change, or knowledge building.
4. Provide any advice or assistance that would help prepare the person for this situation, such as conducting a walk-through of the situation.

Additional information on this technique and the others discussed in this section can be found in Chapter 5 of the Participant's Guide.

Avoid These Coaching Pitfalls

When attempting to implement coaching during this step, be alert to the following pitfalls and take the recommended steps for addressing them:

LEADER'S GUIDE

Giving Fuzzy Feedback on Learning Agility

As I've said, learning agility is a rather complex construct. Making vague comments about a person's "inability to adapt" or the fact that he seems "reluctant to experiment with new ideas" doesn't provide that individual with the type of detailed information he needs to support his development. Instead, try to provide professionals with feedback that helps them to paint a clear picture of the specific behaviors they need to strengthen to support their learning agility. Two examples are provided below:

• "I know that once you are on board with a new change situation, you do a great job in coming up with ideas for ways that we can make that change process more effective. The thing that you may want to work on is how you initially approach those discussions. Several people have commented on the fact that when you first hear about an impending change your immediate, knee-jerk reaction is to complain about the situation or to write it off as simply 'another stupid idea from corporate.' My concern is that when people think back to these situations they are going to focus on your initial reaction, rather than the fact that you always come through for everyone at the end. I want to make sure that you are not viewed as being rigid or unable to adapt to change."
• "You and I both know that you have huge expertise in dealing with these types of complex procurement issues, probably more than anyone else on your cross-functional team. At the same time, there are other people on the team who are in a better position to understand the comparative technical capabilities of the vendors who are bidding on this project, while others are in a better position to understand the expectations of our senior stakeholders. Whenever you problem solve with others on your team, try to keep this fact in mind. If you tend to shut them off or challenge them before they have a chance to put their views on the table, you are going to limit the amount of information that you can bring to bear on this problem and will eventually place yourself in a position in which you aren't going to be able to obtain the support you need from everyone."

Setting Fuzzy Learning Goals

The same need for precision occurs when we are setting learning goals with our team members. Whenever possible, set learning goals that target a few selected skills and enable career professionals to gauge their progress on learning. They should be able to understand how you expect them to apply that learning. Here is an example.

LEADER'S GUIDE

If you are going to have a sales rep go on a ride-along with one of the strongest members of your sales team, instead of saying, "I would like you to watch how David handles a sales call with multiple decision-makers," you might say, "During this call David is going to be pitching to the VP of supply chain, as well as the VP of operations and finance. Between now and the call date, I want you to sit down with David and find out what steps he has taken to customize his presentation to the needs of these three executives and how he has prepared to address their very different sets of concerns. During the meeting I would like you to pay particular attention to how he adapts his language as he shifts the conversation from one of these buyers to another and the questions that he is using to draw out the views of each of these individuals. When you get back I would like to hear your reactions and discuss how you can begin to apply what you've learned to the Acme account that you will be working with."

Failing to Integrate Learning with Job Requirements

Another coaching pitfall associated with this development step is not taking the time to help team members understand the connection between learning activities and job requirements. When this connection isn't emphasized, your team members will come to view learning activities as events that lack job relevance, and they won't make the personal investment needed to transform these activities into meaningful developmental experiences. At the same time, they will tend to rush through new work challenges without taking the time to consider how those situations could be used as learning opportunities.

You can avoid this pitfall by (1) asking your team members to set development goals for any learning activities in which they will be involved, (2) converting naturally occurring events to learning opportunities, (3) setting learning objectives for all major job assignments, and (4) setting aside time after key learning activities to stage a debriefing session and find out what your team members have taken away from the learning experience.

Lacking Immediate Opportunities to Apply Learning

Studies have shown that our ability to retain a new skill is directly related to having opportunities to practice, and receive feedback on, our performance as soon as possible after the event. Retention is directly related to the time delay we experience between learning and on-the-job application. For this reason, if you are making someone on your team responsible for mastering a new software application and then training others on your team on that application, use the estimated start time for software conversion as your basis for determining when you would send that team member to training. Whenever possible, look for ways to implement this kind of "just-in-time" learning for your team members.

Dwelling on the Negative

When conducting debriefing sessions, it is easy to fall into the habit of focusing on what went wrong. In most cases, and particularly when you are coaching an exceptional performer, your team member's attention will be all too quickly drawn to those aspects of the work challenge that he didn't handle well. Ask someone to provide a self-audit of how she delivered a presentation or to observe herself on videotape as she attempts to try out a new communications skill, and chances are that the individual's attention will immediately go to everything that she did poorly. While we all learn a lot from our mistakes, recent research suggests that we actually learn a lot more from our successes than we do from our failures. In fact, a research study at MIT reported in the July 2010 issue of *Neuron* found that changes actually show up at the neurological level. That is, we process information more efficiently when we draw that information from a success, rather than from a failure.

The implication of this research is that, when you are providing a team member with coaching about a recent on-the-job learning experience, it is important to call that person's attention to what he learned from the experience, to even small improvements in competencies, and to anything he feels he can take away from the experience that might be readily transferable to new work situations. Here are some coaching comments that can focus a team member's attention on successes:

- "I know that this situation presented you with a lot of new challenges, but looking back on it what was the one thing you felt good about in terms of what you learned?"
- "What was most surprising to you about what you took away from this situation?"
- "Can you think of one work situation that you will be better prepared to handle more effectively in the future as a result of this learning?"
- "Philosopher Friedrich Nietzsche once said, 'That which does not kill us makes us stronger.' How are you stronger as a result of having completed this learning experience?"

LEADER'S GUIDE

Reference

"Learning substrates in the primate prefrontal cortex and striatum: Sustained activity related to successful actions." (2009). Mark Histed, Anitha Pasupathy, and Earl Miller. *Neuron, 63*, 244–253.

CHAPTER SEVEN

COACHING OTHERS ON BRAND MANAGEMENT

What a Personal Brand Communicates

Your personal brand can be thought of as that combination of behaviors, appearance, and communication patterns that others readily associate with you. Your personal brand can also be viewed as:

- The overall reputation that you have established both with others inside your organization and with key external contacts, such as customers, suppliers, or board members
- Those adjectives that these individuals would be most likely to use when describing you to others
- Your unique personal signature, the way that others come to know and define you

When a brand is very strong or weak, a person's brand signature spreads out before him like the shock waves of an earthquake, establishing a defining context for the expectations that others come to set for him. Over time, people who have never even met us begin to form strong positive or negative expectations about us based on the personal brands that we have developed. The phrase "your reputation precedes you" nicely sums this up. Brand management, however, is more than just "image management." It also involves being sensitive to how our behaviors impact

LEADER'S GUIDE

other people and come to shape our reputations as organizational leaders. Furthermore, brand management requires that we fully understand how the reputations we forge over time significantly affect our ability to accomplish things through others.

Chapter 6 of the Participant's Guide shows professionals how to better understand the personal brands that they have established in their organization and the steps that they can take to strengthen their brands. In this final chapter of the Leader's Guide we will take a look at the coaching actions that you can take to help others become more effective in personal brand management. [As a side-note, if the subject of branding is new to you, you may find it helpful to read the first few pages of Chapter 6 of the Participant's Guide before proceeding on with the rest of this chapter.]

The Challenges Faced by Career Professionals

The Problem of Brand Bias

It is very human to focus on those parts of ourselves that we like the best. When it comes to brand management, this means paying attention to brand attributes that have worked especially well for us in the past and that are reflective of our personal values. Following this line of thought, a work professional may take pride in the fact that she has gained a reputation for being a tenacious problem solver who can work with complex issues. Unfortunately, she may focus so much of her attention on this aspect of her brand that she is totally unaware that others also view her as difficult to work with and as someone who is prone to conflict. In the same way, another individual may feel good about the fact that he is regarded as being a warm and friendly person who works well with others across the organization. At the same time, this professional may fail to realize that, while others appreciate his agreeable disposition, they also view him as being somewhat unreliable, with a reputation for quite often failing to keep his commitments.

This problem of brand bias is sometimes exacerbated by well-intended managers who pay attention to certain aspects of a team member's brand while ignoring others. A common example of this is the manager who continually praises an employee for getting results, while saying little about the fact that the team member has difficulty maintaining productive work relationships. Another contributing factor is when an over-protective manager shields a team member from criticism or concerns that are voiced by other managers. Finally, some professionals pay close attention to how they present themselves to senior executives, yet are relatively complacent when it comes to considering how they present themselves to "the unwashed masses," that is, their peers and direct reports. In this situation, while the professionals may learn how to manage upward more effectively, they fail to learn how to build a base of influence at their own level.

Not Knowing When and How to Change One's Brand

When Honda, Toyota, and Hyundai introduced cars into the U.S. market, they realized the need to first establish a foothold at the lower end of the auto market by focusing their sales and brand strategy on inexpensive subcompacts. They then continued to migrate up the marketing food chain, to eventually go after the market for sedans, SUVs, and other luxury vehicles. All of these auto dealers were smart enough to understand that each change in market position required associated changes to their brand strategies.

In the same way, as professionals strive to advance in leadership roles they must understand how to adapt their personal brands to meet the different expectations of each management level. While some professionals understand the importance of making these transitions, others assume that the behaviors and personal characteristics that helped them to become successful in the past are what they need to carry forward into the future. Such individuals have difficulty understanding that at each organizational level a different set of unspoken leadership norms and expectations comes into play.

Consider the non-managerial professional who establishes a strong reputation as being a knowledgeable technical performer and independent problem solver. If this person hopes to advance to a first-line management position she will need to make changes to her brand. Her promotional success will be based less on her ability to independently tackle tough work challenges and more on her ability to establish a reputation as a strong team leader. If a few years later this same professional seeks out a middle management position, she will have to develop a personal brand that conveys that she is someone who can influence others, such as the heads of other departments, even when she has no direct authority over those other individuals.

Failing to Understand That Small Things Matter

In attempting to strengthen their brands, a third challenge career planners face is assuming that, if the big things are working well, the small things

LEADER'S GUIDE

don't matter. They fail to realize that one's personal brand is not entirely about performance results. It also includes the many small things we do and say that present to everyone with whom we come in contact a composite image of ourselves as leaders and human beings.

I once coached a leader who was so driven to get results that he would push others relentlessly to ensure that they met project milestones and kept commitments on deliverables. Unfortunately, my client's interpersonal approach was very caustic, with the result that he tended to attack or belittle anyone who didn't immediately respond to his email inquiries or who dared to surface concerns regarding potential project hurdles. Over time this leader managed to alienate almost everyone who worked with him, and they in turn found creative ways to keep him at arms length from their projects. While everyone appreciated this leader's intelligence and drive, they were unwilling to put up with the high level of conflict and stress that typically accompanied his involvement in any project.

The fact is that, over time, all of the small things that we say and do shape the way that others see us. Negative examples include:

- Sending a flaming email or voicemail in a moment of anger
- Ignoring requests for support by peers
- Taking calls or playing with your iPhone during staff meetings
- Working for weeks on a project, only to send out a sloppy document because you have ignored final editing for grammar and spelling

    Positive examples include:

- Working late in order to help someone who is faced with an urgent deadline
- Attempting to head off an impending conflict with someone, rather than have an issue surface later during a staff meeting
- Sharing credit on a project with less visible support staff
- Taking the lead on helping others manage an onerous change project

How You Can Help

Make the Connection Between Behaviors and Brands

Individuals often have difficulty understanding how all of their behaviors come together to leave others with an overall impression of who they are as people and how they operate as professionals. One of the most important coaching roles you can play is to help your team members get a clearer grasp of their most dominant brand attributes or those behaviors that tend to characterize them in the minds of others.

One tool you can use for doing this is the Personal Brand Matrix introduced in Chapter 6 of the Participant's Guide. The matrix helps individuals identify both those *task-based attributes* that are associated with how they are viewed as competent performers and those *people-based attributes* that speak to how others view them as people. Chapter 6 also provides readers with suggestions for strengthening each of these brand attributes. I recommend that you review this section of the Participant's Guide and then use the matrix as a vehicle for reaching alignment with your team members on the most critical areas for improvement.

Keep Them Focused on the "How" as Well as the "What"

In the previous chapter, I discussed how important it is to use stage-setting discussions to encourage team members to view job assignments and other job challenges as learning opportunities. Use these stage-setting discussions to help career planners understand how critical job assignments can be used to strengthen their brands. As an example, if your team member has developed a reputation for staunchly defending "tried and true" solutions to problems at the expense of innovative ideas, discuss the importance of remaining open to new ideas and participating in brainstorming during group problem-solving sessions.

You can also help people focus on their brand when performing project debriefings or after-action reviews (AARs). Use questions such as the following to draw the career planner's attention to how she went about getting results:

- "Now that the project is completed, how do you think people feel about your involvement in it?"
- "When people work together on project assignments, they tend to play different roles. Often one person assumes the role of meeting facilitator, while another person takes the lead in generating ideas. Still another may help organize good ideas into action, while there is usually someone who plays the role of 'harmonizer' in helping everyone work through disagreements. How do you think that the other people on this work assignment would describe the principal role that you played in supporting it?"

- "We've talked about how you performed against expected results on this project. Now let's consider it from a different perspective. Looking back, how did you feel you did in terms of managing others' expectations, maintaining good communications, and building good relationships? What kind of impression did you leave in the minds of those who worked with you?"

Look for Opportunities to Showcase Brand Strengths

Another coaching action you can take is to help team members identify work challenges and project assignments that highlight their strengths. Let us assume that you have a team member whose core strengths are her organizational ability and the care with which she manages the details of her work. Work assignments that might showcase these brand strengths could include:

- Place her in a position that involves helping a cross-functional team maintain the project schedule.
- Have her troubleshoot the details of her team's project plan before they present it to senior management.
- Assign her to work with your procurement manager in evaluating the tricky details of an important proposal from a supplier.
- Give her the task of helping you evaluate several of the planning components that have to feed into your annual budget forecasting model.

Any of these work projects would give this team member the "runway" needed to showcase the strongest aspects of her personal brand.

Educate Team Members on Brand Migration

Earlier in this chapter I explained that brand expectations change as we advance from one organizational leadership level to another. Many of these changes have to do with the unwritten rules of conduct or organizational norms that define the exceptional leadership behavior at each management level. An important coaching role is helping team members learn how they need to shift their behavior if they want others to look at them as a "good fit" for the next leadership level.

Case in Point: Jessica

One of my coaching clients, Jessica, was a young, highly intelligent IT professional and newly minted MBA. Jessica had been hired directly from her university to take part in her employer's accelerated leadership development program. Throughout her first year with the company, Jessica had made several presentations to her manager and her manager's manager. During these presentations her bosses were very impressed with her work. They also noticed a few characteristics of her delivery style that, at the time, they didn't comment on. Specifically, Jessica tended to employ a rather informal, conversational style in her delivery. During these sessions she also tended to use a lot of non-words: "So . . . like the new software platform that we want to purchase. . . . is like . . . you know. . . ." Because she approached her work with a high amount of energy, whenever Jessica discussed an aspect of her work that she deeply cared about, she tended to talk very rapidly and would sometimes fidget nervously in front of the group.

Now I know that all of this seems trivial, but when Jessica made her first presentation to her senior managers, all of these characteristics came together to leave her audience with the impression that she was "immature," "unsure of herself," and "lacking executive presence." Through practice sessions in coaching, we quickly turned this situation around. The fact is, however, her manager could have prevented this problem from developing if he had just met with her in advance of this important presentation to discuss how her delivery style needed to be adapted to the expectations of her senior-level audience.

Avoid These Coaching Pitfalls

When attempting to implement coaching during this step, be alert to the following pitfalls and take the recommended steps for addressing them:

Being Reluctant to Conduct Difficult Conversations

Conversations about performance are easy. Less easy are conversations that involve image management; yet quite often I have seen a professional's brand image erode because that person has never been given feedback about interpersonal behaviors or social skills.

LEADER'S GUIDE

Case in Point: Tony

One of my coaching clients, Tony, was an incredibly adept leader when it came to knowing his field, which was online marketing. The problem was that, although Tony had advanced very quickly through leadership levels, he still conducted himself as he did a few years ago when he was fresh out of college. The most noticeable problem was that Tony's overall appearance was very shabby. He would walk into an important meeting wearing a wrinkled shirt that looked as if it had been slept in the night before. On the few days that he wore a tie (and he worked in a very conservative business environment in which ties and sports coats were mandatory for certain events), it tended to be loud and tacky. Tony was also a very big and hefty individual who had gained a lot of weight during the previous two years and simply hadn't bothered to update his wardrobe. As a result, he looked as if he had been squeezed into some of his clothes. Another issue was that when Tony became excited about a topic he would talk too loudly and make grandiose gestures to illustrate his points, an idiosyncrasy that became more noticeable on those occasions when he "loosened up" during organizational social gatherings.

Once again, these behaviors might seem trivial to you. My point is, however, that social norms that are unimportant to one organization can be very important to leadership survival in another. In my client's case, at the time Tony entered coaching he was being sized up for consideration for a very senior leadership role. Unfortunately, some executives who didn't know him well were hesitant to take this step. Their assumption—right or wrong—was that a leader who was this sloppy in his personal appearance and general demeanor might also be slipshod when it came to his work.

Tony was a very receptive coachee. When we had a frank talk about why I had been called in as a coach, he was a bit shell-shocked. Five minutes into our conversation, he asked me, "Why didn't my manager ever talk to me about this?" Why indeed.

The fact is that many managers feel uncomfortable having conversations that involve sensitive topics or are somewhat personal. However, our assumption here is that the person you are coaching wants to prepare herself to take on broader leadership responsibilities in your organization. If you don't sit down and have a chat with her about how professional expectations change across leadership levels and organizational settings (such as making the shift from field to corporate positions), you can leave a good performer confused and frustrated about his or her inability to advance in your company.

Underestimating the Importance of First Impressions

The pitfall that we just reviewed is closely related to the second one, managing first impressions. When we meet someone for the first time, we notice a number of small behaviors that either leave a favorable or unfavorable impression on us. Over time, however, these small quirks fade into the background as we come to know the person underneath. The danger is that eventually we are likely to forget about the first impressions that our team members leave with others in the organization. One way to correct for this tendency is to follow up with your people to find out how they initially present themselves to other managers.

Not long ago an associate of mine asked me for this kind of feedback on one of his direct reports. I told him that, while she appeared to be a very friendly and outgoing person, I was concerned about her ability to think through issues in a thoughtful and studied way. In terms of first impressions, I observed someone who talked very fast, sometimes over-talking me during our conversations. There were also occasions when she would jump ahead and try to anticipate where our conversation was headed, with the result that she would interject a comment that wasn't really relevant. When my associate received this feedback he was initially surprised, but later acknowledged that he realized that this was characteristic of her conversational style. However, during the several years that they had worked closely together he had long since phased it out of his awareness.

When providing coaching, always keep in mind that people tend to form first impressions very quickly and, once formed, these impressions are difficult to change. Give some careful thought to the first impressions that your team members present to other leaders in your organization and provide them with help and advice on how to make the most of these "first contact" moments.

LEADER'S GUIDE

ABOUT THE AUTHOR

Robert Barner, Ph.D., has more than twenty-five years of applied experience within the field of organization and leadership development. As a senior OD/LD executive, he has directed high-potential development and coaching for organizations in such sectors as manufacturing, engineering, aerospace, biotech, media, franchising, and hospitality. He received his Ph.D. in organization development from the Fielding Graduate Institute. Currently, Dr. Barner holds the position of associate director for Southern Methodist University's Department of Dispute Resolution and Counseling within the university's Annette Caldwell Simmons School of Education and Human Development.

Over the past twenty years Dr. Barner has also presented to several international conferences on the subject of executive coaching. He has been a contributor to several academic and business texts and has published more than fifty articles within academic and professional journals. Dr. Barner currently serves as a reviewer for two academic journals.

His five previous books on team building and leadership have been translated into German, Norwegian, and Estonian and distributed throughout North America, Europe, Scandinavia, and India.

In addition to his academic responsibilities, Dr. Barner is also the owner of Plano Executive Advisory Services, a consulting company that focuses on the assessment, development, and coaching of high-potential leaders. Additional information on workshops related to the subject of accelerated leadership development can be obtained by contacting Dr. Barner at robert.barner@planoadvisory.com, or by visiting his company website at www.planoadvisory.com.

INDEX

Page referenced followed by *fig* indicate illustrations; followed by *t* indicate tables.

A

Accelerating development: coaching role in developing plan for, 186, 196–197, 203–204; creating development plan for, 12–13, 39–54, 84; examining possibility of, 10–11; identifying developmental gaps for, 17–36, 186, 188–189, 191; leveraging development assignments for, 186, 205–216; targeted and disciplined approach of, 11–12. *See also* Career professionals; Career targets; Development; Next Steps

Accelerating on-the-job learning: acceleration = agility + efficiency, 85–90; calibrating learning requirements, 221–222; Case in Point: Kirk on, 115–116; coaching approach to, 187, 221–229;

coaching pitfalls to avoid for, 226–229; exploiting available avenues for learning, 90–98, 219; increasing the efficiency of your learning for, 98–115; Next Steps for, 116–120; thought experiments for, 224–225. *See also* Learning agility

Actions. *See* Development actions

Activity-based development model: Case in Point: Randy on applying, 42–44*t*; description of, 40*fig*

Adaptability: how others gauge your, 145; related to learning agility, 16, 143; strategies for improving your, 143–148

Adaptable leadership strategies: Brand Application Table, 154*t*; conveying receptiveness to new ideas, 147–148; establishing your reputation as change agent, 144–147; managing stress, 143–144

Aerobic exercise, 103–104

After-action review (AAR), 110–111, 116, 225–226, 235

Aging with Grace (Snowdon), 107

American Society for Training and Development (ASTD), 4–5

Anticipatory guidance feedback, 52

Apple, 123

Aronson, Elliot, 109

Assessment: comparative performance expectations, 31–33; development gap, 190–191; of development plan robustness, 199–200; learning agility, 87–88, 218–219, 222–223; representative career tradeoffs, 19–20, 191–192; value of skills to your career target, 55*t*

Assessment instruments: CHOICES, 86–87, 88, 222; LTR (leadership talent

review), 10; Questions You
Can Ask to Evaluate Your
Learning Agility, 117–119,
222
Assignments. *See* Development
assignments
Assumption testing, 108–109

B

Behaviors: adaptable, 143–148,
154*t*; connection between
personal brand and,
234–235; first impressions of,
127–129; as job demand
element, 24–26; related to
learning agility, 16; seven
shifts in leadership, 24–25;
sustained impressions of,
128*fig*, 129–130
Big picture, 22–23
Biorhythms, 104–105
Blind spots, 185–186
BPO (business process
outsourcing) project:
leadership competencies
developed through, 71–72;
matching development
assignment to, 71
Brain Application Table,
154*t*–156*t*
Brain plasticity, 106
The Brain That Changes Itself
(Doidge), 107
Brain-derived neurotrophic
factor (BDNF), 103
Brand Application Table,
154*t*–156*t*
Brand bias, 232–233
Brand migration, 236–237
Brands: importance of
distinctive, 122–123; the 3Cs
of, 123, 158. *See also* Personal
brands
Building relationship strategies,
140–141
Burt, Ronald, 89, 90

C

Calibrating learning
requirements, 98–100

Career Accountability Model:
clarifying roles using the,
179; coachee's
responsibilities, 180*fig*;
coach's responsibilities,
180*fig*–181
Career myopia, 190
Career planning: using accurate
information to base, 191;
coaching questions to ask
about, 189–190; effective gap
assessment as part of,
190–191. *See also* Career
targets; Development
planning; Development plans
Career professionals: challenges
for leveraging development
assignments, 205–206;
development plan challenges
faced by, 197–198;
development as tool to
retain, 169; failing to
integrate learning with job
requirements of, 228;
"Golden Child Syndrome,"
194–195; guidelines for
coach-provided feedback to,
181–185; misconception
regarding false expectations
of, 171–172; on-the-job
learning challenges faced by,
218–221; organizational
changes creating
development gap challenges
for, 188–189; personal brand
of, 123–159, 187, 231–239;
why development is a
priority, 166–169. *See also*
Accelerating development;
Development; Organizations;
Skills/competencies
Career target assignments:
conduct three informational
interviews, 35–36; describe
your ideal, 34–35;
Informational Interview
Form, 37
Career targets: assessing value of
skills to your, 55*t*; Case in
Point: Tom on assessing,
20–21; clarifying job demand
features, 23–31; coaching

approach to identifying, 186;
coaching pitfall of projecting
your own, 192–194;
comparative performance
expectations and, 31–33;
crucible metaphor of, 23–24;
how coaches can help
formulate, 189–192; keeping
the big picture in mind,
22–23; matching your
personal priorities to, 19–21;
organizational changes and
adaptation of, 189; taking
aim at your, 17–19. *See also*
Accelerating development;;
Career planning
Career tradeoffs: assessing your
priorities in relation to,
19–20, 192–193; considering
representative, 19–20
Carter, Jimmy, 98
Cases in Point: Carlos, 48–49;
Carol, 220–221; Charlotte,
201; Jamie, 32–33; Jessica,
237; Ken, 81–83; Kirk,
115–116; Paul, 53–54;
Randy, 42–44*t*; Sandra, 153,
157; Tom, 20–21; Tony,
238–239
Center for Creative Leadership,
199
Change agent reputation,
144–147
Change agility, 86, 87, 218
Change Management Grid,
147
Change. *See* Organizational
change
Charan, Ram, 191
CHOICES, 86–87, 88, 222
Cirque du Soleil, 123
Closing the gap: balancing
career target and personal
priorities, 19–21; career
target identification, 17–19;
coaching approach to, 186;
created by organizational
changes, 189; identifying job
demands, 23–33; keeping big
picture in mind, 22–23; Next
Steps for, 34–36. *See also*
Developmental gaps

Coachees. *See* Career
professionals
Coaching conversations: avoid
dwelling on the negative,
229; avoiding fuzzy
communication, 202;
avoiding giving fuzzy
learning agility feedback,
227; framing the dialogue,
175–176; listening
component of, 176–177;
making best use of questions
in, 177–178; reluctance to
conduct difficult, 237–239;
why and how of unpacking
terms, 178–179. *See also*
Communication
Coaching relationships:
addressing blind spots,
185–186; Career
Accountability Model,
179–181; clarifying roles in
the, 179–181; framing the
dialogue to build, 175–176;
guidelines for development
feedback, 181–185; how to
make best use of questions,
177–178; listening to build,
176–177; unpacking terms to
build, 178–179. *See also*
Managerial coaching
Cognitive diversity: actions
engaging organization parts
to improve, 68*t*; desire to
increase skills for, 63;
evaluating your skills for,
119; leadership development
experiences to increase, 208;
suggested actions within
current job to improve, 67*t*
Communication: avoiding fuzzy
coaching, 202; different
audiences requiring different
strategies for, 152; email and
voicemail, 138, 141–142;
making best use of coaching
questions, 177–178;
managing difficult
conversations, 141; muzzling
your complaints, 144; of a
personal brand, 231–232;
responding to requests,

141–142, 151–152;
"structural holes" in
organizational, 89; unpacking
the terms to clarify, 178–179.
See also Coaching
conversations; Listening
Communicator strategies: Brand
Application Table, 156*t*;
directing phone conferences,
138; general communicator
image, 136–137; managing
email and social networks,
138–139, 141–142; for
managing meetings, 137–138
Competencies. *See* Skills/
competencies
Complaining, 144
"Cooking school" philosophy,
11
Crucible metaphor: of career
target, 23; job demands as
heart of, 23–24

D

Death by project overload pitfall,
215–216
Decision making: coaching
conversations to help with,
190; SWOT matrix on, 145;
testing your assumptions for,
108–109
Descartes, René, 103
Descriptive feedback, 182
Developing expertise beyond
function: actions engaging
organization parts to
improve, 68*t*; assignments to
improve skills, 66, 208; desire
to increase skills for, 63;
organization-wide
development actions, 69*t*;
outside organization
development actions, 70*t*;
suggested actions within
current job to improve, 67*t*
Development: avoiding
"scattershot" approach to, 9;
benefits of self-direct, 8–10;
"cooking school" philosophy
of, 11; identifying gaps in,
17–36, 186, 188–189, 191;

ineffective incremental, 168;
keeping pace with change
through, 9; matching
learning options with needs
for, 120; planning essentials
for, 38–57; reasons for
prioritizing, 166–169;
self-directed, 8–10, 94–95,
220; sink-or-swim, 168–169,
214. *See also* Accelerating
development; Career
professionals; Managerial
coaching
Development actions: improving
skills by engaging
organization parts, 68*t*;
improving skills with
organization-wide, 69*t*;
improving skills through
outside organization, 70*t*;
improving skills within
current job, 67*t*; supporting
your development planning,
56–57. *See also* Next Steps
Development assignment
categories: developing
expertise beyond your
function, 65, 67*t*, 68*t*, 208;
influencing without
authority, 63, 67*t*, 68*t*, 208;
managing change, 63, 67*t*,
68*t*, 208; managing through
to execution, 65, 67*t*, 68*t*,
208; suggestion development
actions related to, 67*t*–68*t*,
208; taking a broader
perspective, 65, 67*t*, 68*t*;
thinking strategically, 64, 67*t*,
68*t*, 208; working across silos
and functions, 64, 67*t*, 68*t*,
208; working with diverse
groups of people, 64, 67*t*,
68*t*, 119, 208; working
through messy problems, 63,
67*t*, 68*t*, 208. *See also*
Leveraging development
assignments
Development assignment
management: coach role in
leveraging assignments, 186,
205–216; defining success
measures, 77; establishing

test points, 76; obtaining
feedback, 77–79
Development assignment review:
Case in Point:Ken on,
81–83; step 1: reflect, 79–80;
step 2: solicit feedback,
80–81; step 3: consolidate
lessons learned, 81
Development assignments:
career target, 34–37; Case in
Point: Ken on, 81–83; coach
pitfall of pushing too much
for, 216; coaching step of
leveraging, 186, 205–216;
following up the, 212–214;
identifying what you want to
take away from, 62–66;
managing the, 76–79,
211–212; matching project
lifecyles to, 71–72; questions
to ask regarding, 60–61;
reviewing the, 79–81;
selecting, 207–209; seven
criteria for selecting/
evaluating, 61–62, 208;
staging the, 73–75, 209–211;
template for establishing
success measures, 77; why
they often disappoint, 58–59.
See also Leadership skills
development; Next Step
assessments
Development models: activity-
based, 40*fig*, 44*fig*; Case in
Point: Randy on applying,
42–44*fig*; needs-based, 41*fig*,
44*fig*, 120; outcomes-based,
41, 42*fig*, 44*fig*
Development planning: action
steps to support your, 56–57;
Case in Point: Carlos on,
48–49; Case in Point:
Charlotte on, 201; Case in
Point: Paul on, 53–54; Case
in Point: Randy on, 42–44*t*;
coaching pitfall of premature,
194; essentials of good,
38–54; how to leverage your
strengths, 54–56, 200–201;
taking a systems approach to,
203–204. *See also* Career
planning

Development plans: accelerating
development through a,
12–13; actionable nature of,
39, 47–48; alignment of, 40,
48–49; assessing robustness
of, 199–200; coaching
approach to building, 186,
196–197; feedback basis of,
40, 49–54; five characteristics
of good, 39–40; focused and
precise, 39, 45–47;
importance of constructing a,
38–39; linking organization
performance requirements
with, 198–201; performance
outcomes, 39, 40–44*t*;
Project Management Plan,
84
Developmental coaching, 166.
See also Managerial
coaching
Developmental gaps: in
competencies/interpersonal
skills, 191; identifying, 17–36,
186; professional challenges
related to, 188–189. *See also*
Closing the gap
Difficult conversations: coaching
pitfall of avoiding, 237–239;
skills for managing, 141
Directing phone conferences,
138
Disney brand, 123
Doidge, Norman, 107
Dragon Dictation (DD), 140
Drotter, Steve, 191
Dweck, Carol, 105

E

The Economist, 90
Edison, Thomas, 89
Eichinger, Robert, 86, 87
Email: avoiding wars, 141–142;
smart management of,
138–139
Employee assistance program
(EAP), 170
Employees. *See* Career
professionals
Evaluative feedback, 182
"Executive presence," 45

F

Facebook: mobile accounts for,
140; networking using, 89,
100; smart management of,
138
Feedback: anticipatory guidance,
52; avoid dwelling on the
negative, 229; avoiding
giving fuzzy learning agility,
227; Case in Point: Paul on,
53–54; from co-workers and
internal customers, 200;
descriptive versus evaluative,
182; development plan based
on collective, 40, 48–49;
guidelines for coach-
provided, 181–185;
guidelines for soliciting,
50–52; in-process, 52;
obtaining development
assignment, 77–79;
performance, 52; reviewing
assignments by soliciting,
80–81; strengthening your
personal brand using,
126–127, 130; 360-degree
surveys, 173; tips of getting
useful, 15; on your learning
ability, 116–117
Feedback guidelines for coaches:
1: don't overdo it, 182; 2: ask
before you tell, 182; 3:
provide descriptive feedback,
not evaluative feedback, 182;
4: focus on the future not
past, 182–183; 5: provide
feedback in learning
situation, 183–184; 6: break
large feedback chunks into
bits, 184; 7: keep feedback
targeted and precise, 184; 8:
don't make yourself judge
and jury, 184–185
Feedback guidelines for
participants: 1: solicit
feedback from wide range of
providers, 50–51; 2: set the
stage, 51; 3: unpack fuzzy
language, 51; 4: ask
context-defining questions,
52; 5: ask for three types of

feedback, 52; 6: avoid debate, 52
Fielding Graduate University, 4
First impressions: illustrated diagram of, 128*fig*; as personal brand layer, 127–129; underestimating the importance of, 239
Fixed intelligence theory, 105–107
Following up assignments, 212–214
Formal education, 93–94, 220
Fortune magazine, 90
Fuzzy communication pitfall, 202
Fuzzy learning agility feedback, 227
Fuzzy learning goals, 227–228

G

"Golden Child Syndrome," 194–195
Good communicators: Brand Application Table, 156*t*; directing phone conferences, 138; email and social networks management by, 138–139; general strategies for image, 136–137; meeting management by, 137–138
Gossip-mongers, 141

H

Hagerman, Eric: first subheading, 103; second subheading, 88; third subheading, 99
Harvard University, 107
"Heir apparent syndrome," 203
Honda, 233
Hyundai, 233

I

Image-lag perspectives, 132–134
Impact, related to learning ability, 16
Improving project planning, 150
In-process feedback, 52
Incremental development, 168

Influencers: description of, 150–151; improving your image as, 151–153; "white space" management by, 151; without authority, 63, 66, 67*t*–70*t*
Influencing without authority: actions engaging organization parts to improve, 68*t*; assignments to improve skills, 66, 208; desire to increase skills for, 63; organization-wide development actions, 69*t*; outside organization development actions, 70*t*; suggested actions within current job to improve, 67*t*
Informational Interview Form, 37
International Forum for Visual Facilitators, 5
Interpersonal skills, 191
IQ (intelligence quotient) theories, 105–107

J

Job assignments. *See* Development assignments
Job demands: description of, 23; first element: leadership behavior, 24–26; heart of the crucible metaphor of, 23–24; organizational culture impact on, 27–28; organizational strategic priorities impact on, 28–29; organizational structures impacting, 30; questions identifying your career target unique, 26; second element: organizational context, 27–30; third element: performance expectations, 31–33

K

Kabat-Zinn, Jon, 109–110, 144
Korn/Ferry International, 86, 87

L

Langer, Ellen, 107
"Larks," 104
Leadership: eight key development experiences listed for, 208; how your people are reflection of your, 167; LTR (leadership talent review) to assess, 10. *See also* Development assignment categories
Leadership behavior: adaptable, 143–148, 154*t*; connection between personal brand and, 234–235; first impressions of, 127–129; as job demand element, 24–26; related to learning agility, 16; seven shifts in, 24–25; sustained impressions of, 128*fig*, 129–130
The Leadership Pipeline (Charan, Drotter, and Noel), 24, 25, 191
Leadership skills development: developing expertise beyond your function, 65, 67*t*, 68*t*, 208; influencing without authority, 63, 67*t*, 68*t*, 208; managing change, 63, 67*t*, 68*t*, 208; managing through to execution, 65, 67*t*, 68*t*, 208; suggestion development actions related to, 67*t*–68*t*, 208; taking a broader perspective, 65, 67*t*, 68*t*; thinking strategically, 64, 67*t*, 68*t*, 208; working across silos and functions, 64, 67*t*, 68*t*, 208; working with diverse groups of people, 64, 67*t*, 68*t*, 119, 208; working through messy problems, 63, 67*t*, 68*t*, 208. *See also* Development assignments; Skills/competencies
Leadership talent review (LTR), 10
Learning: AAR (after-action review) for, 110–111, 116, 225–226, 235; calibrating

requirements for, 98–100, 221–222; challenges faced by career professionals, 218–221; different avenues for, 91–97, 219–221, 223–226; exploiting available avenues for, 90–98, 219; failing to integrate job requirements and, 228; increasing efficiency of your, 98–116; lacking immediate opportunities to apply, 228–229; naturally occurring events opportunities for, 112–113, 226; self-directed, 8–10, 94–95, 220–221

Learning agility: adaptability component of, 16, 143; assessing your own, 87–88, 218–219, 222–223; avoid giving fuzzy feedback on, 227; CHOICES instrument for evaluating, 86–87, 88, 222; description of, 88, 217–218; four major components of, 86, 87, 218; getting feedback on your, 116–117; how to strengthen your, 88–90; learning factors/behaviors related to, 16; Next Steps for increasing, 116–120; question to evaluate your, 117–119; Questions You Can Ask to Evaluate Your Learning Agility, 117–119, 222. *See also* Accelerating on-the-job learning; Skills/competencies

Learning avenues: Case in Point: Carol, 220–221; formal education, 93–94, 220; organizational training, 91–92, 220; practice runs, 97–98; professional conferences, 92–93, 220; self-directed learning, 8–10, 94–95, 220–221; shadowing and modeling, 95–97, 220, 223–224

Learning efficiency: AAR (after-action review) to increase, 110–111, 116,

225–226, 235; becoming a mindful learner to increase, 107–110; best use of your learning style for, 111–112; biorhythms and, 104–105; calibrating your learning requirements, 98–100, 221–222; Case in Point: Kirk on increasing, 115–116; eliminating self-imposed constraints, 105–107; employing prompting and stimulus control for, 113–116; making use of naturally occurring events for, 112–113, 226; mining your social networks for information for, 100–103; physical exercise to increase your, 103–104; understanding four levels of learning mastery, 99t–100

Learning experiences, 118

Learning goals: avoiding fuzzy, 227–228; need for precision in setting, 227

Learning management system (LMS): description of, 81–82; networking to gather information on, 100; reviewing a development assignment on launching a, 81–83

Learning mastery levels, 99t–100

Learning styles, 111–112

The Lessons of Experience (Center for Creative Leadership), 199

Leveraging development assignments: challenges facing career professionals requiring, 205–206; coaching step of, 186; following up the assignment, 212–214; managing the assignment to maximize, 76–79, 211–212; selecting the assignment element of, 207–209; seven criteria for selecting/ evaluating and, 61–62, 208; staging the, 73–75, 209–211. *See also* Development assignment categories

Leveraging technology, 140

Leveraging your strengths: assessing value of skills to career target, 55t; breaking down skill area for your success, 54–56; Case in Point: Charlotte, 201; coaching facilitation of, 200–201; value of development plan for, 56

LinkedIn, 100, 138

Listening: lead-in to facilitate, 176–177; non-judgmental, 176. *See also* Communication

Lombardo, Michael, 86, 87

Lominger International, 86

M

Making assumptions pitfall, 215

Malleable intelligence theory, 105–106

Managerial coaches: addressing blind spots, 185–186; characteristics of, 172–173; clarifying coaching roles, 179–181; formulating career target role by, 189–192; framing the dialogue, 175–176; how to give development feedback, 181–185; listening by, 176–177; making best use of questions, 177–178; misconceptions about coaching and, 170–172; why and how of unpacking terms, 178–179

Managerial coaching: applying five steps of, 186–187; implementing, 175–187; misconceptions about, 170–172; performance, transitional, and developmental, 165–166; pitfalls to avoid, 192–195, 202–204, 214–216, 226–229, 237–239; reasons for prioritizing development in, 166–169; understanding your role as coach, 169–174.

See also Coaching
relationships; Development;
Developmental coaching;
Managerial coaching steps
Managerial coaching
misconceptions: 1: coaching
is therapy, 170; 2: coaching
is same as performance
management, 170–171; 3:
good coaches have all the
answers, 171; 4: coaching is
taking responsibility for
other's career success, 171; 5:
coaching raises false
expectations of employees,
171–172
Managerial coaching pitfalls:
being reluctant to conduct
difficult conversations,
237–239; chewing their food
for them, 215; death by
project overload, 215–216;
dwelling on the negative,
229; fuzzy communication,
202; giving fuzzy feedback
on learning agility, 227;
"Golden Child Syndrome,"
194–195; "heir apparent
syndrome," 203; lacking
immediate opportunities to
apply learning, 228–229;
making assumptions, 215;
not taking a systems
approach, 203–204;
premature development
planning, 194; projecting
your own career priorities,
192–194; pushing too
much, 216; setting fuzzy
learning goals, 227–228;
sink-or-swim scenarios, 214;
underestimating importance
of first impressions, 239
Managerial coaching steps:
accelerate on-the-job
learning, 187, 217–229;
building the plan, 186,
196–197; identify the gap,
186, 188–189, 191;
leveraging development
assignments, 186, 205–216;
manage your personal

brand, 187, 231–239.
See also Managerial
coaching
Managers: brand bias
exacerbation by, 232–233;
"Golden Child Syndrome,"
194–195; "heir apparent
syndrome" pitfall, 203; how
employees are reflection of
leadership of, 167; sink-or-
swim development approach
by, 168–169, 214. *See also*
Senior executives
Managing assignments: coaching
support for, 211–212;
defining success measures,
77; establishing test points,
76; obtaining feedback,
77–79
Managing change: actions
engaging organization parts
to improve, 68*t*; assignments
to improve skills, 66; Change
Management Grid, 147;
desire to increase skills for,
63; organization-wide
development actions, 69*t*;
outside organization
development actions, 70*t*;
suggested actions within
current job to improve, 67*t*
Managing expectations,
148–149
Managing through to execution:
actions engaging
organization parts to
improve, 68*t*; assignments to
improve skills, 66, 208; desire
to increase skills for, 63;
organization-wide
development actions, 69*t*;
outside organization
development actions, 70*t*;
suggested actions within
current job to improve, 67*t*
Meetings: improving your brand
by management of, 137–138;
with senior-level executives,
142–143
Mental agility, 86, 87, 218
Mindful learners, 107–110
Mindful Learning (Langer), 107

"Mindful mediation," 109–110
Mindfulness for Beginners (Kabat-
Zinn), 110, 144
*Mindset: The New Psychology of
Success* (Dweck), 105
Mobile technology, 140
Modeling: coach-provided,
223–224; learning through,
95–97, 220
Muzzling your complaints, 144
Myopic perspectives, 132–134
MySpace, 138

N

National OD Network, 5
Naturally occurring events,
112–113, 226
Needs-based development
model: Case in Point: Randy
on applying, 42–44*t*;
description of, 41*fig*;
matching learning options to
development needs, 120
Neiman Marcus, 122
Neuron (publication), 229
New ideas: conveying your
receptiveness to, 147–148;
learning agility for
responding to, 117
Next Step assessments: 1:
describe your ideal career
target, 34–35; 2: conduct
three informational
interviews, 35–36. *See also*
Development assignments
Next Steps: accelerating your
leadership development, 83;
accelerating your learning,
116–120; building your plan,
56–57; challenge to take the,
14; for identifying your
brand, 157–159;
strengthening your learning
agility, 116–120; tips for
facilitating process of, 15;
understanding your career
target, 17–36. *See also*
Accelerated leadership;
Development actions
Nietzsche, Friedrich, 229
Noel, Jim, 191

O

On-the-job learning. *See* Accelerating on-the-job learning
Organizational change: adaptation of career targets due to, 188–189; development for keeping pace with, 9; evaluating your adaptation to, 117–118; improving skills for managing, 63, 66, 67*t*–70*t*; reputation as agent for, 144–147; three change perspectives on, 146*fig*; tools for effective management of, 147
Organizational cultures: indicators of, 27; job demands and different, 27–28; personal brand and social norms of, 238–239; questions for identifying, 29
Organizational training, 91–92, 220
Organizations: conducting information al interviews of leaders in, 35–37; EAP (employee assistance program) of, 170; matching development plans with performance requirements of, 198–201; performance expectations of, 31–33; strategic priorities of, 28–29; "structural holes" in communication of, 89; structures of, 30. *See also* Career professionals
Organized professional strategies: Brand Application Table, 154*t*; leverage technology, 140; organize your work space, 139
Outcomes-based development model: description of, 41, 42*fig*; Randy's application of, 42–44*fig*
"Owls," 104

P

Participants. *See* Employees
Paulus, Paul, 64
People agility, 86, 87, 218
People-based attributes, 131*fig*, 235
Performance coaching, 165
Performance expectations: assessment comparative, 31–32; Case in Point: Jamie on, 32–33; as job demand element, 31
Performance feedback, 52
Performance outcomes: activity-based development model on, 40*fig*; Case in Point: Randy on planning for, 42–44*fig*; connecting your professional growth to, 40–41; as development plan essential, 39
Personal brand discovery: overcoming image-lag and myopic perspectives for, 132–134; Personal Brand Matrix used for, 130–136, 235; work success/problems and associated attributes, 134*t*–136
Personal Brand Matrix: coaching help to use the, 235; illustrated diagram of, 131*fig*; people-based attributes, 131*fig*, 235; personal brand discovery using, 134–136; task-focused attributes of, 130–131*fig*, 235; understanding where you fit in the, 130–132
Personal brand strategies: as adaptable leader, 143–148, 154*t*; as good communicator, 136–138, 156*t*; as influencer, 150–153, 156*t*; as organized professional, 139–140, 154*t*; as results-driven performer, 148–150, 155*t*; as team player, 140–143, 155*t*
Personal brands: Case in Point: Jessica, 237; Case in Point:

Sandra, 153, 157; Case in Point: Tony, 238–239; coaching approach to managing, 187, 231–239; coaching pitfalls related to, 237–239; creating opportunities to leverage your, 153; description of your, 124; discovering your, 132–136; educating team members on migration of, 236–237; failing to understand that small things matter, 233–234; feedback to strengthen your, 126–127, 130; first impressions layer of, 127–129, 239; focusing on the "how" as well as "what," 235–236; looking for opportunities to showcase strengths of, 236; making the connection between behaviors and, 234–235; negative actions that hurt your, 234; Next Steps for your, 157–159; not knowing when and how to change one's, 233; people-based attributes, 131*fig*, 235; problem of brand bias, 232–233; sustained impressions layer of, 128*fig*, 129–130; taking responsibility for your, 127; task-focused attributes, 130–131*fig*, 235; the 3Cs of, 123, 158; understanding the attributes of, 125–127; understanding the value of a, 124–125; what it communications, 231–232. *See also* Brands; Reputations
Personal priorities: Case in Point: Tom on matching priorities to, 20–21; coaching pitfall of projecting your own, 192–194; matching your career target to, 19–20, 191–192
Perspective, related to learning ability, 16

Phone conferences, 138
Pitfalls. *See* Managerial coaching
pitfalls
Planning. *See* Development
planning
Plus/Delta Technique, 108
Practice runs, 97–98
Priorities: balancing career
targets and personal, 19–21,
191–192; coaching pitfall of
projecting your own career,
192–194; meeting senior
stakeholder's possible
conflicting, 190–191; reasons
for managerial coaching,
166–169; of results-driven
performer, 149–150
Professional conferences, 92–93,
220
Project Management Plan, 84
Projects: avoiding coaching
pitfall of overloading,
215–216; BPO (business
process outsourcing), 71–72;
improving skills for planning,
150; plan for managing, 84
Prompts: Case in Point: Kirk on
using, 115–116; increasing
learning efficiency using,
114–115

Q

Questions You Can Ask to
Evaluate Your Learning
Agility, 117–119, 222

R

Ratey, John, 103
Reagan, Ronald, 98
Reputation: establishing change
agent, 144–147; impact of
your, 125, 231. *See also*
Personal brands
Responding to requests, 142,
151–152
Results agility, 86, 87, 218
Results-driven performer
strategies: Brand Application
Table, 155*t*; improving

project planning, 150;
managing expectations on
assignments, 148–149; set
and act on priorities,
149–150
Results-focused, 118
"The Résumé Test," 89,
119–120
Reviewing assignments: Case in
Point: Ken on, 81–83; step 1:
reflect, 79–80; step 2: solicit
feedback, 80–81; step 3:
consolidate lessons learned,
81
Risk taking: related to learning
ability, 16; of sink-or-swim
development, 168–169
ROI (return on investment), 150
Run the Gauntlet technique, 147

S

Scenario Forecasting, 147
Scope and learning ability, 16
Self-directed development:
benefits of, 8–10; Case in
Point: Carol, 220–221;
options for, 94–95, 220
Self-discovery, 8–9
Self-insight, 16
Senior executives: ability of
influencer to fit in with, 152;
delivering a presentation to,
77; guidelines for soliciting
feedback from, 50–52;
meeting conflicting priorities
of different, 190–191; team
player strategies when
meeting with, 142–143.
See also Managers
Sense-making skills, 118–119
Setting priorities, 149–150
Shadowing: coach-provided,
223–224; learning through,
95–97, 220
Sink-or-swim development:
coaching role in, 214;
unwanted risk of, 168–169
Skills/competencies: assessing
value to your career target,
55*t*; development actions to

improve, 67*t*–70*t*; identifying
development gap in
competencies/interpersonal,
191; lacking immediate
opportunities to apply new,
228–229; leveraging your
strengths, 54–56, 200–201;
people-based attributes,
131*fig*, 235; task-focused
attributes, 130–131*fig*, 235;
understanding organizations
requirements for specific,
198–201. *See also* Career
professionals; Leadership
skills development; Learning
agility
Smithsonian (publication), 90
Snowdon, David, 107
The Social Animal (Aronson), 109
Social capital, 90
Social network sites: Facebook,
89, 100, 129, 138; LinkedIn,
100, 138; MySpace, 138;
Twitter, 140
Social networks: creating social
capital through, 89–90; do's
and don'ts for managing
your, 102–103; learning how
to mine information through
your, 100–103; strengthening
your personal brand,
138–139; testing capability of
your, 101–102
Society for Human Resource
Management (SHRM), 5
Southern Methodist University,
4
*Spark: The Revolutionary New Science
of Exercise and the Brain* (Ratey
and Hagerman), 103
Staging assignments, 73–75
Stakeholder Analysis Chart, 147
Starbucks, 122
Stimulus control: Case in Point:
Kirk on using, 115–116;
increasing learning efficiency
using, 113–114
Strategic priorities: job demands
impacted by organization,
28–29; questions for
identifying, 29

Stress management, 143–144
Sustained impressions, 128*fig*, 129–130
SWOT matrix, 145
Systems approach, 203–204

T

Taking broader perspective: actions engaging organization parts to improve, 68*t*; assignments to improve skills, 66, 208; desire to increase skills for, 63; organization-wide development actions, 69*t*; outside organization development actions, 70*t*; suggested actions within current job to improve, 67*t*
Task-focused attributes, 130–131*fig*, 235
Team player strategies: avoiding email and voicemail wars, 141–142; Brand Application Table, 155*t*; building relationships, 140; managing difficult conversations, 140–141; responding to requests, 142, 151–152; when meeting with senior-level executives, 142–143
The Team Troubleshooter (Barner), 108, 145, 147, 151
Template for establishing success measures, 77
Testing assumptions, 108–109
Thinking strategically: actions engaging organization parts

to improve, 68*t*; assignments to improve skills, 66, 208; desire to increase skills for, 63; organization-wide development actions, 69*t*; outside organization development actions, 70*t*; suggested actions within current job to improve, 67*t*
Thought experiments: description of, 224; example of conducting a, 224–225
3Cs of brand, 123, 158
360-degree surveys, 173
Toyota, 123, 233
Transitional coaching, 165–166
Treats and Opportunities Analysis, 147
Twitter, 140

U

University of Chicago, 89
University of Massachusetts Medical School, 109
University of Texas, 64
U.S. Army, 110

V

Voicemail wars, 141–142

W

Wal-Mart, 122
"What if" scenarios, 224–225
White-space management: coaching priority for, 167–168; influencers' skills for, 151

Work success/problem brand, 134*t*–136
Working across silos and functions: actions engaging organization parts to improve, 68*t*; assignments to improve skills, 66, 208; desire to increase skills for, 63; organization-wide development actions, 69*t*; outside organization development actions, 70*t*; suggested actions within current job to improve, 67*t*
Working with diverse groups: actions engaging organization parts to improve, 68*t*; assignments to improve skills, 66, 208; desire to increase skills for, 63; evaluating your skills for, 119; organization-wide development actions, 69*t*; outside organization development actions, 70*t*; suggested actions within current job to improve, 67*t*
Working through messy problems: actions engaging organization parts to improve, 68*t*; assignments to improve skills, 66, 208; desire to increase skills for, 63; organization-wide development actions, 69*t*; outside organization development actions, 70*t*; suggested actions within current job to improve, 67*t*

Pfeiffer Publications Guide

This guide is designed to familiarize you with the various types of Pfeiffer publications. The formats section describes the various types of products that we publish; the methodologies section describes the many different ways that content might be provided within a product. We also provide a list of the topic areas in which we publish.

FORMATS

In addition to its extensive book-publishing program, Pfeiffer offers content in an array of formats, from fieldbooks for the practitioner to complete, ready-to-use training packages that support group learning.

FIELDBOOK Designed to provide information and guidance to practitioners in the midst of action. Most fieldbooks are companions to another, sometimes earlier, work, from which its ideas are derived; the fieldbook makes practical what was theoretical in the original text. Fieldbooks can certainly be read from cover to cover. More likely, though, you'll find yourself bouncing around following a particular theme, or dipping in as the mood, and the situation, dictate.

HANDBOOK A contributed volume of work on a single topic, comprising an eclectic mix of ideas, case studies, and best practices sourced by practitioners and experts in the field.

An editor or team of editors usually is appointed to seek out contributors and to evaluate content for relevance to the topic. Think of a handbook not as a ready-to-eat meal, but as a cookbook of ingredients that enables you to create the most fitting experience for the occasion.

RESOURCE Materials designed to support group learning. They come in many forms: a complete, ready-to-use exercise (such as a game); a comprehensive resource on one topic (such as conflict management) containing a variety of methods and approaches; or a collection of like-minded activities (such as icebreakers) on multiple subjects and situations.

TRAINING PACKAGE An entire, ready-to-use learning program that focuses on a particular topic or skill. All packages comprise a guide for the facilitator/trainer and a workbook for the participants. Some packages are supported with additional media—such as video—or learning aids, instruments, or other devices to help participants understand concepts or practice and develop skills.

- *Facilitator/trainer's guide* Contains an introduction to the program, advice on how to organize and facilitate the learning event, and step-by-step instructor notes. The guide also contains copies of presentation materials—handouts, presentations, and overhead designs, for example—used in the program.

- *Participant's workbook* Contains exercises and reading materials that support the learning goal and serves as a valuable reference and support guide for participants in the weeks and months that follow the learning event. Typically, each participant will require his or her own workbook.

ELECTRONIC CD-ROMs and web-based products transform static Pfeiffer content into dynamic, interactive experiences. Designed to take advantage of the searchability, automation, and ease-of-use that technology provides, our e-products bring convenience and immediate accessibility to your workspace.

METHODOLOGIES

CASE STUDY A presentation, in narrative form, of an actual event that has occurred inside an organization. Case studies are not prescriptive, nor are they used to prove a point; they are designed to develop critical analysis and decision-making skills. A case study has a specific time frame, specifies a sequence of events, is narrative in structure, and contains a plot structure—an issue (what should be/have been done?). Use case studies when the goal is to enable participants to apply previously learned theories to the circumstances in the case, decide what is pertinent, identify the real issues, decide what should have been done, and develop a plan of action.

ENERGIZER A short activity that develops readiness for the next session or learning event. Energizers are most commonly used after a break or lunch to stimulate or refocus the group. Many involve some form of physical activity, so they are a useful way to counter post-lunch lethargy. Other uses include transitioning from one topic to another, where "mental" distancing is important.

EXPERIENTIAL LEARNING ACTIVITY (ELA) A facilitator-led intervention that moves participants through the learning cycle from experience to application (also known as a Structured Experience). ELAs are carefully thought-out designs in which there is a definite learning purpose and intended outcome. Each step—everything that participants do during the activity—facilitates the accomplishment of the stated goal. Each ELA includes complete instructions for facilitating the intervention and a clear statement of goals, suggested group size and timing, materials required, an explanation of the process, and, where appropriate, possible variations to the activity. (For more detail on Experiential Learning Activities, see the Introduction to the *Reference Guide to Handbooks and Annuals*, 1999 edition, Pfeiffer, San Francisco.)

GAME A group activity that has the purpose of fostering team spirit and togetherness in addition to the achievement of a pre-stated goal. Usually contrived—undertaking a desert expedition, for example—this type of learning method offers an engaging means for participants to demonstrate and practice business and interpersonal skills. Games are effective for team building and personal development mainly because the goal is subordinate to the process—the means through which participants reach decisions, collaborate, communicate, and generate trust and understanding. Games often engage teams in "friendly" competition.

ICEBREAKER A (usually) short activity designed to help participants overcome initial anxiety in a training session and/or to acquaint the participants with one another. An icebreaker can be a fun activity or can be tied to specific topics or training goals. While a useful tool in itself, the icebreaker comes into its own in situations where tension or resistance exists within a group.

INSTRUMENT A device used to assess, appraise, evaluate, describe, classify, and summarize various aspects of human behavior. The term used to describe an instrument depends primarily on its format and purpose. These terms include survey, questionnaire, inventory, diagnostic, survey, and poll. Some uses of instruments include providing instrumental feedback to group members, studying here-and-now processes or functioning within a group, manipulating group composition, and evaluating outcomes of training and other interventions.

Instruments are popular in the training and HR field because, in general, more growth can occur if an individual is provided with a method for focusing specifically on his or her own behavior. Instruments also are used to obtain information that will serve as a basis for change and to assist in workforce planning efforts.

Paper-and-pencil tests still dominate the instrument landscape with a typical package comprising a facilitator's guide, which offers advice on administering the instrument and interpreting the collected data, and an initial set of instruments. Additional instruments are available separately. Pfeiffer, though, is investing heavily in e-instruments. Electronic instrumentation provides effortless distribution and, for larger groups particularly, offers advantages over paper-and-pencil tests in the time it takes to analyze data and provide feedback.

LECTURETTE A short talk that provides an explanation of a principle, model, or process that is pertinent to the participants' current learning needs. A lecturette is intended to establish a common language bond between the trainer and the participants by providing a mutual frame of reference. Use a lecturette as an introduction to a group activity or event, as an interjection during an event, or as a handout.

MODEL A graphic depiction of a system or process and the relationship among its elements. Models provide a frame of reference and something more tangible, and more easily remembered, than a verbal explanation. They also give participants something to "go on," enabling them to track their own progress as they experience the dynamics, processes, and relationships being depicted in the model.

ROLE PLAY A technique in which people assume a role in a situation/scenario: a customer service rep in an angry-customer exchange, for example. The way in which the role is approached is then discussed and feedback is offered. The role play is often repeated using a different approach and/or incorporating changes made based on feedback received. In other words, role playing is a spontaneous interaction involving realistic behavior under artificial (and safe) conditions.

SIMULATION A methodology for understanding the interrelationships among components of a system or process. Simulations differ from games in that they test or use a model that depicts or mirrors some aspect of reality in form, if not necessarily in content. Learning occurs by studying the effects of change on one or more factors of the model. Simulations are commonly used to test hypotheses about what happens in a system—often referred to as "what if?" analysis—or to examine best-case/worst-case scenarios.

THEORY A presentation of an idea from a conjectural perspective. Theories are useful because they encourage us to examine behavior and phenomena through a different lens.

TOPICS

The twin goals of providing effective and practical solutions for workforce training and organization development and meeting the educational needs of training and human resource professionals shape Pfeiffer's publishing program. Core topics include the following:

Leadership & Management
Communication & Presentation
Coaching & Mentoring
Training & Development
E-Learning
Teams & Collaboration
OD & Strategic Planning
Human Resources
Consulting

What will you find on pfeiffer.com?

- The best in workplace performance solutions for training and HR professionals

- Downloadable training tools, exercises, and content

- Web-exclusive offers

- Training tips, articles, and news

- Seamless on-line ordering

- Author guidelines, information on becoming a Pfeiffer Partner, and much more

Discover more at www.pfeiffer.com